CW00363446

Steps in UNDERSTANDING MATHEMATICS

T. WARREN & C. J. COX

JOHN MURRAY

Acknowledgements

The authors are grateful for advice received from Dr B. J. Vowden (University of Kent), Carl Schyberg and Tina Bouldin (The King Ethelbert School), the editors at John Murray, the assessors of the manuscript, the many pupils and teachers who helped trial the material, and last but not least our families. A detailed list of credits appears on page 272.

First published 1989
by John Murray (Publishers) Ltd
50 Albemarle Street, London W1X 4BD

Reprinted 1991, 1993

Printed in Great Britain by
Cambridge University Press

British Library Cataloguing in Publication Data

Steps in understanding mathematics (SUM).
1. Mathematics – For schools
510

ISBN 0-7195-4452-1 Bk.3: Pupils'

About this book

This is the third book of **Steps in Understanding Mathematics**, a course for GCSE Mathematics. This book will prepare you for the 14+ assessment required by the National Curriculum.

There are 35 chapters, divided into:

- **To remind you** . . . to revise ideas met earlier in your course.
- **Points to discuss** . . . to give you the chance to talk about the mathematics and to see how it links with everyday life.
- **Exercises** to give you practice at different kinds of questions and improve your understanding of the mathematics.
- **Extension work** (boxed) at the end of each chapter to give you a challenge with harder problems.

New ideas are clearly explained, and there are examples throughout to show you how to use the mathematics.

The book also includes:

- **Take a break**—puzzles and games for you to try.
- **Assignments**—projects and investigations.
- **Information for aural tests**—to use when your teacher gives you an aural test.
- **Summaries** of the ideas met in each chapter, to help you study and revise.
- **Glossary** giving the meaning of mathematical words which you will meet in the course.

Your teacher will also give you **worksheets** during the course for projects, practical work, homework and assessment.

Contents

1 Base ten: the denary system

● To remind you . . .

- **Spacing numbers**
  Fifteen thousand million in figures is 15 000 000 000.
  Note the small spaces every three figures in numbers of more than four figures.

- **Columns**
  This abacus shows the number 27 345 (twenty-seven thousand, three hundred and forty-five). The beads at the top of the abacus represent 2 ten-thousands, 7 thousands, 3 hundreds, 4 tens and 5 units.

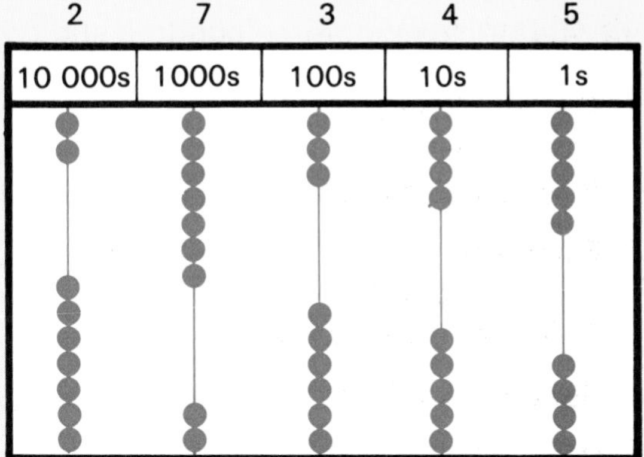

Fig. 1:1

▶ Points to discuss . . .

1. What do the following terms mean?
   digits   e.g.   perimeter   multiple
   place value

2. What do we mean by
   find the sum of
   find the product of?

3. Our number system is based on ten. Why do you think this is?

4. Could we base a number system on five? If so, how?

5. How would you show the numbers 450, 7309, and 20 810 on an abacus?

6. People from planet Kor use a number system based on four. What are the number headings on the abacus from planet Kor?

1 Draw an abacus showing the number 45 604.

2 Write in figures:

(a) thirty (b) ninety-three (c) six hundred and one

(d) two thousand, three hundred and twenty

(e) forty-two thousand, four hundred and six

3 In the number 7523 the 7 stands for 7 thousands. What does the figure 5 stand for in:

(a) 53 (b) 605 (c) 9523 (d) 56 123?

4 What do the abbreviations AD and BC mean when we write AD 1990 and 100 BC?

You don't have to copy the sentences!

5 Figure 1:2 gives some facts. Write the numbers in words, and write in full any abbreviations.

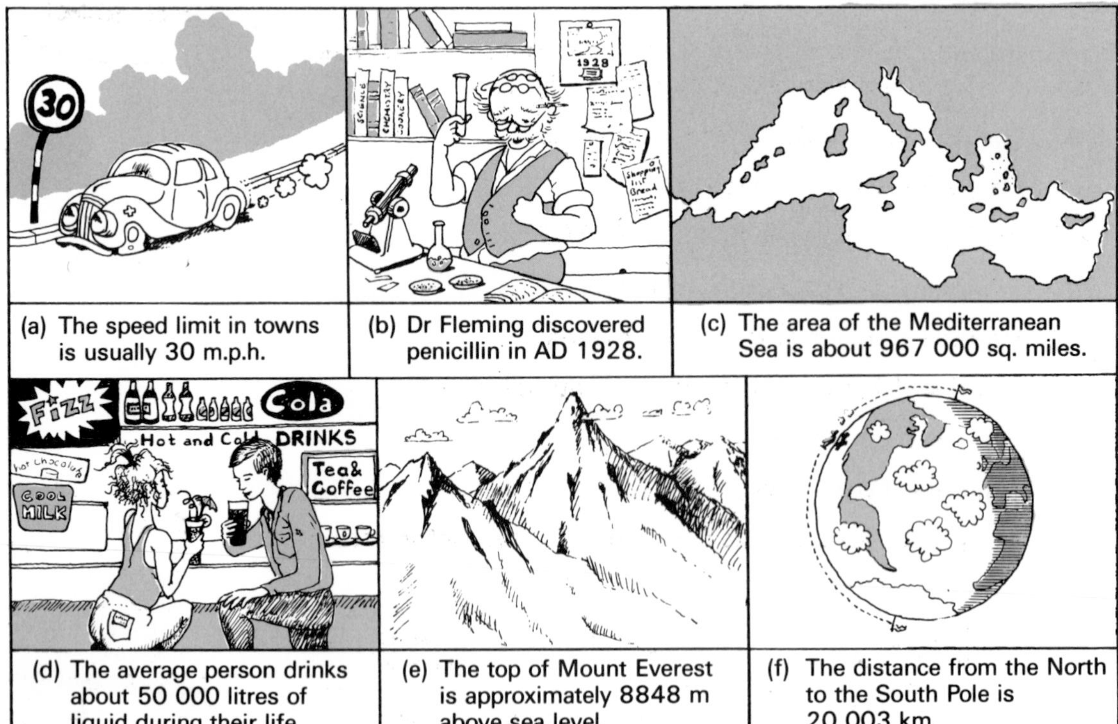

(a) The speed limit in towns is usually 30 m.p.h.

(b) Dr Fleming discovered penicillin in AD 1928.

(c) The area of the Mediterranean Sea is about 967 000 sq. miles.

(d) The average person drinks about 50 000 litres of liquid during their life.

(e) The top of Mount Everest is approximately 8848 m above sea level.

(f) The distance from the North to the South Pole is 20 003 km.

Fig. 1:2

6 Write in figures:

(a) ninety-nine thousand

(b) two hundred thousand and nine

(c) seven hundred and fifty thousand, four hundred and eight

(d) six million, one hundred thousand and twelve

7 Solve these clues to the word puzzle in Figure 1:3 and write down the answers.

Fig. 1:3

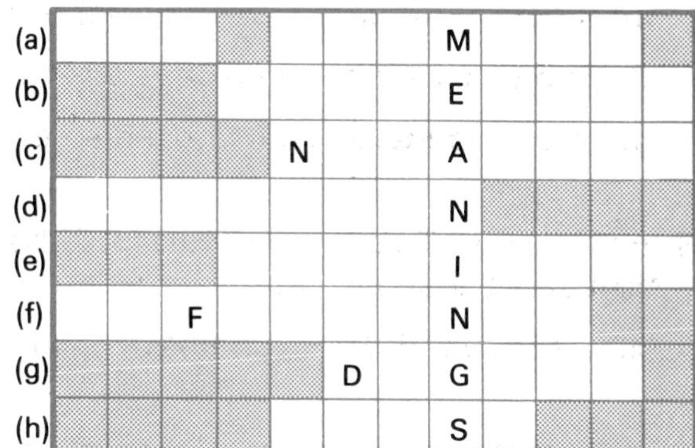

(a) e.g. (two words)

(b) ∴ is shorthand for this.

(c) −4 is a . . . number.

(d) Sometimes called 'sharing'.

(e) 6, 12 and 18 are some . . . of 6.

(f) 'Find the . . . between 75 and 59' means 'Work out 75 − 59'.

(g) 2356 has four of these.

(h) In $8 + 9 \times 7$ the multiplication is done . . .

DO NOT WRITE ON THIS BOOK!

8 The answers to this question are given in Figure 1:4. Link up each part with its answer. For example, (a) H.

(a) 'Find the sum of 9, 10 and 12' means . . .

(b) The perimeter of a shape is . . .

(c) The figure in the tens column of 9567 is . . .

(d) The area of a rectangle is found by . . .

(e) 'Find the product of 8 and 31' means . . .

(f) 1, 3, 5 and 7 are the first four . . . numbers.

(g) +5 is a . . . number.

(h) 4^2 is a short way to write . . .

(i) The symbol = means 'is equal to'. The symbol ≠ means . . .

A multiplying the length by the width	**B** 6	**C** 'is not equal to'
D positive	**E** 4 × 4	**F** multiply 8 and 31 to obtain 248
G the distance around it	**H** add them to find the total	**I** odd

Fig. 1:4

Worksheet 1A may be used here.

9 Copy and complete the number squares in Figures 1:5 to 1:7.
Try to do all the working out in your head.

+	6	8	12	18	25
10	16	18			
17					
22					
31					
35					

Fig. 1:5

−	30	38	45	50	52
20	10	18			
15					
22					
29					
25					

Fig. 1:6 Subtract the side numbers from the top numbers.

×	8	11	15	20	25
7	56	77			
11					
10					
20					
15					

Fig. 1:7

Worksheet 1B may be used here.

2 Line graphs

We are bombarded with information from television, radio, newspapers, magazines, and books. Graphs are often used to show the information.

1 How do facts and figures help us to obtain a clearer picture of things?

2 In what different ways are facts and figures presented in the media?

In this chapter we look at line graphs. Bits of information are plotted on the graph as points. The points are then joined together by curved or straight lines to show the trend.

Example The graph below shows the growth of Thomas from birth to five years old.
The points marked with a cross show Thomas's height when it was measured on his birthday each year. A line has been drawn through these points.
Note that we can find Thomas's approximate height *between* the whole years. For example, the dashed line shows that he was about 95 cm tall when he was three and a half years old.

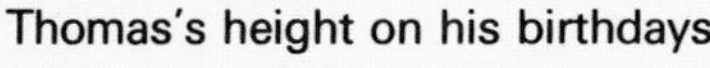

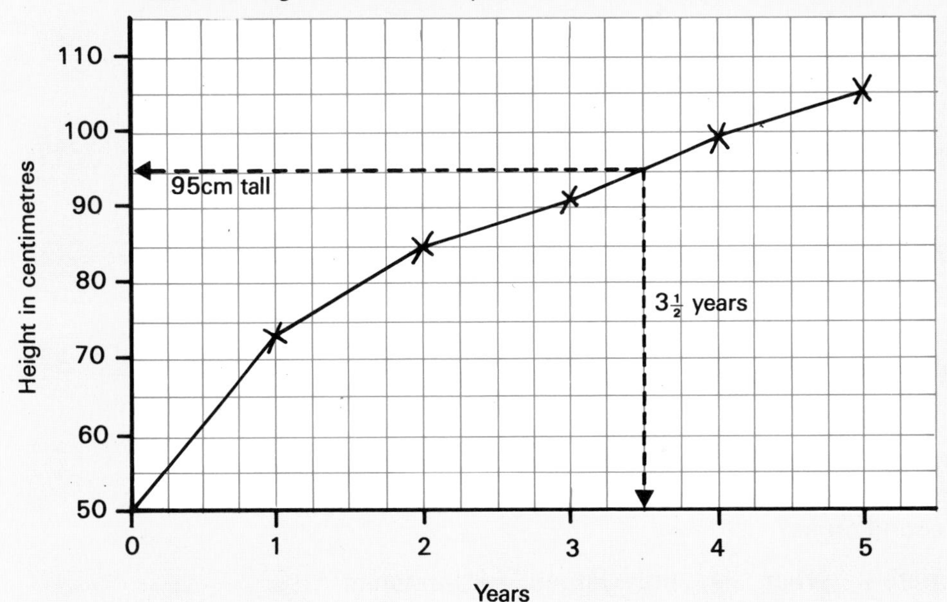

Fig. 2:1

Example This graph shows the numbers of people attending eight football matches.
By joining the eight crosses we make the graph easier to understand. We cannot find values between the points on this graph because the matches are only played weekly.

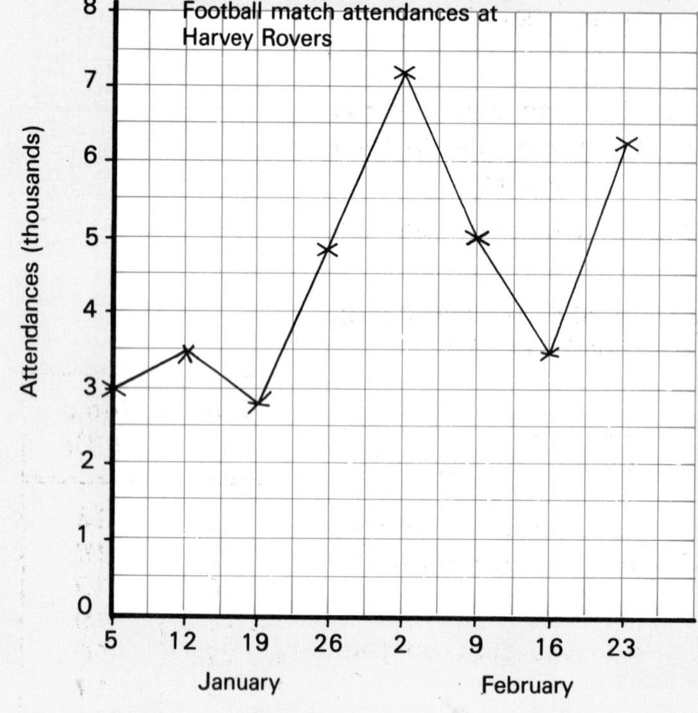

Fig. 2:2

1 (a) In Figure 2:1 (page 5) one year has been divided into smaller units. What does one smaller unit represent?

(b) Approximately how tall was Thomas at birth?

(c) About how tall was Thomas at 4 years 3 months?

(d) Approximately how old was Thomas when he was 90 cm tall?

2 (a) In Figure 2:2 how many people are represented by two units of the vertical axis?

(b) The first cross shows that on 5th January 3000 people attended the match. What attendance figure is shown by the second cross?

(c) Approximately what is the largest attendance recorded?

3 Teresa decided to draw a line graph of her marks (out of 20) for maths homework one term. She numbers the weeks 1 to 10. The table shows her marks.

Week	1	2	3	4	5	6	7	8	9	10
Mark	18	16	13	14	17	18	19	18	19	20

(a) Draw a line graph for Teresa. 5 mm squared paper is best for this. You decide what scales to use on each axis, but put weeks along the *horizontal* axis.

(b) Can you use this graph to find values between the points you plotted?

(c) Describe briefly how Teresa's marks changed during the term. Should she be pleased with herself?

4 Joseph plots the temperature of his classroom every hour from 8 a.m. to 4 p.m. one day. This is how he records it.

Time	Temp. (°C)
8	13
9	18
10	19
11	19
12	20
1	17
2	18
3	20
4	18

(a) Draw a line graph to illustrate Joseph's readings. Choose your own scales, but put time on the *horizontal* axis.

(b) Can you use the graph to find values between your plotted points?

(c) Estimate the room temperature at
(i) 2:30 (ii) 8:30 (iii) 10:30

(d) What do you think happened between noon and 1 p.m.?

5 A disease called myxomatosis killed many British rabbits in the 1950s. This table shows the effect on the number of rabbits of Archer's farm.

Year	1950	1951	1952	1953	1954	1955	1956	1957	1958	1959
Rabbit population to nearest 100	900	1000	700	400	200	100	200	300	300	400

(a) Draw a line graph to show how the number of rabbits changed. Use scales:
Horizontal: Year, 1 cm to each year
Vertical: Number of rabbits, 1 cm to 100 rabbits

(b) Describe what happened to the number of rabbits on the farm from 1950 to 1959.

6 Using 5 mm squared paper draw axes:
Horizontal: Purchase price (£1000s), 2 cm to 10 units, from 10 to 100
Vertical: Fee (£s), 2 cm to 10 units, from 40 to 100

When a person wants to buy a house, a surveyor is asked to look at it to check for any faults. The surveyor charges a fee according to how much the house is costing the buyer. The fees are shown in the table on the right.

Draw a line graph to illustrate the fees.

Purchase price	Fee
£12 000	£40
£15 000	£45
£20 000	£50
£25 000	£55
£30 000	£60
£40 000	£65
£50 000	£75
£60 000	£80
£70 000	£85
£80 000	£85
£90 000	£90
£100 000	£100

Source: Halifax Building Society

7 Answer the questions in Figure 2:3.

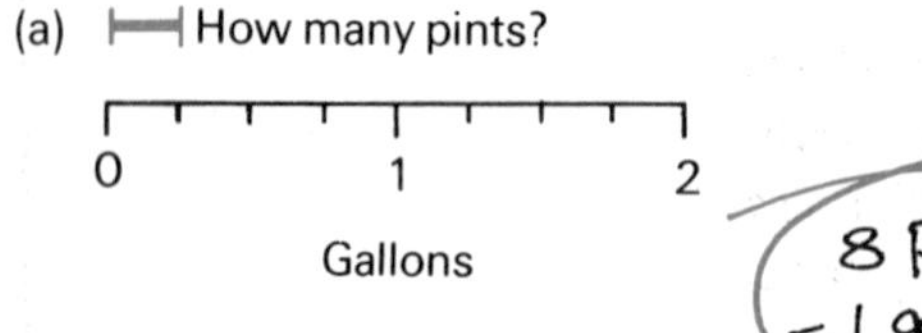

8 pints = 1 gallon

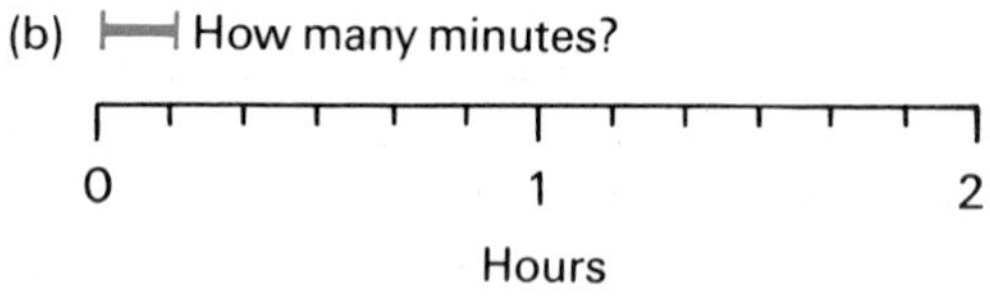

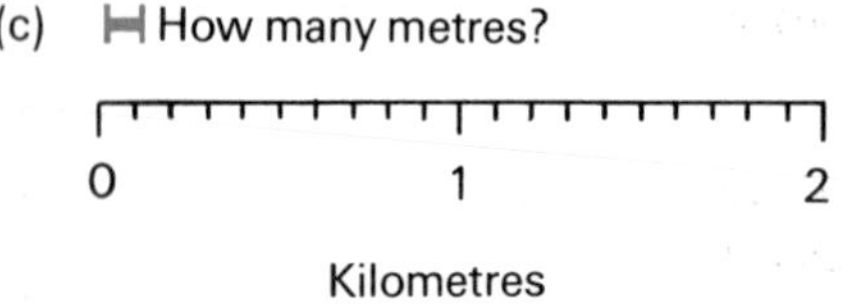

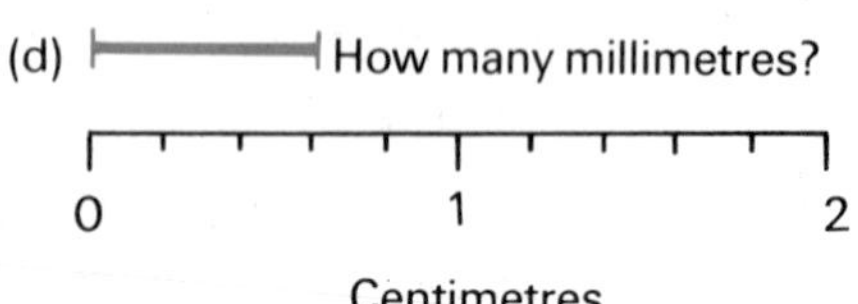

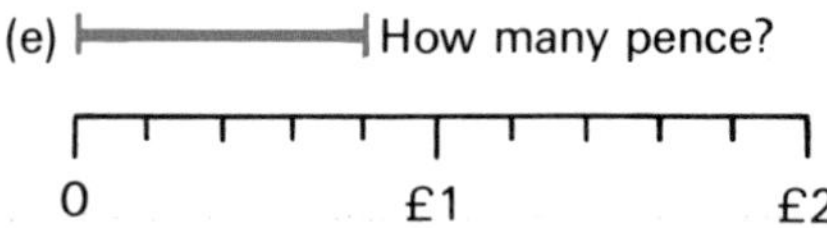

Fig. 2:3

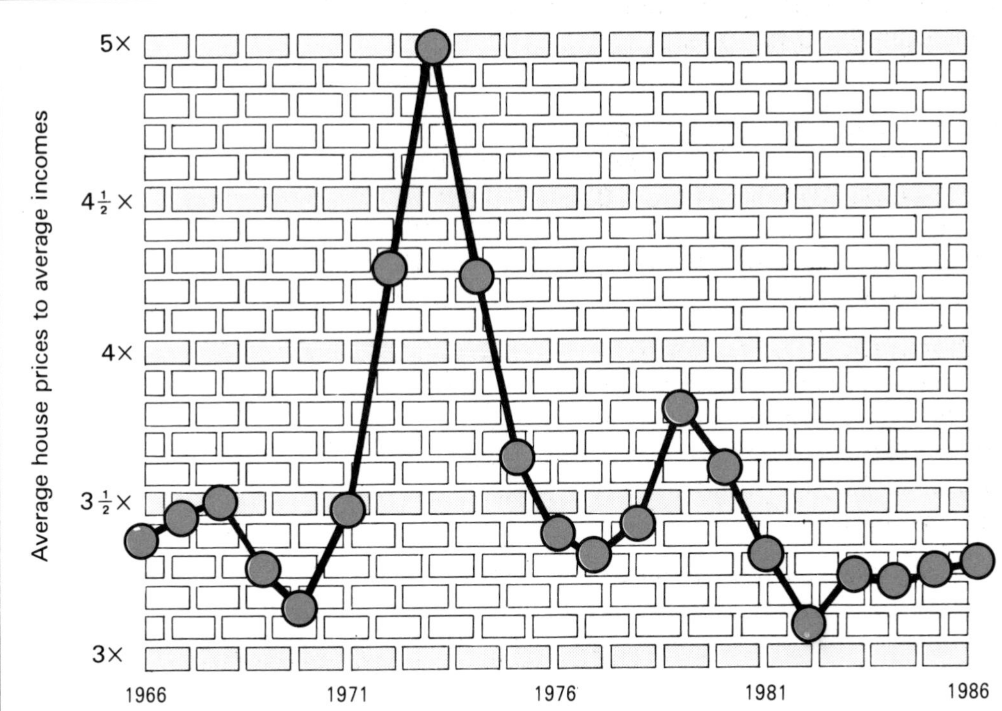

Source: The Building Societies Association

Fig. 2:4

8 Figure 2:4 appeared in the *Which?* magazine in March 1987. It shows how dear an average house was compared to average yearly pay from 1966 to 1986. For example, in 1971 an average house cost about $3\frac{1}{2}$ times the average yearly pay.

(a) Look at the year scale. Is it easy to read? Give your reasons.

(b) Look at the vertical scale. Is it easy to read? Give your reasons.

(c) When would people have found it most difficult to borrow enough money to buy a house? (This is called 'getting a mortgage'.)

(d) Try to draw a better version of this graph.

Worksheets 2A and 2B may be used here.

3 Types of number

Some Indian people of the Amazon jungle have no number system. The closest the Nambiquara tribe have to a number is a word meaning 'to be two alike'!

▶ Point to discuss . . .

What difference would it make to your life if there were no numbers?

● To remind you . . .

- **Even and odd numbers**

  Even numbers will divide exactly by 2. Odd numbers will not.

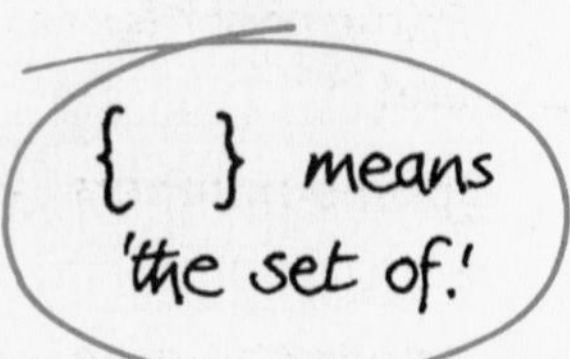

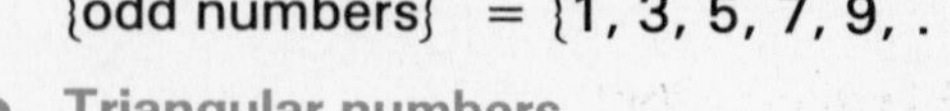

{even numbers} = {2, 4, 6, 8, 10, . . .}
{odd numbers} = {1, 3, 5, 7, 9, . . .}

- **Triangular numbers**

  Triangular numbers may be represented by a triangle of dots (Figure 3:1).

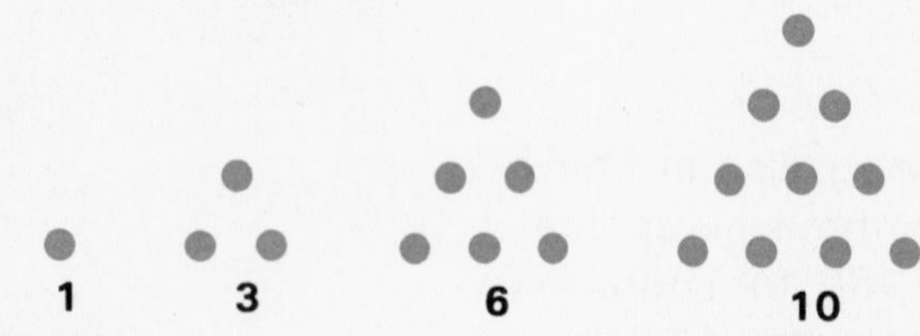

Fig. 3:1

Triangular numbers are made by adding counting numbers:

1 = 1
3 = 1 + 2
6 = 1 + 2 + 3
10 = 1 + 2 + 3 + 4

- **Square numbers**

  Square numbers may be represented by a square of dots (Figure 3:2).

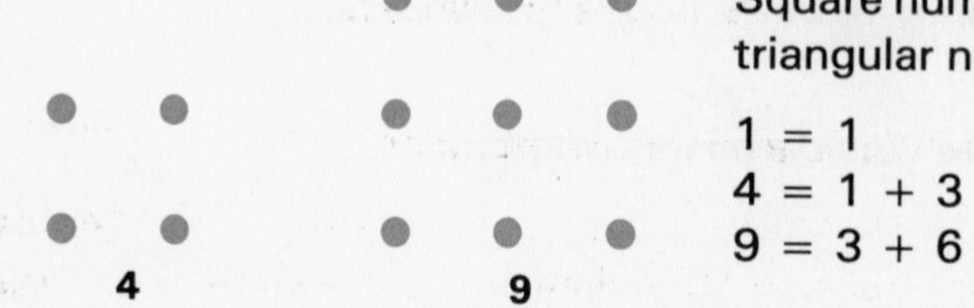

Fig. 3:2

Square numbers are made by adding triangular numbers:

1 = 1
4 = 1 + 3
9 = 3 + 6

- **Integers**
  Integers are the positive and negative (+ and −) whole numbers, and usually include zero.

  Negative numbers must have a minus sign in front of them.
  Positive numbers may have a plus sign in front of them.

  Integers may be shown on a number line (Figure 3:3).

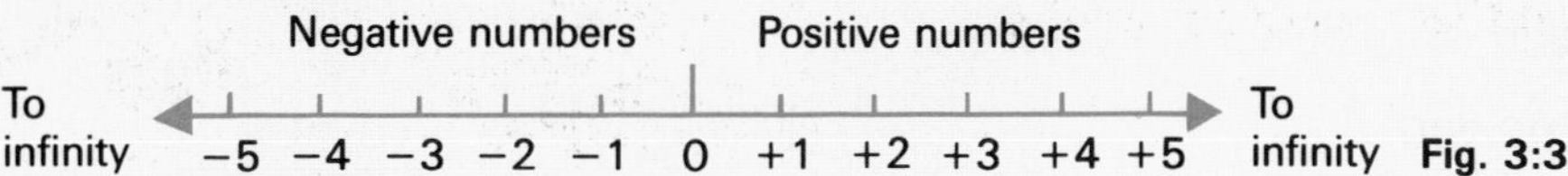

Fig. 3:3

- **Prime numbers**
  Prime numbers can only be divided exactly by themselves and by 1.

  {prime numbers} = {2, 3, 5, 7, 11, 13, 17, 19, 23, . . .}

- **Infinity**
  All the above sets of numbers are infinite. This means that they go on for ever.

1 What is an infinite set of numbers?

2 Are the following sets infinite?

(a) {pupils in your school}

(b) {grains of sand on Hastings Beach}

(c) {3, 6, 9, 15, 18, . . .}

3 Numbers are used to identify houses. Write down five other examples of the use of number.

4 Draw a square to illustrate that 16 is a square number.

5 Draw dots to illustrate that 21 is a triangular number.

6 Draw a number line from −10 to +10 inclusive.

7 Describe in words: {2, 4, 6, 8, 10, . . .}.

8 Why are there no even prime numbers except for the number 2?

9 How many digits has the telephone emergency number?

10 Solve these clues to the word puzzle in Figure 3:4 and write down the answers.

(a) Having no end.

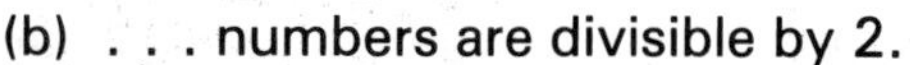

(b) . . . numbers are divisible by 2.

(c) {. . ., −3, −2, −1, 0, 1, 2, 3, . . .}

(d) 2 is the only even . . . number.

(e) . . . numbers are formed by adding counting numbers.

(f) A . . . number is made by multiplying a number by itself.

(g) The . . . of 8 and 5 is 40.

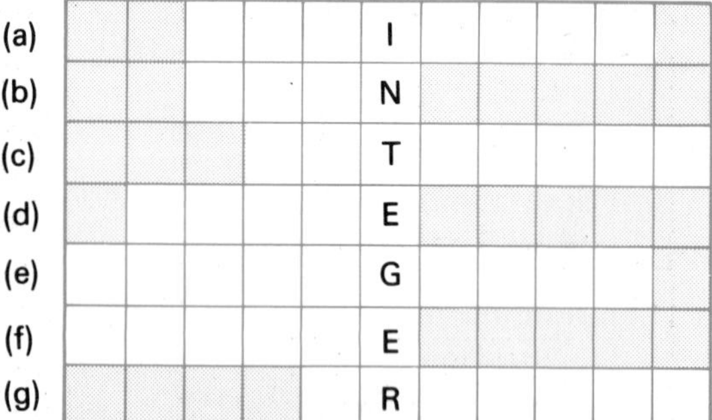

Fig. 3:4

11 What kind of numbers result when two consecutive triangular numbers are added together?

12 Write down the next five square numbers after 9.

13 Say whether each of the following numbers is prime or is not prime.

(a) 31 (b) 99 (c) 101 (d) 81 (e) 53

14 Write the numbers from 1 to 10 inclusive.

(a) Which of the numbers is both prime and triangular?

(b) Which of the numbers is both odd and a square?

(c) Which two numbers are both even and triangular?

(d) Write the sum of all the prime numbers in the list.

(e) Write the product of the two largest triangular numbers in the list.

15 Each of the pictures in Figure 3:5 is associated with one word and one number from the two lists below. Link each picture with the correct word and number. For example, (a) Pontoon and 21.

Words	Century Triplets Pontoon Quadruped Score Dozen Gross Bull Baker's dozen
Numbers	20 100 13 50 21 4 12 3 144

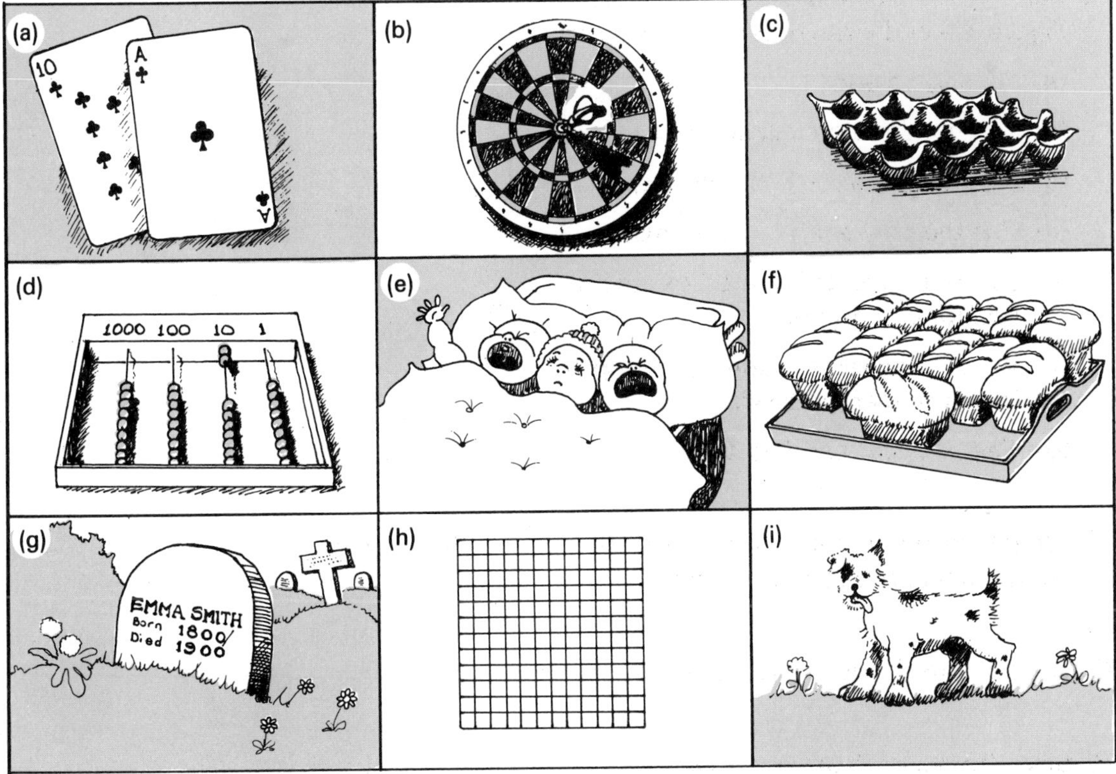

Fig. 3:5

Worksheet 3 may be used here.

16 Using only the digits 2, 3, 4, 8 and 5, and using each digit not more than once in each part, write:

(a) the largest possible five-digit number

(b) the smallest possible four-digit number

(c) the smallest possible four-digit number that is divisible by 3

(d) the largest possible two-digit prime number (NEA)

4 Addition and subtraction: which operation?

It is just as important to know *which* of the four rules (+ , − , × , ÷) to use as *how* to use them.

▶ Points to discuss . . .

1 Which of the four rules is being used in each part of Figure 4:1?

Fig. 4:1

2 Find at least four other everyday examples where you need to use one of the four rules, saying which one you would use.

● To remind you . . .

- **Estimation**

  An estimated answer can help you to notice errors.

Example In adding 53, 8 and 101, Andras incorrectly wrote this.

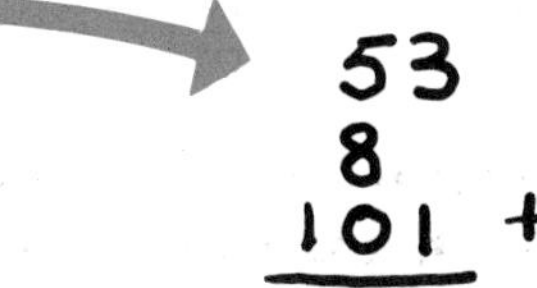

An estimated answer of
50 + 10 + 100 = **160**
would have shown Andras that his answer was wrong.

Only use a calculator in this exercise when you cannot work out the answer without it.

1 Write down the letter of the correct answer. For example, (a) B.

(a) 23 × 10 =
A 203 B 230

(b) 4500 is . . . tens.
A 450 B 45

(c) 37 × 100 = . . .
A 3700 B 370

(d) 15 × 200 = 15 × 2 × 100 = 30 × 100 = . . .
A 3000 B 300

(e) Find the difference between 83 and 45 means . . . them.
A add B subtract C divide

(f) The product of 23 and 12 is 276. A product is the result of . . .
A addition B subtraction C multiplication

(g) Find the sum of 8, 12 and 34 means . . . them.
A add B subtract C multiply

2 With practice you can learn to add quite large numbers in your head. You may well find your own way of doing the following examples.

Example Add 134 to 245.

Think:	Add the hundreds	100 + 200 = 300.
	Add the tens	30 + 40 = 70,
		making 370.
	Add the units	4 + 5 = 9,
		making **379.**

Example Subtract 70 from 232.

Think: From 70 to 100 is 30.
From 100 to 232 is 132, making **162** altogether.

Work these out in your head, just writing down the answer.

(a) 15 + 25 (b) 23 + 15 (c) 33 + 46

(d) 300 + 50 + 9 (e) 50 − 15 (f) 64 − 18

(g) 90 − 63 (h) 110 − 27

3 In addition and subtraction be careful to put the figures in the correct columns.

Example 810 + 9 + 5070

Write this down as:

```
  8 1 0
      9
5 0 7 0 +
-------
5 8 8 9
```

Example 743 − 19

Write this down as:

```
7 4 3
  1 9 −
-----
7 2 4
```

Find:

(a) 8 + 12 + 135 (b) 501 + 17 + 4

(c) 1537 + 23 + 109 (d) 281 − 120

(e) 426 − 207 (f) 308 − 129

4 Which sign, + or −, should be written instead of each star?

(a) Vera has £20. She gives £7 to Lucy. Vera now has £20 * £7.

(b) Monika has fifteen cows, five of which each give birth to a calf. Monika now has 15 * 5 animals.

(c) The four sides of a field measure 135 m, 87 m, 123 m and 96 m. In walking around the field Tom walks 135 m * 87 m * 123 m * 96 m.

(d) John has 54 matchbox labels. He swops 16 with Winston for a football and gets 23 more from a shop. John now has 54 * 16 * 23 matchbox labels.

(e) Susan has 35 cassettes at the start of a year. During the year she loses 9 cassettes, buys 17 and gives away 12. Susan now has 35 * 9 * 17 * 12 cassettes.

5 Work out the answers to question 4.

6 Here are some jumbled-up words connected with addition and subtraction. Rearrange the letters to find the words.

(a) ismun (b) keat aayw (c) dad
(d) ttcarbus morf (e) ceenffreid
(f) ums fo (g) ulps

7 Timothy was given these questions for homework.

(a) 165 + 8 + 23 (b) 674 + 20 469
(c) 842 − 261

He got all of them wrong! Find and describe his errors.

```
165          674          842
  8           20          261−
  23+        469+         ----
----         ----         681  ✗
268  ✗       1163 ✗
```

See me

8 The mileometer in Figure 4:2 shows the total distance the car has travelled.

(a) What is the maximum mileage the mileometer can show?

(b) How much further would the car have to travel to show the maximum mileage?

Fig. 4:2

9 The mileometer recordings for four different cars are shown in Figure 4:3.

(a) What is the total mileage for the four mileometers?

(b) What is the difference between mileometers:
(i) A and B (ii) A and C (iii) A and D?

(c) Give approximations for all four mileages:
(i) to the nearest 10 miles
(ii) to the nearest 50 miles.

A 0 2 8 2 3
B 0 3 7 6 9
C 0 0 6 5 6
D 3 8 9 0 1

Fig. 4:3

10 Find the sum of nine thousand and eighteen, and three thousand one hundred.

11 A reservoir gains and loses the following amounts of water (in litres) in a week.

Mon.	Tues.	Wed.	Thurs.	Fri.	Sat.	Sun.
+10 801	−5497	−12 806	−809	+3005	+18	−2500

What is the total gain or loss at the end of the week?

12 The route map in Figure 4:4 represents nine towns and the roads joining them. The numbers show distances in miles.

Ann Lewis, a sales rep, wants to visit all nine towns. She starts and finishes at Atford.

(a) Copy the route map. Write down a route Ann could take.

(b) Find the total distance Ann will travel if she uses this route.

(c) Try to find the shortest route possible.

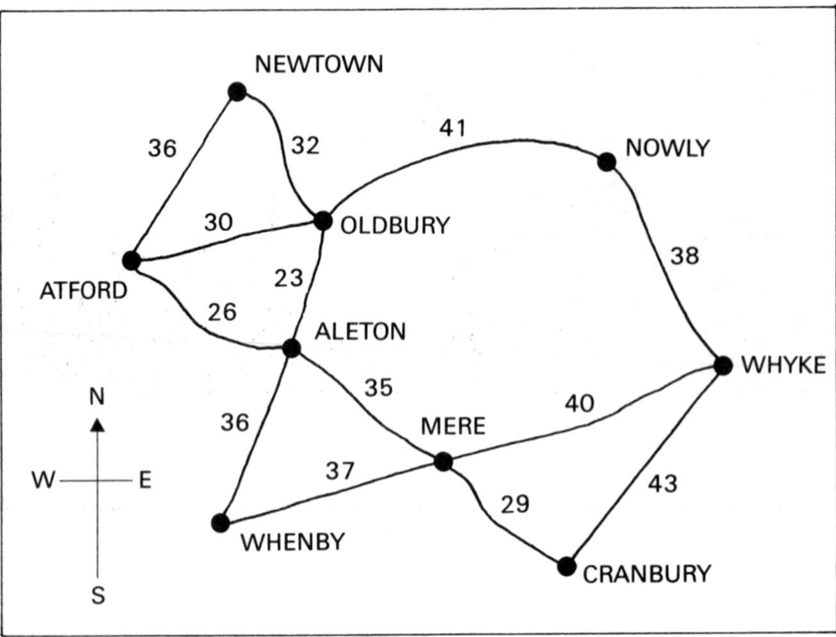

Fig. 4.4

13 In one week a self-employed builder paid out and received the following:

Monday, paid out £53 for cement and ballast
Tuesday, received a cheque for £105
Wednesday, received a tax rebate of £83
Thursday, paid a bill of £123 for hiring equipment
Friday, received cheques for £76·50 and £134·50

How much more did he receive than pay out?

14 In an election Thomas received 18 636 votes, Griffiths 12 798 votes and Smith 7876 votes. 79 votes were spoilt. Also, 28 978 people who were entitled to vote did not do so.

(a) How many more votes than Griffiths did Thomas receive?

(b) How many people voted altogether?

(c) Altogether, how many people were entitled to vote? (LEAG)

Worksheet 4 may be used here.

Networks and traversability

Worksheet B1 may be used here.

To remind you . . .

Figure B1:1 has

- 5 nodes
- 9 arcs
- 6 regions

A network is traversable when it can be drawn without lifting your pencil or going over any line twice.

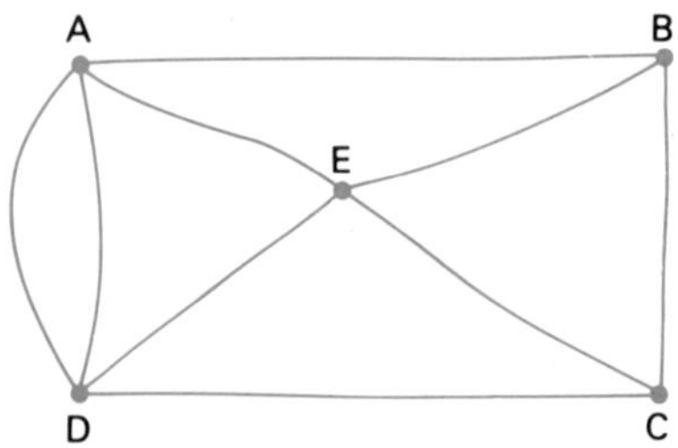

Fig. B1:1

1

(a)

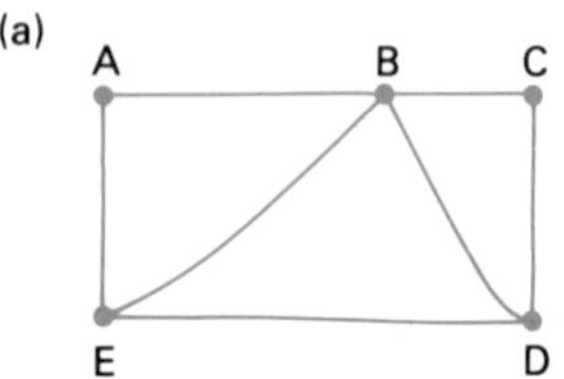

(b)

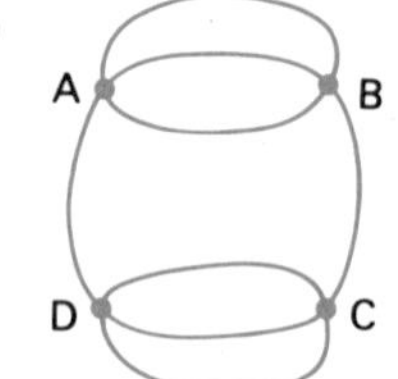

(c)

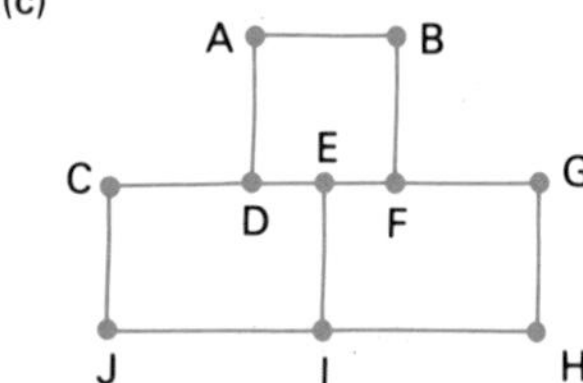

(d)

A B C D E

An ODD node is where an odd number of arcs meet.

An EVEN node is where an even number of arcs meet.

Draw the networks in Figure B1:2. Label the odd nodes O and the even nodes E.

2 Make a table showing how many odd and even nodes each network has.

3 (a) Which of the networks in Figure B1:2 are traversable?

(b) Give a route for each traversable network, like this: A → B → C and so on.

4 Draw some networks of your own. Are they traversable? Challenge a friend!

Chase

This is a game for two players, using one counter each.

Figure B1:3 represents an airline network. Bond (007) can capture Goldfinger (GF) by getting to the same airport.

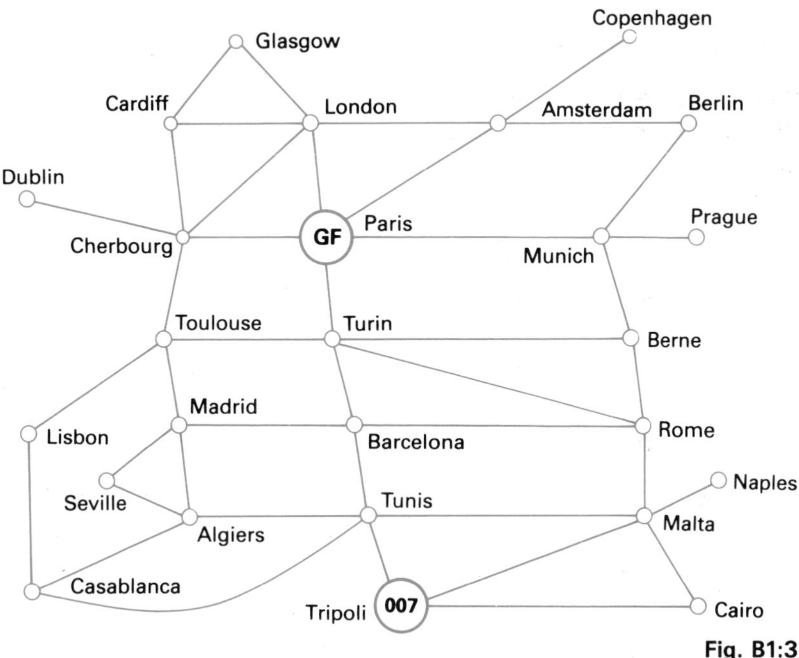

Fig. B1:3

They move one arc at a time. Bond moves first.

5 Pictograms

● To remind you . . .

- **Picture graphs**

A pictogram shows information by pictures or symbols. For example, ten cars may be represented by a drawing of one car. Five cars would then be represented by half a car.

represents 10 cars.

represents 5 cars.

Figure 5:1 shows the numbers of babies born in Bonnypeg each year from 1983 to 1987, correct to the nearest 500.

1983	
1984	
1985	
1986	
1987	

represents 1000 babies

represents 500 babies

Fig. 5:1

The first five questions refer to Figure 5:1.

1 How many babies, to the nearest 500, were born each year?

2 Find the sum of the babies born during the five years.

3 Giving reasons, would you expect the birth-rate to be more, or less, in (a) 1980, (b) 1990?

4 Find the mean number of babies born per year during the five years.

5 Draw a symbol representing 750 babies.

6 Figure 5:2 shows the population of Aber in 1961, 1971 and 1981.

By 1991 it is thought the population will be as shown in Figure 5:3.

(a) How many people lived in Aber in 1961?

(b) How many people will be living there by 1991?

(c) How many more people will be living there in 1991 compared with 1961?

(d) In 1951 there were 1000 people living in Aber. Draw a picture to represent this number. (WJEC)

represents 500 people.

1961	
1971	
1981	

Fig. 5:2

1991	

Fig. 5:3

7 The number of cars using a certain junction from Monday to Friday were:

Monday 80, Tuesday 50, Wednesday 45, Thursday 35, Friday 63,

Draw a pictogram showing, to the nearest ten cars, the numbers of cars from Monday to Friday inclusive.

Use the symbol

for 20 cars

Draw your own symbol for 10 cars

8 Draw a pictogram to show the data in this table.

Customers visiting Ucan Seymore, Optician					
Mon.	Tues.	Wed.	Thurs.	Fri.	Sat.
45	65	15	22	37	60

Use the symbol to represent 15 customers

Worksheet 5 may be used here.

9 1000 school leavers were asked which type of job they would prefer.

To the nearest five their answers were as follows:

Clerical/shop	250	Forces/police/fire service	175
Engineering/industrial	150	Newspapers/radio etc.	100
Welfare/social	200	Catering/hotels	125

(a) Show this data clearly in:

(i) a line graph (ii) a stick graph (iii) a pictogram.

(b) Which kind of graph do you think shows the data best? Give your reasons.

6 Multiplication and division: which operation?

▶ Points to discuss . . .

1 How could you find 79 × 59 without using the ☒ key?

2 If you press 8 ☒ 2 ☒ 5 then ⊟, what have you multiplied 8 by altogether?

3 What calculator sequence will find out how many 20p pieces make £5?

4 How could you find 84 ÷ 7 without using the ⊞ key?

● BODMAS

If there are two or more operations to carry out in a problem the order to use can be remembered as BODMAS.

Brackets first,
Of next (use × for 'of'),
Division and Multiplication next,
Addition and Subtraction last.

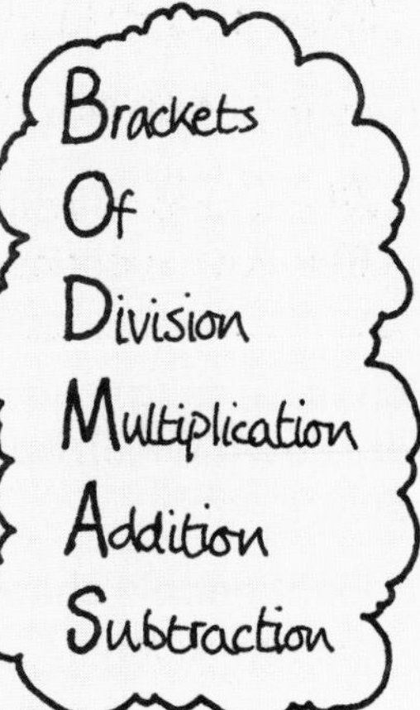

6

Scientific calculators usually follow BODMAS, but more basic calculators usually do not.

Try 3 ⊞ 4 ⊠.

If your calculator now displays 7, it has not followed BODMAS. Why not?

Try these:

(a) $5 + (18 - 3) + 40 \div 5$
The correct answer is **28.**

(b) $\frac{1}{2}$ of $80 - 30 \div 10$
The correct answer is **37.**

1 Link up each statement with the correct letter A to J from Figure 6:1.

(a) A sign for 'is approximately equal to' is . . . or . . .

(b) $202 \div 2$ is not 11. It is . . .

(c) $89 \times 0 =$ . . . (two possible letters)

(d) $0 \div 89 =$ . . . (two possible letters)

(e) The order of operations can be remembered as . . .

(f) Brackets should be dealt with . . .

(g) An approximation for 38×42 is . . .

(h) 50×50 contains 2 noughts. The answer is . . .

(i) $360 \div 30$ gives the same answer as $36 \div$ . . .

(j) $606 \div 3$ is not 22. It is . . .

A	nought
B	BODMAS
C	$40 \times 40 = 1600$
D	$\approx$ or $\simeq$
E	2500
F	first
G	101
H	3
I	202
J	0

Fig. 6:1

2 kg is the abbreviation for kilogram. Write in full:

(a) km (b) km/h (c) cm (d) m^2
(e) m.p.h. (f) ml

3 Each of (a) to (g) can be solved by multiplication or division. Write down which operation is needed. Do not work out the answers yet.

(a) Eight people share 32 eggs. How many eggs does each person receive?

(b) A flower bed contains 9 rows of 12 plants. How many plants are there in the bed?

(c) Seven people equally shared £791. How much did each receive?

(d) Fence panels are 6 feet wide. How many panels are needed to make a fence 264 feet long?

(e) A car is moving at 50 km/h. How long will it take to travel 950 km?

(f) Trees cover $\frac{1}{4}$ of a 400 m^2 garden. What area do the trees cover?

(g) A square has a perimeter of 96 cm. How long is one side?

4 Work out the answers to question 3.

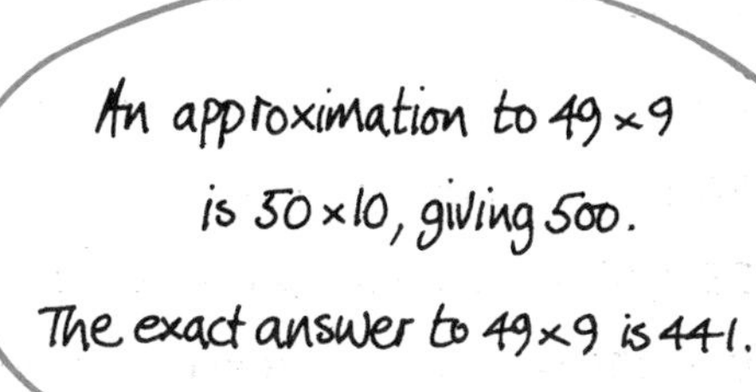

5 Give approximate answers and exact answers to:

(a) 38 × 9 (b) 78 × 39

(c) 105 × 32 (d) 79 × 41

6 Evaluate (find exact answers):

(a) 121 ÷ 11 (b) 100 ÷ 4

(c) 200 ÷ 8 (d) 515 ÷ 5

(e) 404 ÷ 2 (f) 3030 ÷ 15

7 This bottle contains 100 ml of medicine. Joan takes the medicine each day for 14 days. What is the amount of medicine then left in the bottle? (LEAG)

Fig. 6:2

8 Solve these clues to the word puzzle in Figure 6:3 and write down the answers.

(a) Order of operations.

(b) cm in full.

(c) Repeated subtraction.

(d) ml in full.

(e) Brackets are dealt with . . .

(f) Dividing.

(g) An . . . answer helps to avoid errors.

(h) 85 × 0 gives this.

(a)					D						
(b)					I						
(c)					V						
(d)					I						
(e)					S						
(f)					I						
(g)	A				O						
(h)					N						

Fig. 6:3

9 Describe two ways in which you could use a calculator to check that 417 × 27 = 11 259.

HINT
8×9 = 72
9×8 = 72
72÷8 = 9

10 To find a remainder when using a calculator is quite difficult. The example shows one way of doing it.

Example Find the remainder when 89 is divided by 6.

89 ÷ 6 = gives 14·833 333 . . .

The whole number part of the answer is 14.

14 × 6 = 84

So the remainder is 89 − 84 = 5.

Answer: 89 ÷ 6 is **14 remainder 5** or **$14\frac{5}{6}$**.

Write two answers (as in the example) for:

(a) 55 ÷ 9 (b) 124 ÷ 7 (c) 408 ÷ 5

(d) 809 ÷ 2 (e) 8164 ÷ 9

11 In May, 9563 copies of the newspaper *Local Scene* were sold each weekday (Monday to Saturday). How many copies were sold in May?

12 Frances Drake took a leap year and 29 days to sail round the world. How many (a) days, (b) hours, did her journey take?

MAY					
Sun.	1	8	15	22	29
Mon.	2	9	16	23	30
Tues.	3	10	17	24	31
Wed.	4	11	18	25	
Thurs.	5	12	19	26	
Fri.	6	13	20	27	
Sat.	7	14	21	28	

Fig. 6:4

13 (a) 5000 apples are packed into boxes. How many apples will be left over if the apples are packed:
(i) 12 to a box (ii) 24 to a box (iii) 48 to a box?

(b) It takes a minute and ten seconds to pack 4 boxes, each containing 12 apples. How long will it take to pack 5000 apples? (Do not include the apples left over.)

14 To find the digit sum of a number, add the digits until you finish with a single digit.

Example 4128 → 4 + 1 + 2 + 8 = 15 → 1 + 5 = **6**

- Even numbers divide exactly by 2.
- Numbers with a digit sum of 3, 6 or 9 divide exactly by 3.
- Numbers ending in 0 or 5 divide exactly by 5.
- Even numbers with a digit sum of 3, 6 or 9 divide exactly by 6.
- Numbers with a digit sum of 9 divide exactly by 9.

NOTE Read the arrow → as 'becomes'.

Copy this table. Fill it in to show if the numbers divide exactly by 2, 3, 5, 6, 9 or 10.

÷	36	48	60	72	90	108	125	150	180	209
2	✓									
3	✓									
5	✗									
6	✓									
9	✓									
10	✗									

Fig. 6:5

15 100 people are going to a bonfire party.

(a) How many times must the recipe in Figure 6:6 be cooked so that each person can have a good portion of chilli con carne?

(b) How many chilli peppers are needed?

(c) How many 0·43 kg tins of kidney beans are needed?

Chilli con carne for 4

450 g minced beef
2 onions
2 green chilli peppers
400 g tomatoes
2 teaspoons tomato purée
200 ml stock
1 teaspoon chilli powder
400 g kidney beans

Fig. 6:6

16 A couple take out a mortgage of £18 600 to help them buy a flat. Allowing for tax relief they will have to pay back £48 300 over 25 years.

(a) What will be their yearly repayment over the 25 years?

(b) What will be their monthly repayment over the 25 years?

(c) How much is their weekly repayment to the nearest £?

17 (a) $(508 \times 36) + (508 \times 14)$

(b) $(4596 \times 379) - (3596 \times 379)$

(LEAG)

NOTE
There is an easy way of doing question 17. Can you find it?

18 Mark Brown made this graph (Figure 6:7) to help him check how much petrol his car was using.

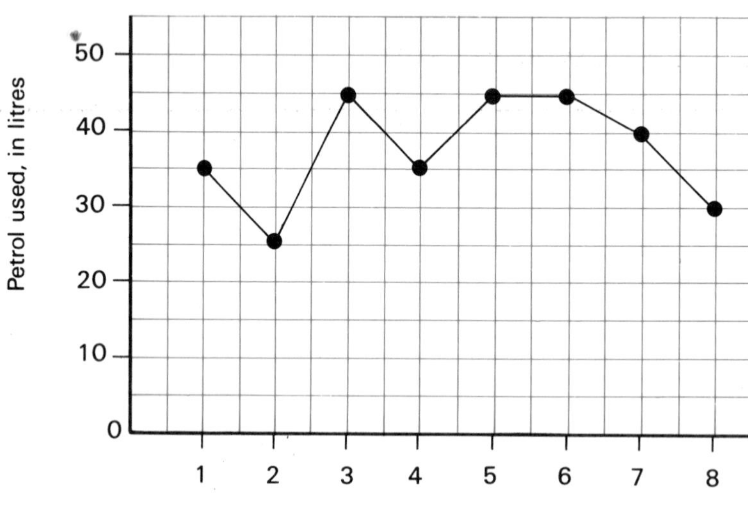

Fig. 6:7

(a) How much petrol did he use altogether in the eight weeks?

(b) Petrol for the eight weeks cost him £135·00. How much did one litre of petrol cost?

Worksheet 6 may be used here.

19 A van travelled 35 789 miles in one year. On average it used one gallon of petrol to cover 23 miles.

(a) How many gallons of petrol were needed to cover 35 789 miles? (Give your answer to the nearest whole number.)

(b) What was the cost of the petrol if one gallon cost £1·79?

20 Evaluate:

(a) 23 000 ÷ 500 (b) 23 000 ÷ 250

(c) 23 000 ÷ 125 (d) 23 000 ÷ 25

(e) Describe a method, other than division, for finding the answers to parts (b), (c) and (d).

21 How many thousands are there in 90 000 000?

7 Time

The Sun is a ball of fire. The temperature at its centre is about 15 000 000 °C. To the same scale as the photo, the Earth is about the size of a full stop.

As you walk home from school at about 3 m.p.h. the Earth upon which you walk is hurtling round the Sun at about 66 000 m.p.h.

At the same time the Earth is also turning. A tree on the equator is moving at about 1000 m.p.h. Great Britain is moving at approximately 600 m.p.h.

An eclipse of the Sun

▶ Points to discuss . . .

1 What unit of time is related to the Earth going round the Sun?

2 Every fourth year is a leap year of 366 days. Why?

3 What unit of time is related to the Earth turning about its own axis?

4 If the Earth is moving at such great speeds why do we not feel dizzy?

5 How does the 24-hour clock system work?

6 What examples of the use of the 24-hour clock can you think of?

A Yes	B 22nd December	C 30
D 1901 to 2000	E Big Ben	F 10
G April 1st	H 720	I 12 noon

Fig. 7:1

1 The answers to this question are given in Figure 7:1. Link up each part with its answer.

(a) The name of the largest bell in this tower. ⟶

(b) The number of seconds in 12 minutes.

(c) 1984 was a leap year. Will AD 2000 be a leap year?

(d) The official start of winter.

(e) Midday.

(f) The number of days in each of April, June, September and November.

(g) The 20th century.

(h) The number of years in a decade.

(i) A day of fools.

Fig. 7:2

2 Why are some days called **bank** holidays?

3 Five students took part in a sponsored swim, which started at 9:30 a.m. The students took the following times:

Bob 50 min Mary 1 h 10 min Nita 1 h 25 min
Hayley 2 h 55 min Tom 3 h 42 min

Give the time each student finished.

4 Carol is studying for an exam. She made this timetable for her revision. Copy and complete it.

Day	Start	End	Time taken
Wed.	9:30 a.m.		2h 30min
Thurs.	9:20 a.m.	12 noon	
Fri.	10:05 a.m.	12:50 p.m.	
Sat.	10:45 a.m.	2:20 p.m.	
Sun.		5 p.m.	4h 40min

Fig. 7:3

5 Write, in both figures and words, the times shown on these clocks.

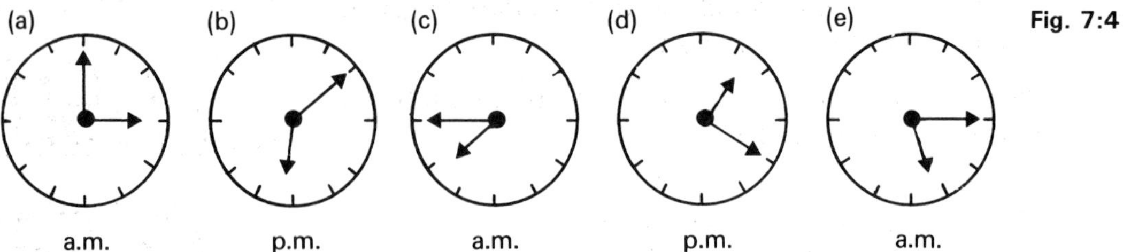

Fig. 7:4

6 If clocks (a), (c) and (e) in Figure 7:4 are 20 minutes fast, write down the correct times in figures and words.

Write your answers like this:
(i) 3 a.m.
(ii) three o'clock in the morning

7 Calculate the differences in times between clocks:
(i) (a) and (c) (ii) (b) and (d) (iii) (c) and (e)

8 3rd May 1986 can be written as 3.5.86. Write in figures:

(a) 8th October 1986 (b) 30th December 1986

(c) 23rd July 1990 (d) 2nd May 1999

9 Write in full:

(a) 9.4.78 (b) 24.6.90 (c) 10.3.92

(d) 28.12.86 (e) 28.2.95

10 The abbreviation a.m. is short for *ante meridian* which means 'before midday.' What is the abbreviation for *post meridian* and what does it mean?

11 **Example** 7:30 a.m. is 0730 in the 24-hour clock system.
7:30 p.m. is 1930 in the 24-hour clock system.

Write the times shown on the clocks below:

(i) in a.m. or p.m. time (ii) in 24-hour clock time

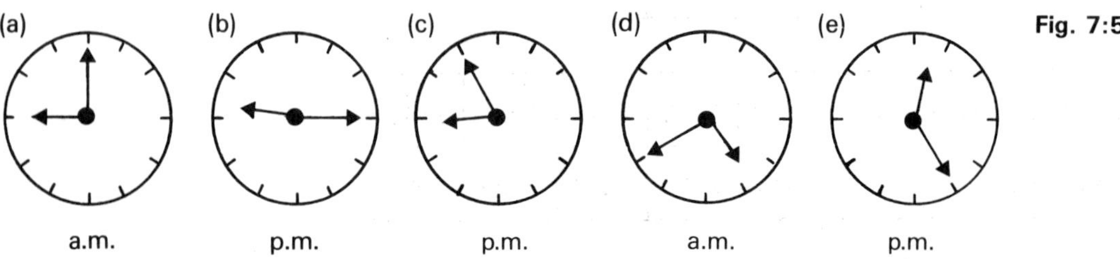

Fig. 7:5

12 (i) Some digital clock times are given on the right. Write the times as a.m. and p.m. times.

(ii) Write the times that would be on the clock faces 20 minutes before the times shown.

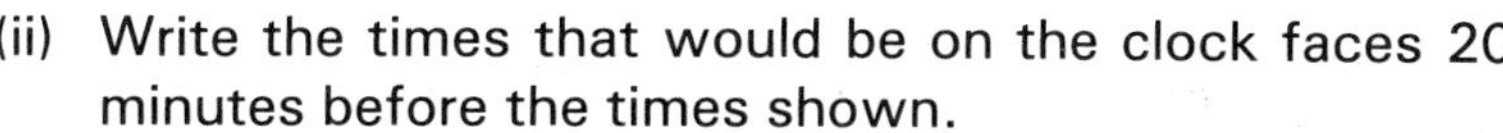

(iii) Write the times that would be on the faces 1 hour 5 minutes after the times shown.

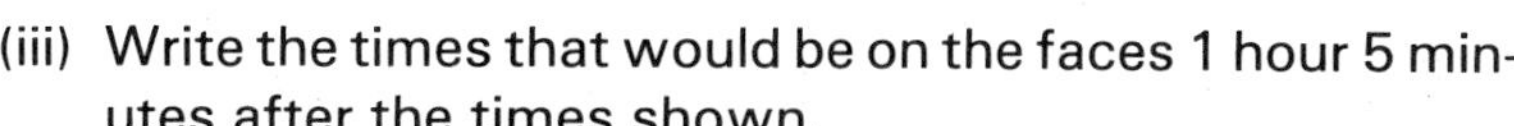

(a) 

(b) 

(c) 

(d) 

Fig. 7:6

13 Which of the following were leap years?

1920 1931 1939 1944 1960 1966 1984

14 1st January 1985 was a Tuesday, but 1.1.1986 was a Wednesday, and 1.1.1987 was a Thursday.

(a) Use the numbers 365 and 7 to explain why New Year's Day is on a different day of the week each year.

(b) What day of the week is New Year's Day, 1989?

15 Explain the meaning of the words 'British Summer Time'.

16 **Example** Paula catches a train at 1535 and arrives home at 1915. How long has she taken?

Written method

h	min		h	min	
19	15	→	18	75	
15	35		15	35	−
			3	**40**	

19h 15min was changed to 18h 75min so that the 35 minutes could be subtracted

Mental method 1535 to 1600 is 25 minutes;
to 1900 makes 3 hours 25 minutes;
another 15 minutes to 1915 makes
3 hours 40 minutes altogether.

Swansea	1445	1545	1645	1745	1845
London (Paddington)	1724	1833	1929	2039	2139

London (Marylebone)	1839	1850	1915	1940	2030	2130
High Wycombe	1921	1944	2000	2034	2122	2222

Denise must travel by train from Swansea and arrive in High Wycombe before 2100. She must allow at least 20 minutes to get from Paddington to Marylebone.

Use the train timetable on page 35.

(a) Find the last train Denise can catch from Swansea.

(b) Find the earliest time at which she can then arrive at High Wycombe.

(c) Find the time she will take from leaving Swansea to arriving at High Wycombe.

(d) If Denise misses her train at Swansea and catches the next train, find her time of arrival at High Wycombe.

(LEAG)

17 Andrew and Shobana reserved a 14-day holiday for themselves and their two children aged 9 and 3 at the Seanear Hotel for the period 17th to 30th July. They wished to fly from Manchester Airport. In addition they booked

(i) a separate bathroom,
(ii) accommodation with a sea view, and
(iii) insurance cover at £4·60 extra per person.

Calculate the total cost of the holiday using the table below.

Basic prices in £s per person for Heathrow departures

Date periods	2 May–29 May		30 May–26 June		27 June–24 July		25 July–21 Aug		22 Aug–18 Sept	
Number of days	7	14	7	14	7	14	7	14	7	14
Seawash Hotel	212	410	222	435	224	438	218	430	212	410
Seanear Hotel	172	330	180	350	180	350	189	360	170	330
Seafar Hotel	150	290	158	306	162	315	162	315	150	290

Children up to age 4 at **half price** (basic prices only)	A 14-day booking covering two date periods will be charged at the **lower** 14-day charge.	**Additional charges** Separate bathroom: £1.25 per day Sea view: £1.10 per person per day Insurance: £4.60 per person Manchester Airport: £15 extra per person

Worksheet 7 may be used here.

The following questions refer to the BBC television programmes shown in Figure 7:7.

18 What is the **total** time covered by:

(a) the BBC 1 programmes

(b) the BBC 2 programmes?

19 Rewrite the BBC 1 programme times using the 24-hour clock system.

20 Which programme on BBC 2 lasts for

(a) 50 minutes

(b) 55 minutes

(c) 20 minutes?

BBC1 ▮▮ TODAY AT A GLANCE ▮▮ BBC2

BBC1		BBC2	
8.55	Play School	9.0	Pages from Ceefax
9.15	Umbrella		
9.30	This Is the Day		
10.0	Asian Magazine	10.0	The Water Babies
10.30	Carnival of the Animals		
10.55	Two-Way Stretch	11.30	The Charlie Brown and Snoopy Show
		11.55	Windmill
12.25	Carry On Jack	12.55	No Limits
1.55	News	1.55	Oh Yes I Am... Oh No You're Not
1.58	Weather for farmers		
2.00	EastEnders	2.50	Music in Camera
		3.20	Thinking Aloud
3.30	The Great Safari Bird Rally		
4.0	Aled Jones and Friends	4.0	The Pyrates
4.40	The Railway Children	5.25	Testament to the Bushmen
		6.15	Tomorrow's World 21st Birthday Special
6.25	News and Weather		
6.35	Songs of Praise		
7.15	Last of the Summer Wine	7.15	Madama Butterfly
7.50	Tootsie		
9.45	News and Weather	9.45	Sophie's Choice
10.0	New World		
12.10-12.15	Weather	12.10	Cricket: Fourth Test
		12.35-12.55	Classic Ghost Stories

Fig. 7:7

8 Calculators

A Using a calculator

The calculator is a small computer.

Charles Babbage, an Englishman, designed the first programmable computer in 1834. He never saw it built because the parts could not be made accurately enough. Babbage's computer was designed to work at **one addition per second.**

In the 1940s a special computer named ENIAC (for short) was built in America. ENIAC had 18 000 valves and was so big it occupied several rooms. It could carry out **5000 additions per second.**

A computer in the 1940s

In the 1980s a 'silicon chip' was developed that could carry out **400 000 operations per second.** It was about this size: ▬ .

Supercomputers are now being developed that will be able to carry out more than **10 000 000 000 calculations per second.** Other research is aimed at developing a computer that can **'think'**, rather than just calculate at a tremendous speed.

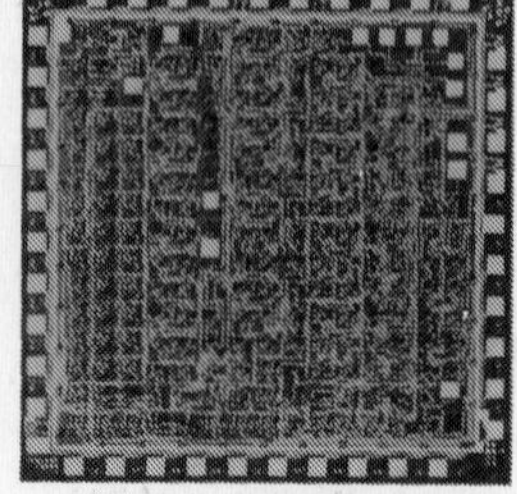

A microchip

1 Check the following answers.

(a) 905 + 9 + 2536 = 3450

(b) 879 × 234 = 205 686

(c) 64 009 ÷ 253 = 253 (d) 83·14 × 9·5 = 789·83

(e) £53·09 × 37 = £1964·33

(f) 89 − 456 + 600 = 233

2 Choose the correct answer, **A** or **B**.

(a) £5 + 85p should be keyed in as
A 5 ⊞ 85 B 5 ⊞ 0·85

(b) From 8000 subtract 35 should be keyed in as
A 35 ⊟ 8000 B 8000 ⊟ 35

(c) Find the sum of 83 and 47 should be keyed in as
A 83 ⊠ 47 B 83 ⊞ 47

(d) Find the product of 39 and 1·5 should be keyed in as
A 39 ⊠ 1·5 B 39 ⊞ 1·5

3 Choose the better approximation.

(a) 37 × 53 A 30 × 50 B 40 × 50

(b) 397 − 18 A 390 − 20 B 400 − 20

(c) £33·46 + £43·21 A £33 + £43 B £34 + £43

4 Read the following questions and then choose the correct calculation.

	Which calculation?
(a) Tom sold 105 of the 217 stamps in his collection. How many stamps had he left?	A 105 + 217 B 217 − 105 C 105 × 217 D 217 − 100 + 5
(b) Thirty-five people share a win of £215 425 on the pools. How much does each person receive?	A £215 425 ÷ 35 B £215 425 − 35 C £215 425 × 35
(c) Ann receives £4·35 change from a £10 note. This was £2 more than she should have received. How much change should she have had?	A £4·35 − £2 B £10 − £4·35 C £10 − £2 D £10 − £4·35 − £2

(d) The product of two numbers is 2072. One of the two numbers is 56. What is the other number?

A 2072 − 56
B 2072 × 56
C 2072 ÷ 56
D 56 + 2072

(e) Work out the answers for parts (a), (b), (c) and (d).

5 The numbers 1, 2, 3, 4, 6 and 12 all divide exactly into 12. We say that 1, 2, 3, 4, 6 and 12 are the **factors** of 12.

Which of the smaller numbers are factors of the largest number in the following sets?

(a) 2, 3, 5, 7 and 420

(b) 3, 4, 5, 6, 7, 8, 9 and 270

(c) 5, 10, 15, 20, 25, 30, 35, 40, 50 and 10 000

6 A 2p coin is 2 mm (two millimetres) thick. A pile of 2p coins is 12 cm (centimetres) high.

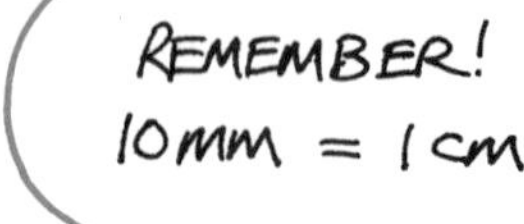

(a) How many coins are there in the pile?

(b) How much are the coins worth?

7 How can we obtain 96 by using the numbers 4, 12, 10 and 5, and any suitable operations?
One way is (4 × 12 × 10) ÷ 5 = 480 ÷ 5 = 96.

Do these using any operations you think are suitable. Think before you press the keys.

(a) Obtain 20 using 2, 5, 7, 10 and 4.

(b) Obtain 400 using 20, 12, 5 and 3.

(c) Obtain 1000 using 3, 6, 10, 10 and 5.

(d) Obtain 1320 using 20, 9, 50, 3 and 24.

(e) Obtain 1296 using 2, 2, 2, 2, 3 and 36.

8 Using each of the figures 1 to 9 once only, write correct multiplication examples, like 432 × 78 = 1659 (though this is wrong!). You will need to think very carefully about what placings are possible. We think there are nine answers; two have the answer 5346 and two have the answer 5796. All the examples have one of the two multiplying numbers starting with a 1.

B Magnus

British Petroleum (BP) Ltd discovered the most northerly oil field in the North Sea in 1974. They named it **Magnus**, after the Viking Saint of Orkney.

To cope with the find BP developed and produced the *Magnus* oil platform. The huge jacket of the production platform is the biggest single steel structure in the world.

Approximately 200 people live and work on the platform, working twelve-hour shifts in a two-week on, two-week off rota.

Facts and figures about *Magnus*

- Height (from sea-bed to top of the flare) — 312 m (≈ 1020 ft)
- Total weight — 70 000 tonnes
- Cost of development — £1 300 000 000
- Depth of sea at site — 186 m (≈ 612 ft)
- Number of piles securing *Magnus* to sea-bed — 36
- Piles are driven into sea-bed down to — 90 m (≈ 300 ft) (approx.)
- May have to withstand wind speed of — over 100 m.p.h.
- May have to withstand waves — 30 m high (≈ 100 ft)
- Length of electrical cable installed — 1680 kilometres
- Depth below sea-bed of oil (approx.) — 2700 m (≈ 9000 ft)
- Quantity of recoverable oil (approx.) — 565 million barrels
- Daily peak production of oil (approx.) — 120 000 barrels

REMEMBER!
m stands for metres.
ft stands for feet.
≈ means 'is approximately equal to'.

Use the information about *Magnus* to answer these questions.

1 How many times higher than a 30 feet high house is:

(a) the overall height of *Magnus*

(b) one of the deepest sea-bed piles

(c) the depth below the sea-bed of the oil?

2 How many 3·5 tonne elephants would equal the weight of *Magnus*?

3 How many £5000 cars could you buy for the cost of developing *Magnus*?

4 The photo shows *Magnus* standing in the Thames! About how high do you think are the Houses of Parliament?

5 (a) How many metres of electrical cable are installed in *Magnus*?

(b) Taking 1 m ≈ 3·29 ft, how many feet of cable are installed?

6 *Magnus* is producing about 120 000 barrels of oil a day. If production carries on without a break how many barrels is this in

(a) a week (b) a year of 365 days?

7 If one barrel sells for £16, what is production worth in

(a) a day (b) a week

(c) in April?

8 If three meals a day per person are served on *Magnus*, approximately how many meals are served in

(a) a day (b) a week (c) a year?

C Solutions by trial and improvement

'Solve' means 'find what number is represented by x'.

Example Solve $x^2 - x = 8$.

First make a sensible estimate of the value of x. An estimate of $x = 3$ gives $3^2 - 3 = 9 - 3 = \mathbf{6}$.
As the answer has to be 8, or near to 8, it is obvious that $x = 3$ is near, but a bit too small.

Try $x = 4$, giving $4^2 - 4 = 16 - 4 = \mathbf{12}$.
$x = 4$ is too big.

Try a number between 3 and 4, say $x = 3{\cdot}5$. Using a calculator: 3·5 [x^2] [−] 3·5 [=] which gives 8·75.
$x = 3{\cdot}5$ is a little too big.

Further trials might be $x = 3{\cdot}4$, $x = 3{\cdot}3$, $x = 3{\cdot}35$ and $x = 3{\cdot}37$.
$x = 3{\cdot}37$ gives 3·37 [x^2] [−] 3·37 [=] 7·9869.
7·9869 is very close to 8, so 3·37 is a satisfactory solution to the equation $x^2 - x = 8$.

Solve these, correct to two decimal places where necessary.

1 $x^2 - x = 6$ **2** $x^2 - x = 12$

3 $x^2 - x = 18$ **4** $x^2 - x = 22$

5 $x^2 + x = 15$ **6** $x^2 + x = 60$

9 Decimal fractions

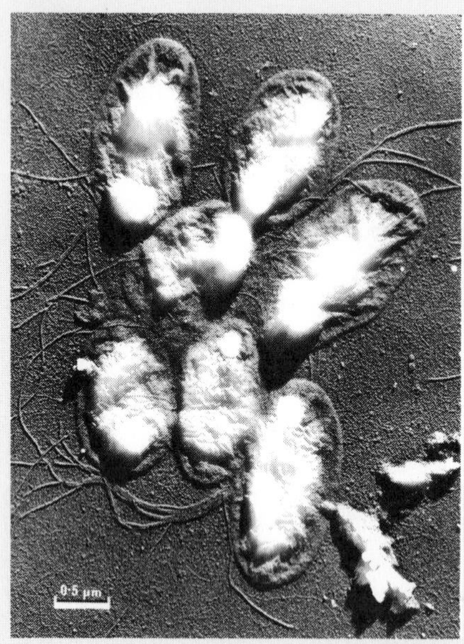

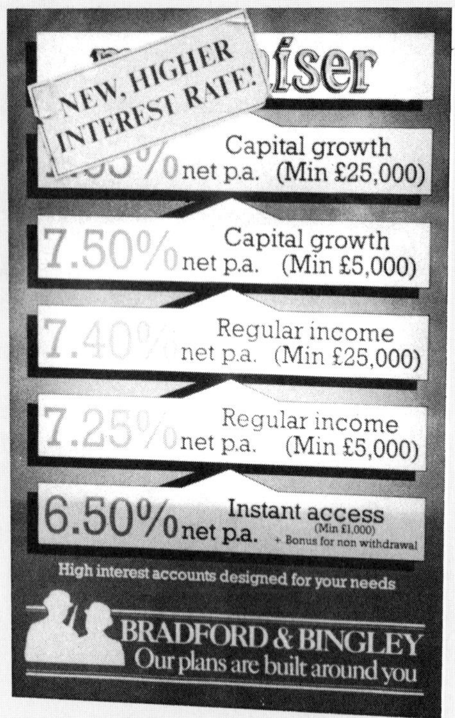

To remind you . . .

- **Place value**

The number 123·456 means

1 hundred + 2 tens + 3 ones + 4 tenths + 5 hundredths + 6 thousandths.

Notice how the place values become ten times **smaller** as we go from **left to right**:

100s → 10s → 1s → $\frac{1}{10}$s → $\frac{1}{100}$s → $\frac{1}{1000}$s.

123·456 is represented in Figure 9:1. Note how much smaller the 6 thousandths are than the 1 hundred.

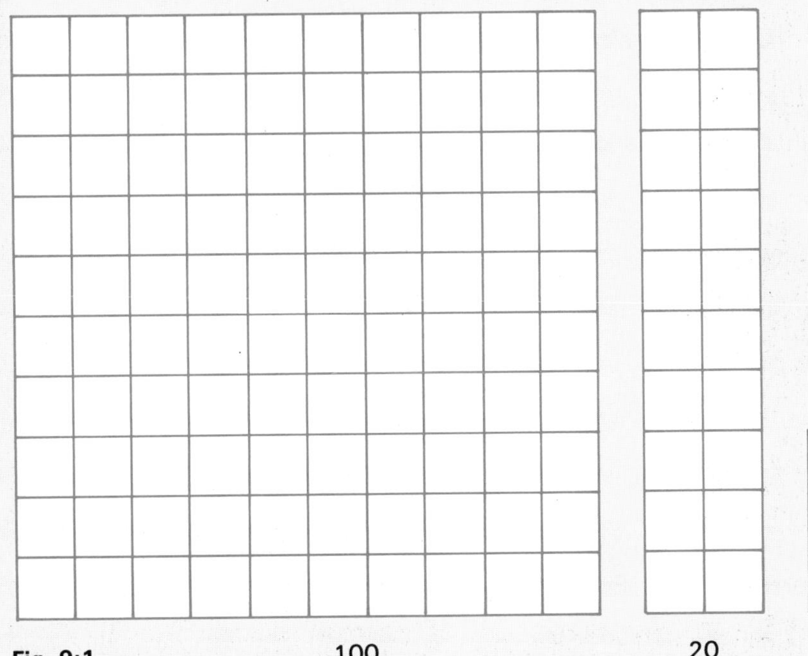

Fig. 9:1

Although you probably use a calculator for most of your decimal arithmetic, it is useful to be able to do simple questions without a calculator.

Example (a) 8·3 + 17·06 + 180

```
   8·30
  17·06
 180·00 +
 ------
 205·36
```

(b) 23 − 5·7

```
 23·0
  5·7 −
 ----
 17·3
```

(c) 8·6 × 200

= 8·6 × 2 × 100
= 17·2 × 100
= **1720**

(d) 8·6 × 2·7

```
   86
   27 ×
  ----
  602
 1720
 ----
 2322 → 23·22
```

9

1 9·37 in words is 'nine point three seven'. Write in words:

(a) 29·37 (b) 45·07 (c) 50·705 (d) 900·06

2 Figure 9:2 contains 100 equal-size squares. We can describe square A as one hundredth or 0·01 of the complete square. Shape B is ten hundredths or 0·10 of the complete square.

(a) In the same way describe shape:
(i) C (ii) D (iii) E
(iv) F (v) G

(b) What decimal part of the whole figure is **not** shaded?

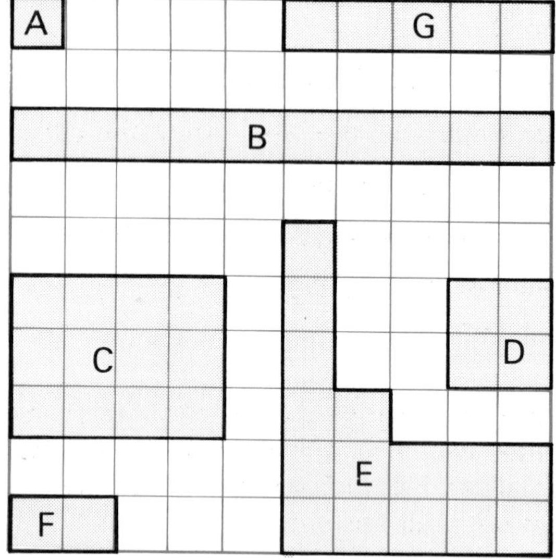

Fig. 9:2

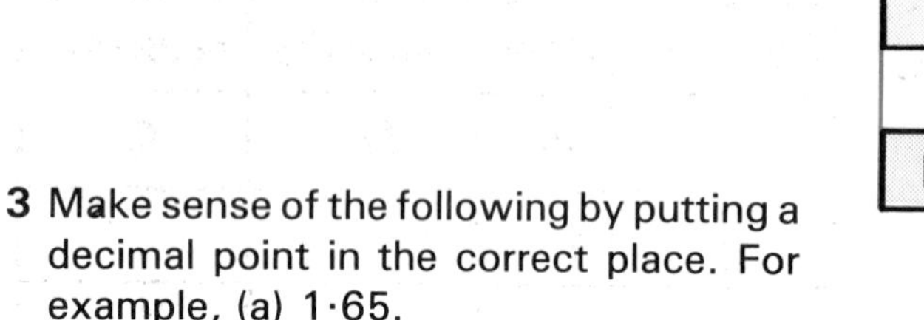

3 Make sense of the following by putting a decimal point in the correct place. For example, (a) 1·65.

(a) The girl was about 165 metres tall.

(b) The pair of shoes cost John £1956.

(c) The classroom was 1345 metres long.

(d) It was a warm day, about 205 degrees Celsius.

(e) Men live on average to be 715 years old.

(f) The elephant weighed 5347 tonnes.

(g) The ant was 53 centimetres long.

(h) The distance around a circle is about 314 times its diameter.

NOTE

A metre is about half the height of a house door.
A tonne is about the weight of a family car.

4 Work out the following.

(a) $5 \cdot 3 + 12 \cdot 9$ (b) $18 + 2 \cdot 35$

(c) $100 \cdot 4 + 1 \cdot 54$ (d) $5 \cdot 6 - 2 \cdot 5$

(e) $9 \cdot 7 - 6 \cdot 8$ (f) $10 - 4 \cdot 6$ (g) $1 \cdot 5 \times 2 \cdot 3$

(h) $23 \times 2 \cdot 6$ (i) $34 \cdot 6 \times 2 \cdot 5$

5 Solve these clues to the word puzzle in Figure 9:3 and write down the answers.

(a) 0·37 is 37 . . .

(b) 0·1 is one . . .

(c) 0.25 and 3.8 are decimal . . .

(d) Separates the whole from the part.

(e) 100 cm equals one . . .

(f) A fraction is a . . . of something.

(g) The 5 in 0·05 is in the second decimal . . .

(a)				D	R					
(b)				E						
(c)	F			C						
(d)				I						
(e)				M						
(f)				A						
(g)				L						

Fig. 9:3

6 Place the following decimal numbers in order of size, beginning with the smallest. Figure 9:4 shows you how to set out your answer.

0·5 2·34 0·49 2·326

2·33 0·51 0·409 2·199

2·201 0·499 2·309 2·3

Units	•	tenths	hundredths	thousandths
0	·	4	0	9
0	·	4	9	

Fig. 9:4

7 (a) The weight of parcel A in Figure 9:5 is 2·6 kg. Give the weights of the other four parcels.

(b) Find the sum of the weights of
(i) parcels A and B (ii) parcels C and E
(iii) all five parcels.

(c) Find the difference between the weights of these parcels:
(i) A and B (ii) D and E (iii) C and E.

A

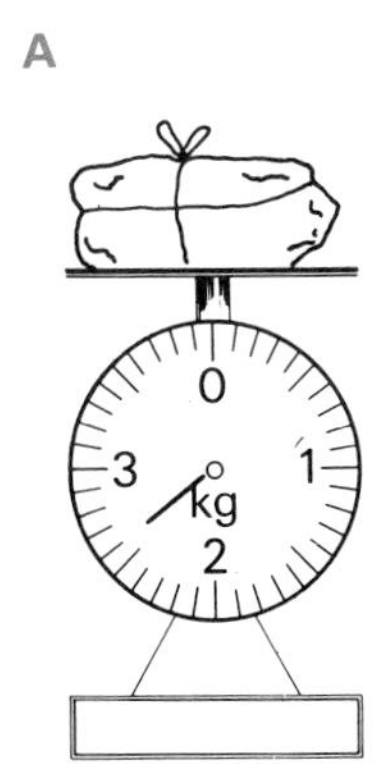

B

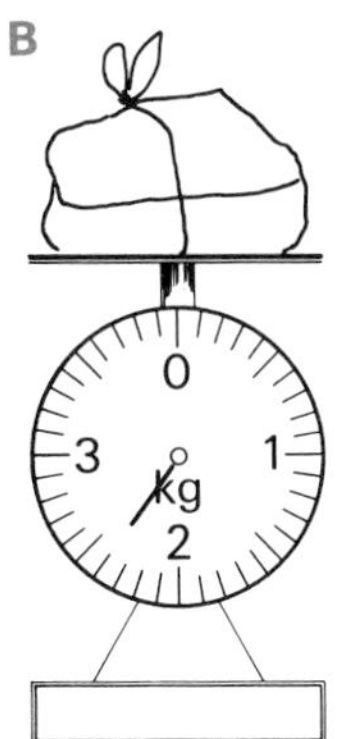

C

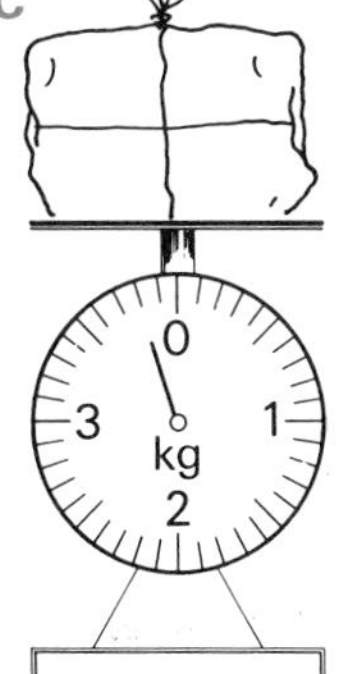

D

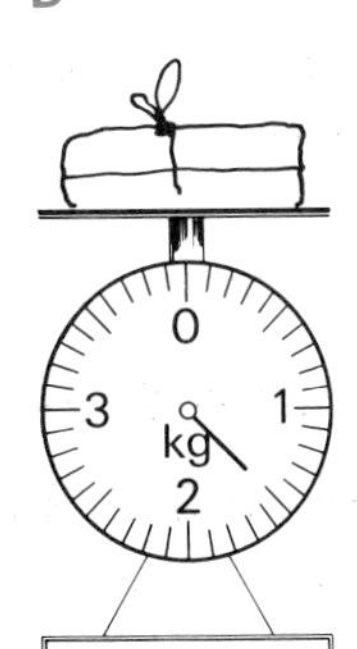

E

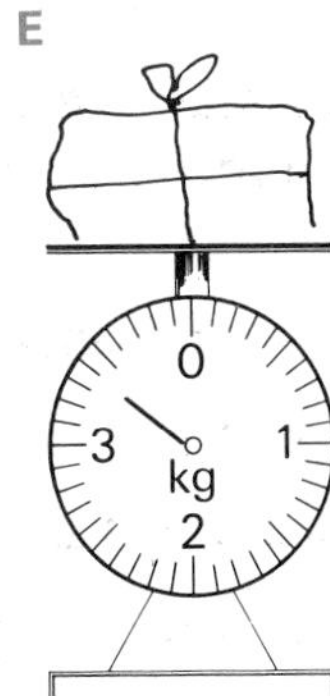

Fig. 9:5

8 Study the example and then copy and complete the table.

Example

- 6·1 × 10 = 6 1· = **61** (move one place for 10).
- 6·1 × 100 = 6 1 0· = **610** (move two places for 100).
- 6·1 × 1000 = 6 1 0 0· = **6100** (move three places for 1000).
- 6·1 × 200 = 6·1 × 2 × 100 = 12·2 × 100 = **1220**.

Number	6	6·1	6·12	61	61·2	0·6	0·61	0·612
× 10							6·1	
× 100						60		
× 20								

9 In 1937 Sydney Wooderson set a world record for running the mile in 4 min 6·4 s. In 1981 Sebastian Coe set a world record for the mile of 3 min 47·3 s. Find the difference between the two times.

10 The symbol $<$ means 'is less than'.
The symbol $>$ means 'is greater than'.
So 0·5 $>$ 0·49 can be read as '0·5 is greater than 0·49'.
Remember that 0·5 = 0·50.

Copy the following and insert the correct symbol $<$ or $>$ or = in the spaces.

(a) 0·5 0·50 (b) 10·4 9·9 (c) 0·07 0·1

(d) 0·905 0·92 (e) 0·810 0·81 (f) 1·07 1·7

(g) 1·001 1·1 (h) 0·006 0·01 (i) 0·3 0·300

11 Work out:

(a) 18 + 23·45 + 108 (b) 56 − 8·32

(c) 2305 + 5·32 (d) 89·2 − 23·7

(e) 23·4 × 4·3 (f) 45·23 × 2·4

12 Given that 6·3 × 14·7 = 92·61, write down the value of:

(a) 6·3 × 1·47 (b) 0·63 × 147 (WJEC)

13 Wendy was ill in hospital. Figure 9:6 shows her temperature at midday over seven days.

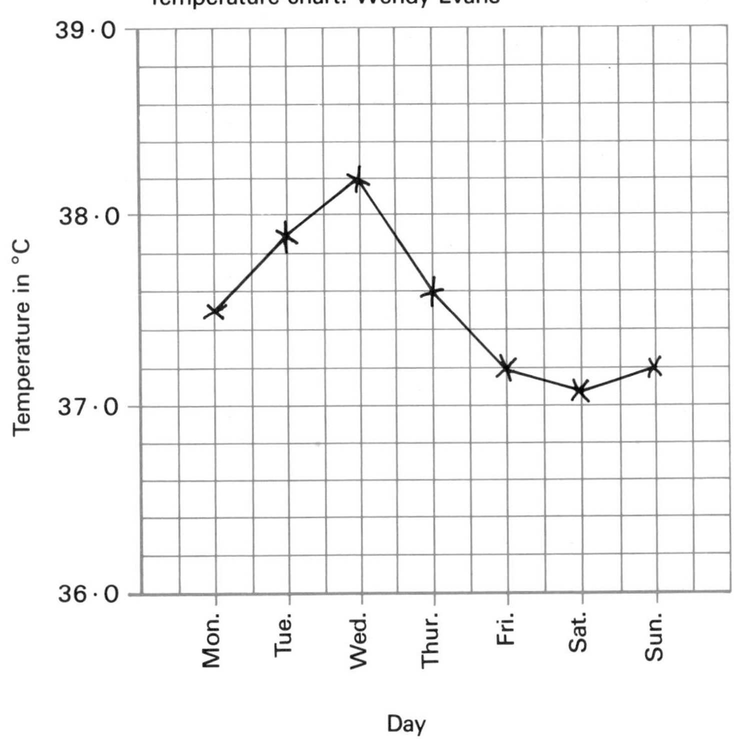

Fig. 9:6

(a) Write down the seven temperatures as decimal numbers. For example, Monday 37·5 °C.

(b) Find the difference between the temperatures on:
(i) Monday and Wednesday
(ii) Wednesday and Friday

14 A motoring organisation estimated that for a car covering 10 000 miles or more per year the average cost per mile was 15·3p.

(a) What would be the total cost for a car covering 10 000 miles? Give your answer in pounds.

(b) What would be the total cost for a car covering 18 400 miles in a year? Give your answer in pounds and pence.

15 It was estimated that during the months of May, June, July and August the water level at a reservoir dropped by an average of 1·23 cm a day. How far did the water level drop during the four months?

16 Copy the following, replacing the stars by the correct numbers.

(a) 6·4 × * = 64 (b) 8·32 × * = 83·2

(c) 7·16 × * = 716 (d) 0·142 × * = 41·2

(e) * × 10 = 61·2 (f) * × 10 = 97·4

(g) * × 100 = 33·1 (h) * × 100 = 1·6

17 Steel bridges will expand by 0·000 011 of their length for every 1 °C rise in temperature.

(a) What would be the expansion of a 1000 feet long steel bridge with a 1 °C rise in temperature?

(b) What would be the expansion of the same bridge with an 8 °C rise in temperature?

10 Conversion graphs

To convert means to change. Figure 10:1 shows a graph to convert between gallons and litres.

▶ Points to discuss . . .

1. How useful is this conversion graph?
2. Suggest ways of improving the graph.
3. What other conversion graphs might be useful?

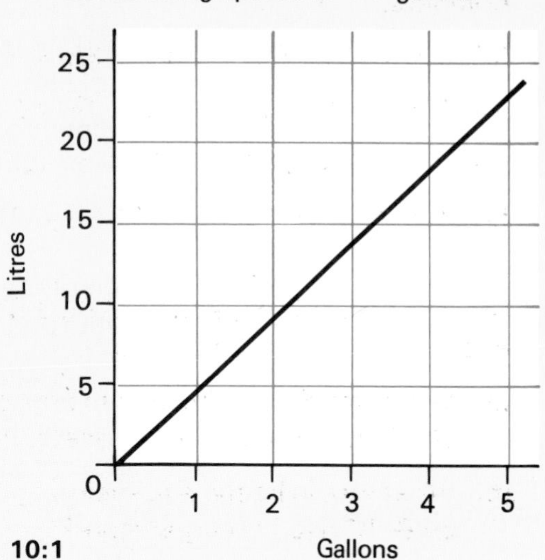

Fig. 10:1

1 10 kilograms is about 22 pounds in weight. 10 kg $\approx$ 22 lb.

(a) About how many lb in weight is:
(i) 20 kg (ii) 50 kg?

(b) Draw a graph for changing pounds to kilograms and kilograms to pounds. Use scales:
Horizontal: 1 cm to 5 kg, from 0 kg to 50 kg.
Vertical: 1 cm to 10 lb, from 0 lb to 110 lb.

Plot the two points (10 kg, 22 lb), (50 kg, 110 lb) and draw a straight line through them.

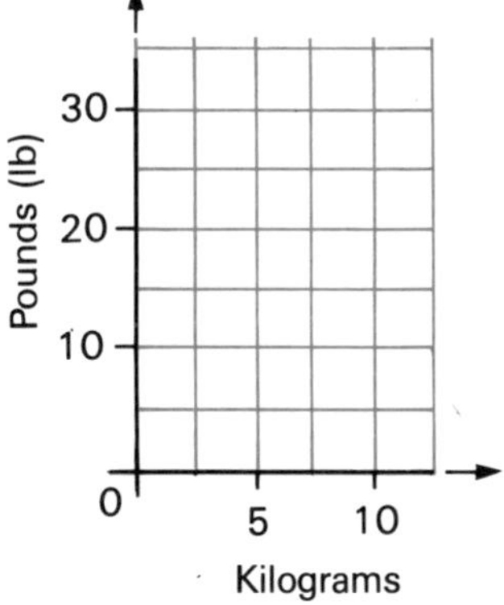

Fig. 10:2

(c) Why is it only necessary to plot two points to draw this graph?

(d) What does 1 millimetre on the vertical axis represent in pounds?

(e) Use your graph to change 20 kg, 30 kg and 35 kg to pounds, correct to the nearest lb.

(f) Use your graph to change 20 lb, 50 lb and 100 lb to kilograms, correct to the nearest kg.

2 On 30th March 1984, 3·70 Deutschmarks (DM) could be changed for £1. Draw a conversion graph for £s and DM. Use scales:

Horizontal: 2 cm to DM 5, from DM 0 to DM 25.
Vertical: 2 cm to £1, from £0 to £5.

Use your graph to change the following sterling amounts to DM. You could check your answers with a calculator.

(a) £2 (b) £5 (c) £3·50 (d) £4·80 (e) 50p

3 These tables show the stopping distances of a car at different speeds on a dry road and on a wet road.

Dry road

Speed in m.p.h.	10	20	30	40	50	60	70	80	90
Stopping distance in feet	15	40	75	120	175	240	315	400	495

Wet road

Speed in m.p.h.	10	20	30	40	50	60	70	80	90
Stopping distance in feet	20	60	120	200	300	420	560	720	900

Draw a graph using scales:
Horizontal axis: 1 cm to 10 m.p.h., from 0 to 90 m.p.h.
Vertical axis: 1 cm to 100 feet, from 0 to 1000 feet.

(a) On the graph plot the nine points from the first table (dry road) and join them with a smooth curve. Label the curve 'Dry road'.

(b) On the same graph plot the nine points from the second table (wet road) and join them with a smooth curve using a different colour. Label the curve 'Wet road'.

(c) From the graph estimate the difference in stopping distances on a wet road and on a dry road at 85 m.p.h.

(d) From the graph estimate the maximum safe speed on a wet road 250 feet from a blind corner. (LEAG)

4 Design a conversion graph for changing temperatures in degrees Celsius to degrees Fahrenheit and vice versa. What are the approximate Celsius temperatures for:

(a) 40 °F (b) 65 °F (c) 80 °F?

0°C = 32°F
100°C = 212°F

Take a break 2

A Look out

Copy this diagram on squared paper. Try to draw four straight lines passing through all nine points without taking your pencil off the paper.

Fig. B2:1

B Seven to five

Move three matchsticks so that there are five small squares instead of seven.

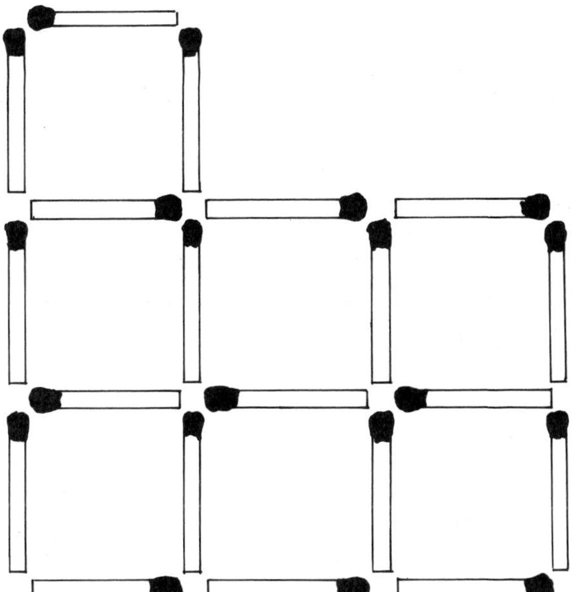

Fig. B2:2

Can you do this by removing two matchsticks or four matchsticks?

C Side-step

This is a game for two players. Use different colours and a ten-by-ten grid.

Each player takes it in turn to put an **X** or an **O** in a square.

The winner is the one who fills four or more adjoining squares in the shape of a triangle, a square or a rectangle (see Figure B2:3). (A diagonal 'rectangle' is not allowed.)

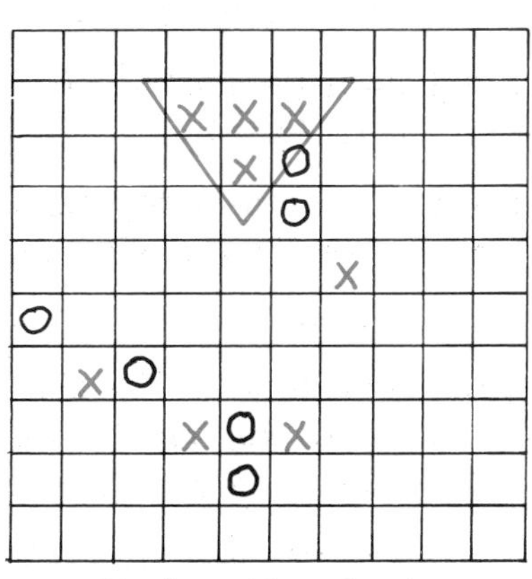

X wins with a triangle.

Fig. B2:3

11 Common fractions: cancelling

To remind you . . .

- $\frac{2}{5}$ (two-fifths) is a common fraction.
  The 5 tells into how many parts a whole one has been divided.
  The 2 tells how many of these parts make up the fraction.
- $2\frac{2}{5}$ is a mixed number. What is it a mix of?

Points to discuss

1 What do we mean when we refer to 'a fraction'?

2 Which is the numerator part and which is the denominator part of a common fraction?

3 Figure 11:1 shows that $\frac{4}{8}$ is the same fraction as $\frac{1}{2}$.
This can be shown by cancelling:

$$\frac{4}{8} \xrightarrow{\text{divide top and bottom by 4}} \frac{\not{4}^{1}}{\not{8}_{2}}$$

Cancel $\frac{45}{60}$.

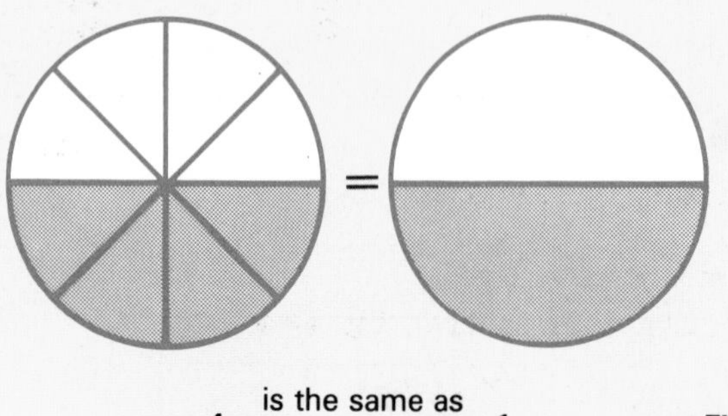

$\frac{4}{8}$ ⟵ is the same as ⟶ $\frac{1}{2}$ **Fig. 11:1**

4 Cancelling is sometimes called 'simplifying' or 'reducing to the lowest terms'.

Reduce to their lowest terms:

$\frac{3}{6}$ $\frac{4}{12}$ $\frac{5}{20}$ $\frac{15}{20}$ $\frac{24}{30}$ $\frac{30}{40}$

$\frac{18}{36}$ $\frac{9}{15}$ $\frac{36}{45}$ $\frac{21}{35}$

A 18	B $\frac{3}{9}=\frac{1}{3}$	C mixed number
D 12	E cancelling	F top number
G $\frac{2}{7}$	H part of something	I $\frac{6}{9}=\frac{2}{3}$

Fig. 11:2

1 The answers to (a)–(i) are given in Figure 11:2. Write down the letter which answers each question. For example, (a) H.

(a) A fraction is a . . .

(b) The numerator is the . . .

(c) Reducing a fraction to its lowest terms means . . .

(d) $\frac{18}{36}$ can be cancelled by dividing both numbers by . . .

(e) Parts A, B and C of Figure 11:3 together total . . . of the whole rectangle.

(f) Parts B, C, D, G, H and I of Figure 11:3 together total . . . of the whole rectangle.

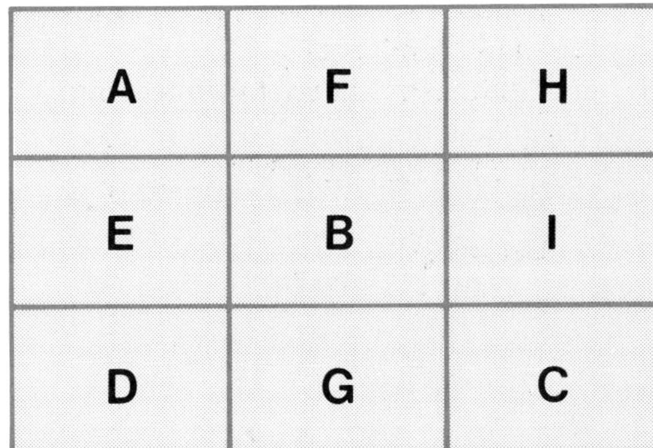

Fig. 11:3

(g) $3\frac{1}{7}$ is called a . . .

(h) The lowest number that will divide exactly by 2 and 3 and 4 and 6 and 12 is . . .

(i) . . . of Figure 11:4 is shaded. 

Fig. 11:4

2 The fraction $\frac{2}{7}$ can be written as 'two-sevenths'.

$\frac{2}{7}$ can be shown as 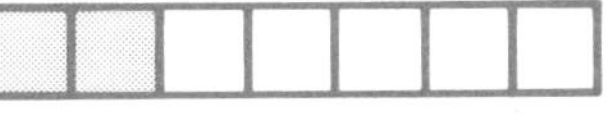

$\frac{5}{7}$ (five-sevenths) of  is unshaded.

Write three sentences like the ones above about:

(a) $\frac{1}{4}$ (b) $\frac{1}{3}$ (c) $\frac{2}{3}$ (d) $\frac{5}{6}$

3 Unscramble the following words.

(a) westol sertm (b) petillum (c) mmoocn

(d) dimxe (e) ifsiplmy

4 $\{\frac{2}{4}, \frac{3}{6}, \frac{2}{6}, \frac{2}{8}, \frac{4}{8}, \frac{3}{9}, \frac{4}{12}, \frac{6}{12}, \frac{3}{12}, \frac{2}{16}, \frac{4}{16}, \frac{8}{16}, \frac{3}{24}, \frac{6}{24}, \frac{18}{24}, \frac{8}{24}\}$

(a) Cancel all sixteen fractions to their lowest terms. For example,

$$\frac{\not{8}^{1}}{\not{24}_{3}} \rightarrow \frac{1}{3}$$

(b) From the set of sixteen fractions list the fractions belonging to sets A, B and C where:

A = {fractions equal to $\frac{1}{4}$}

B = {fractions equal to $\frac{1}{3}$}

C = {fractions equal to $\frac{1}{8}$}

5 $\frac{9}{5}$ is a 'top-heavy' or improper fraction.
$\frac{9}{5}$ as a mixed number is $1\frac{4}{5}$.

Change the following improper fractions into mixed numbers. Cancel if necessary, e.g. $\frac{15}{9} = 1\frac{6}{9} = 1\frac{2}{3}$.

(a) $\frac{5}{4}$ (b) $\frac{7}{3}$ (c) $\frac{19}{5}$ (d) $\frac{21}{9}$ (e) $\frac{25}{10}$ (f) $\frac{18}{12}$

6

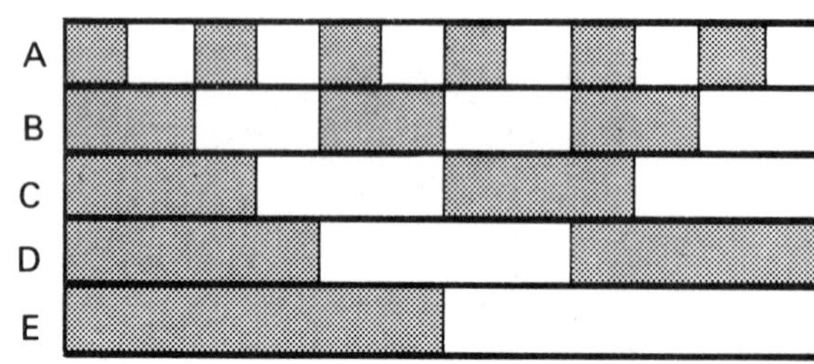

Fig. 11:5

This diagram shows a pattern made up of grey and white tiles. The tiles are five different lengths.

(a) How many tiles are there in:
(i) row A (ii) row B
(iii) row D?

(b) What fraction of each of the five rows is one tile in that row?

(c) What fraction of row D is made up of grey tiles?

7 Seventy-two pupils at Townfield School stay for school dinners. The table shows the results of a survey to find out their first and second choices of meals.

Copy the table and complete the columns showing the fractions.

Meal	First choice	Fraction	Second choice	Fraction
Egg, chips and bacon	36		24	
Steak and kidney pudding	12	$\frac{12}{72} = \frac{1}{6}$	18	
Fish, peas and potatoes	3		6	
Meat pie, beans and potatoes	12		16	
Roast lamb, peas and potatoes	9		8	
Total:	72		72	

8 Simplify:

(a) $\frac{24}{27}$ (b) $\frac{36}{48}$ (c) $\frac{75}{100}$ (d) $\frac{18}{54}$

(e) $\frac{77}{110}$ (f) $\frac{50}{250}$ (g) $\frac{31}{93}$

9 Two different numbers of cubes can be seen here. Some have coloured tops. The others have coloured bottoms.

(a) Write down the two different numbers of cubes.

(b) What fraction of the total number of cubes are the cubes with coloured tops?

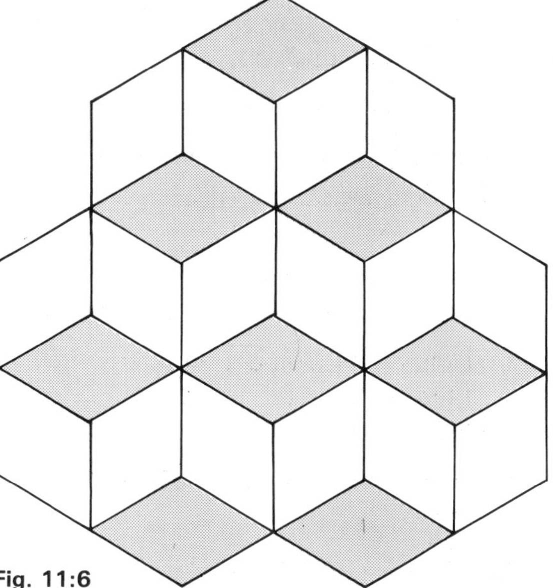

Fig. 11:6

10 A tangram square is shown in Figure 11:7.

(a) Name the different shapes in the square.

HINT
The name for shape C has 13 letters, starts with P and ends with M.

(b) What fraction of the tangram square is each shape?

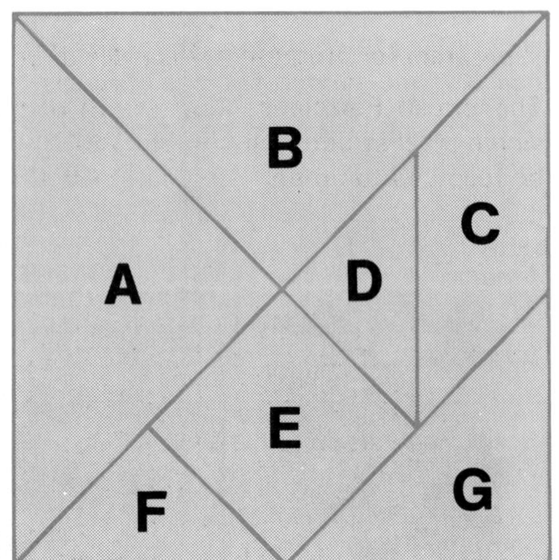

Fig. 11:7

11 A zoo contains two elephants, four tigers, six hyenas, ten wolves, five bears, eighteen monkeys and fifteen snakes. What fraction of the total number of animals is each kind of animal?

12 Flow-charts

A **program** (or programme) is a set of instructions.

The British Petroleum *Magnus* oil platform is the biggest single steel structure in the world. A careful program had to be followed to up-end *Magnus* in the North Sea.

Computers are programmed.

When you were taught how to cross the road safely you were taught a program.

A program must be sensible and well thought out. Its steps can be shown in a **flow-chart**.

Instructions and decisions

Three shapes are used for different things in a program.

- **Start** or **Stop** is inside a running-track shape.
- **Instructions** are inside rectangles.
- **Decisions** (where we need to answer a **question**) are inside diamond shapes.

Start/Stop

Instructions

Decisions

Fig. 12:1

Figure 12:2 shows a flow-chart for the Green Cross Code.

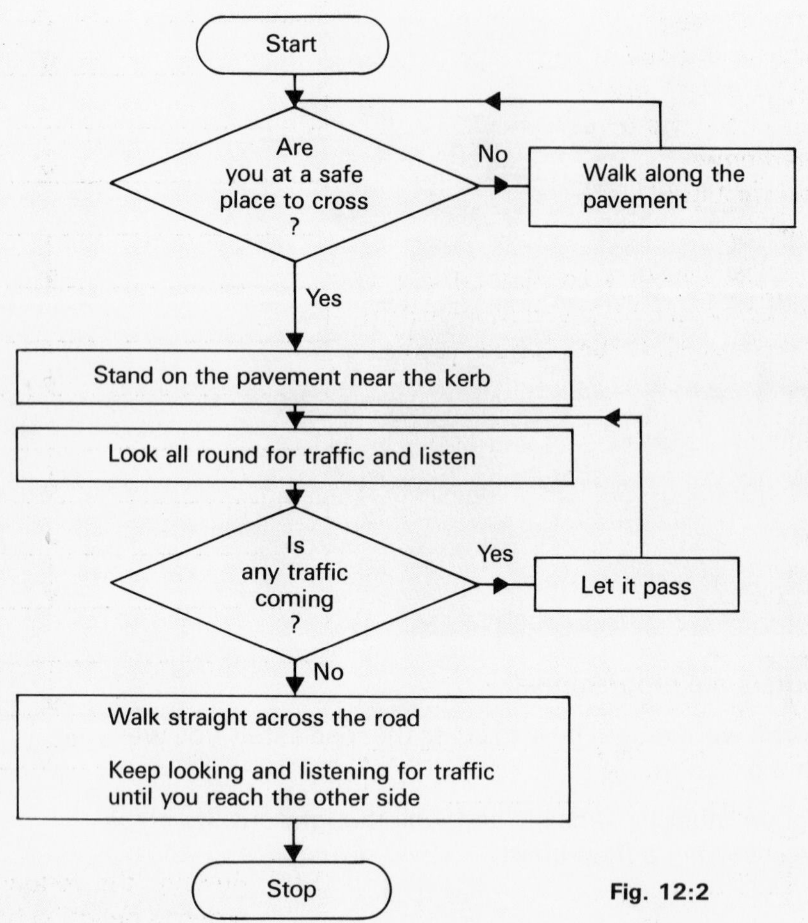

Fig. 12:2

Large blank flow-charts for this exercise are on worksheets 12A and 12B.

1 (a) Rewrite these instructions for washing your face in a sensible order.

Take out plug
Put plug in bowl
Dry face with towel
Run water into bowl
Clean bowl
Replace towel
Wash face

(b) Put your answers to part (a) in the correct boxes of the flow-chart on worksheet 12A. (See Figure 12:3.)

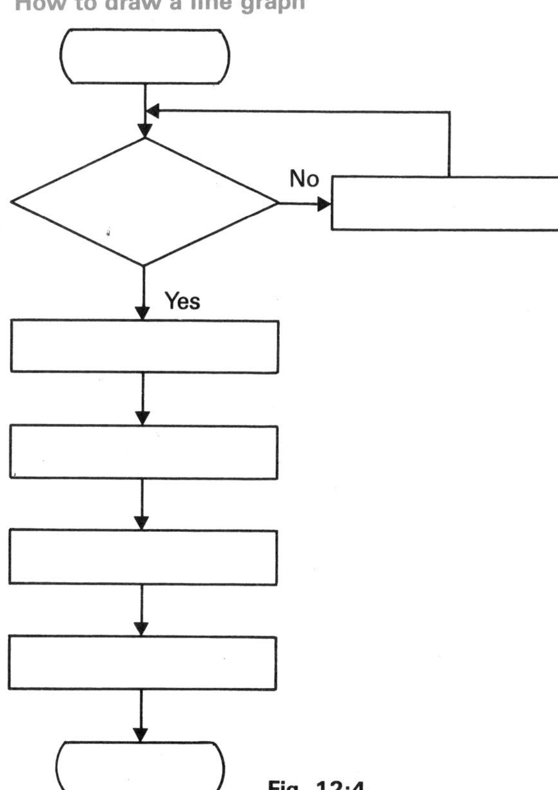

Fig. 12:4

Washing your face

Start

Stop

Fig. 12:3

2 (a) Rewrite the following in a sensible order to describe how to draw a line graph.

Draw the two axes
Examine the information
Stop *Start*
Join the points with a curved or a straight line
Find a sharp pencil and a ruler
Plot the points
Have you a sharp pencil and a ruler?

(b) Put your answers to part (a) in the correct places of the flow-chart on worksheet 12A. (See Figure 12:4.)

3 (a) Rewrite the following in a sensible order to describe how to find the area of a square.

Write the answer in square units
Have you a ruler?
Multiply the length of side by itself
Find a ruler
Measure the length of one side

(b) Put your answers in the correct places of the flow-chart on worksheet 12B. (See Figure 12:5.)

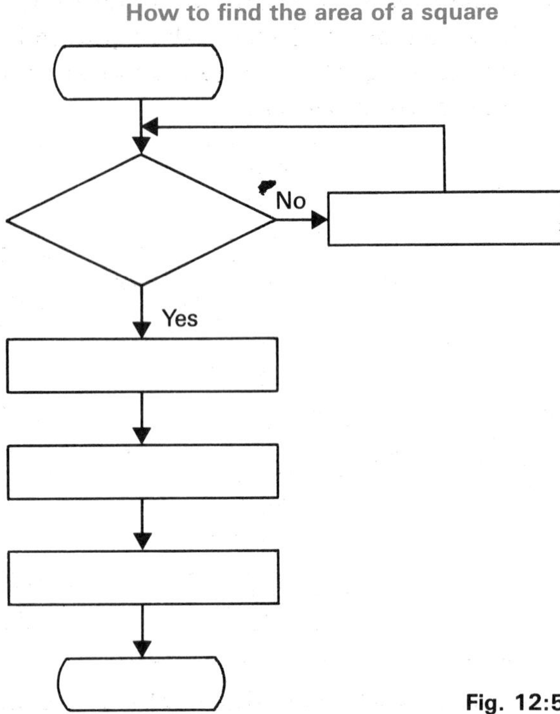

Fig. 12:5

How to check if a number is a prime

Start
Is the number even?
Yes
No
Stop

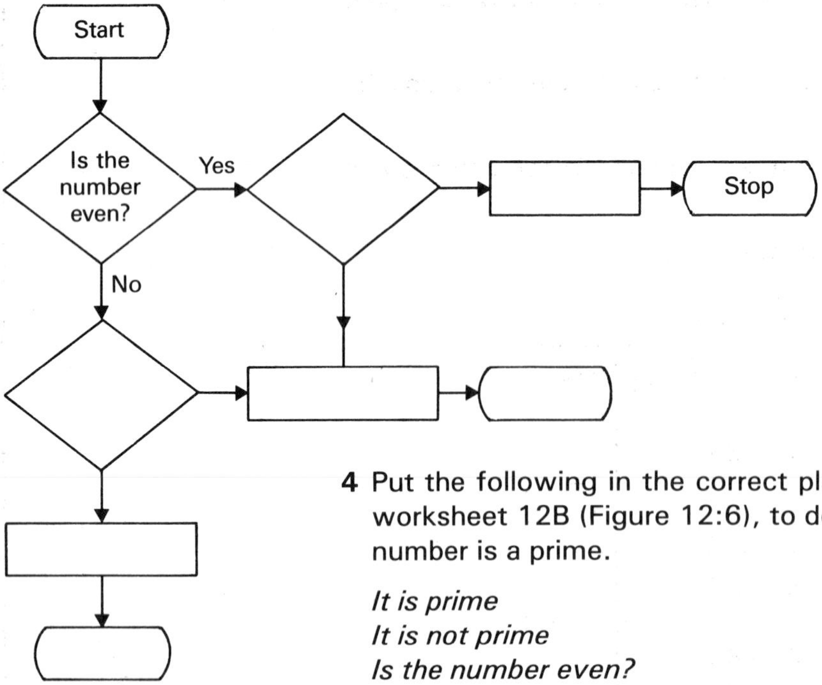

Fig. 12:6

Write 'yes' or 'No' where necessary.

4 Put the following in the correct places of the flowchart on worksheet 12B (Figure 12:6), to describe how to check if a number is a prime.

It is prime
It is not prime
Is the number even?
Can the number be divided exactly by an odd number (other than 1) which is smaller than itself?
Is it 2?
It is prime

5 Floella's moped runs smoothly and is easy to start. Every time she slows down it stalls, the lights fade and the indicators stop flashing. Use the flow-chart in Figure 12:7 to find out what is wrong with it. (SEG)

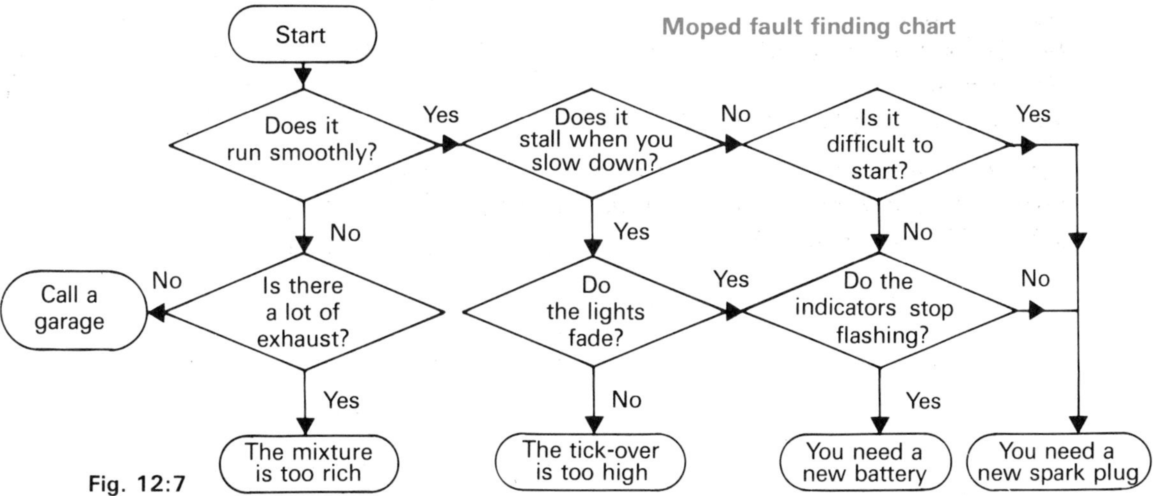

Fig. 12:7

6 The library teacher thought he would put the rules for using the library into a flow-chart. The result is shown in Figure 12:8 on page 64.

(a) John Andrews is in the fifth year. When can he use the library?

(b) Jean Prince is in the second year. When can she use the library?

(c) Copy and complete this table.

Use of library

Surname initial	Years	Days	Time
A to O	1 to 3		
P to Z	1 to 3		
A to O	4 to 6		
P to Z	4 to 6		

Worksheet 12C may be used here.

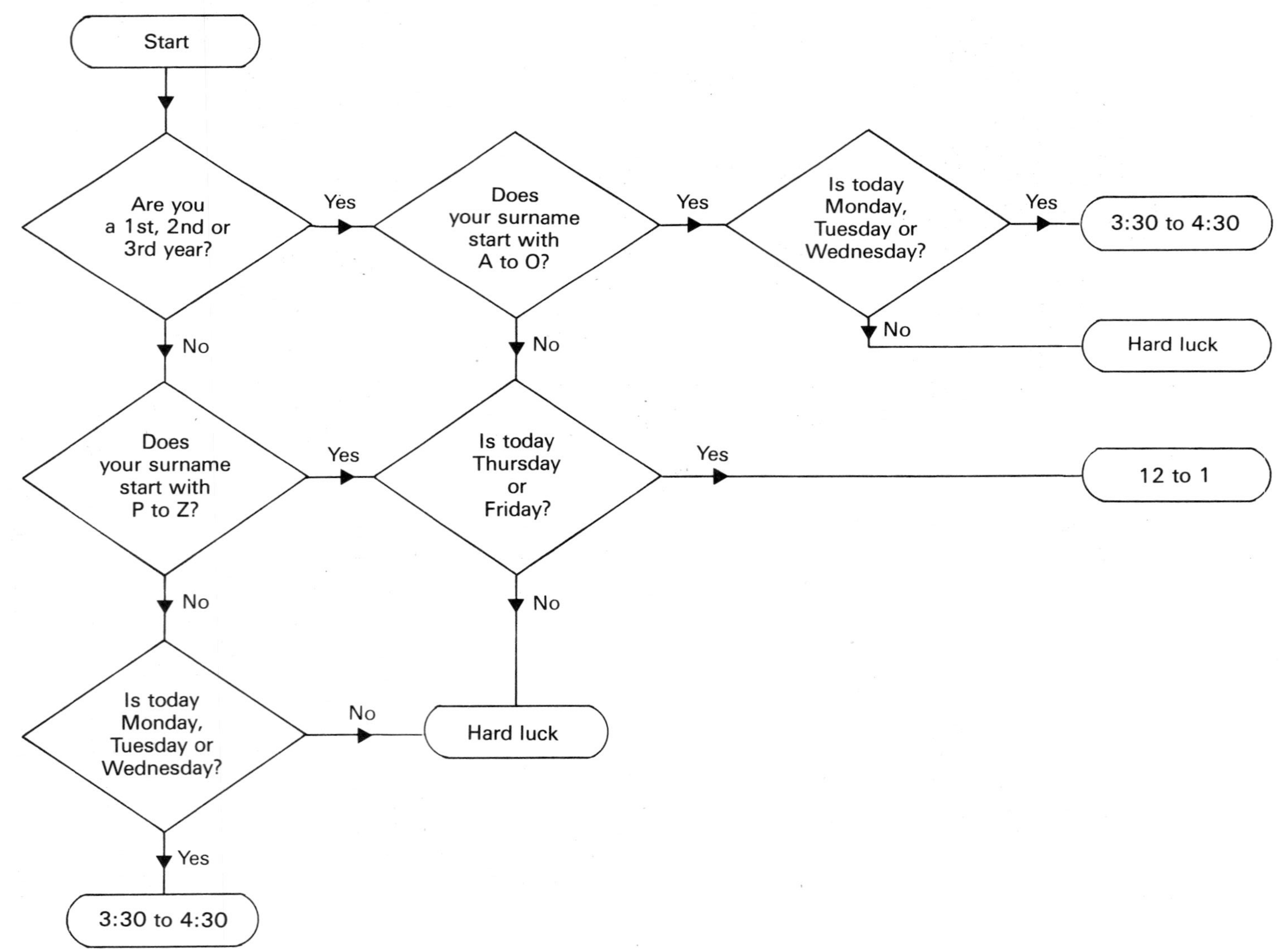
Start
Are you a 1st, 2nd or 3rd year?
Yes
No
Does your surname start with A to O?
Yes
No
Is today Monday, Tuesday or Wednesday?
Yes
No
3:30 to 4:30
Hard luck
Does your surname start with P to Z?
Yes
No
Is today Thursday or Friday?
Yes
No
12 to 1
Hard luck
Is today Monday, Tuesday or Wednesday?
No
Yes
3:30 to 4:30

Fig. 12:8

13 Ratio; enlargement

A Ratio

A ratio compares two quantities.

Examples The ratio of boys to girls in class 3D is 2 : 3 ('two to three'). Figure 13:1 illustrates this.

The ratio of females to males over 75 years old is about 2 : 1.

The number of known crimes in the UK in 1987 compared to 1951 was about 6 : 1.

Pupils in class 3D

Boys	
Girls	

Each symbol represents 5 pupils

Fig. 13:1

▶ Points to discuss . . .

1 Two chain wheels of a bicycle are shown in Figure 13:2. The larger wheel, A, has 36 teeth and the smaller wheel, B, has 12 teeth.

When A turns once, B turns three times. We say that the wheels have a **gear ratio** of **1 : 3**.

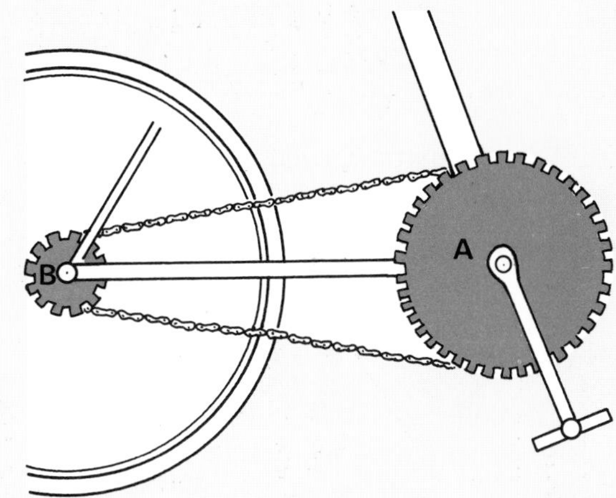

Fig. 13:2

2 Angeli's pay compared to Karl's is in the ratio 4 : 5. Angeli earns £120. What does Karl earn?

Angeli's 4 parts make £120
so one part is £120 ÷ 4 = £30.
Karl's 5 parts are then 5 × £30 = £150.

3 The ratio 15 : 25 can be simplified like a fraction by dividing both numbers, that is by 'cancelling'.

15 : 25 —divide both numbers by 5→ 3 : 5

13

1 (a) Two gear wheels have a ratio of 4 : 1. How many times does the smaller wheel turn for one turn of the larger wheel?

(b) If the smaller wheel turns once, what fraction of one turn will the larger wheel turn?

2 (a) Simplify the ratio 30 : 70.

(b) What is the ratio AB : CD in Figure 13:3?

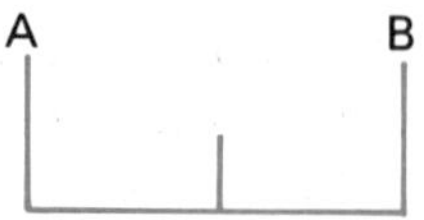

Fig. 13:3

3 (a) Dad earns £150 and Sam earns £50. What is the ratio of Dad's wage to Sam's wage?

(b) What is the ratio of Sam's wage to Dad's wage?

4 The ratio of Julie's age to her mother's age is 1 : 3. Julie is 10 years old. How old is her mother?

5 (a) Gareth's pay compared to Jack's pay is in the ratio 2 : 3. Gareth earns £100. What does Jack earn?

(b) Karen's pay compared to Kirsty's pay is in the ratio 3 : 4. Kirsty earns £160. What does Karen earn?

6 Figure 13:4 shows the ratio of the wages of three girls.

(a) Wendy earns £120. What is Lisa's wage?

(b) Two years ago, the girls' wages were in the same ratio. Tara earned £140 then. How much did Wendy earn?

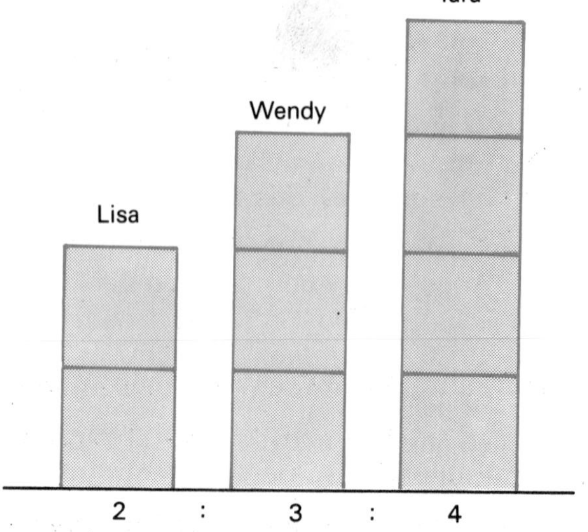

Fig. 13:4

7 A mixture of concrete is made from three parts of sand to one part of cement (and some water). 27 barrowloads of sand are used. How much cement is used?

8 Simplify these ratios.

(a) 6 : 12 (b) 9 : 27 (c) 11 : 55 (d) 18 : 54

(e) 45 : 75 (f) 17 : 34 (g) 42 : 56

(h) 91 : 13

9 The units making up a ratio written with a colon (:) must be the same. For example, to simplify the ratio 2 kg to 500 g we must first change both parts to grams, giving 2000 g : 500 g, which will simplify to 4 : 1.

Simplify the following ratios.

(a) 2 km to 100 m (b) £4·50 to 50p

(c) 3 cm to 15 mm (d) 1 m to 250 cm

(e) £6·00 to 25p (f) 1 kg to 150 g

Worksheet 13 may be used here.

10 Figure 13:5 represents four railway trucks. The ratio of the lengths of the trucks, from left to right, is 1 : 2 : 3 : 4. The ratio AB : CD is 1 : 2.

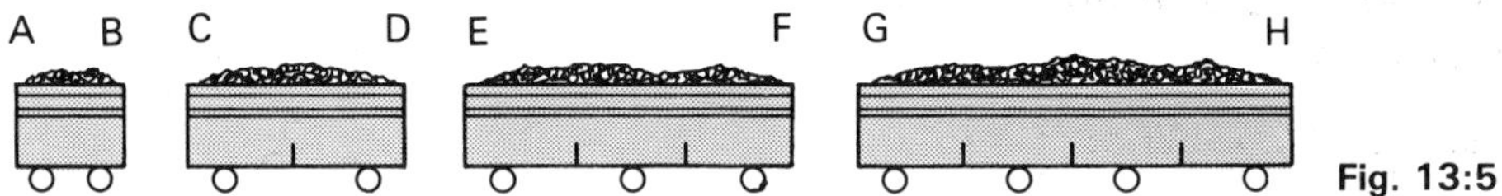

Fig. 13:5

Write down the ratio of:

(a) AB : EF (b) EF : AB (c) CD : GH

(d) GH : CD

11 The trucks can carry loads in proportion to their lengths.

(a) Truck EF can carry 63·75 tonnes. How much can AB carry?

(b) How much can truck GH carry?

B Enlargement

Scale factor

In Figure 13:6 ABCD and $A_1B_1C_1D_1$ are **similar.**
This means they are the same shape but not the same size. The sides of $A_1B_1C_1D_1$ are twice as long as the sides of ABCD.

ABCD has been **enlarged by scale factor 2** to give $A_1B_1C_1D_1$.

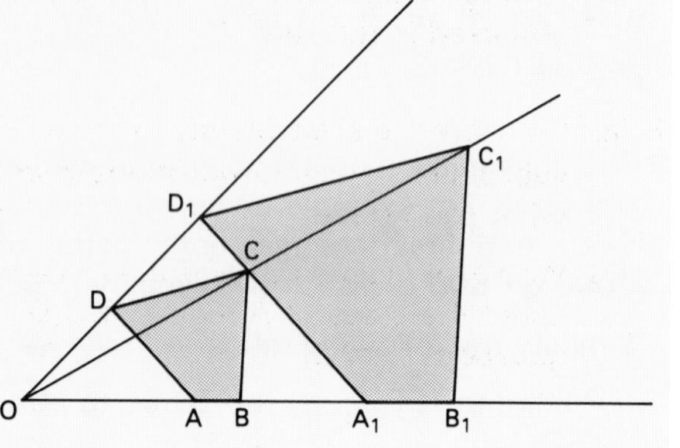

Fig. 13:6

1 Measure OA and OA_1, OB and OB_1, OC and OC_1, and OD and OD_1 on Figure 13:6. Write down what you find.

2 If you wished to enlarge ABCD by **scale factor 3** from centre O to give $A_2B_2C_2D_2$, how long would you make OA_2, OB_2, OC_2 and OD_2?

3 Copy the rays and shape ABCD exactly from Figure 13:6. Draw $A_2B_2C_2D_2$ as an enlargement by scale factor 3 of ABCD from centre O.

4 The word TUB is drawn in Figure 13:7 on 5 mm squared paper. Find the area of each letter in square units.

Fig. 13:7

5 (a) Make a two times enlargement of the word TUB on 5 mm squared paper. Figure 13:8 shows how to start. Make the gaps twice as large as well.

(b) Find the area of each letter in the same square units as you used in question 4.

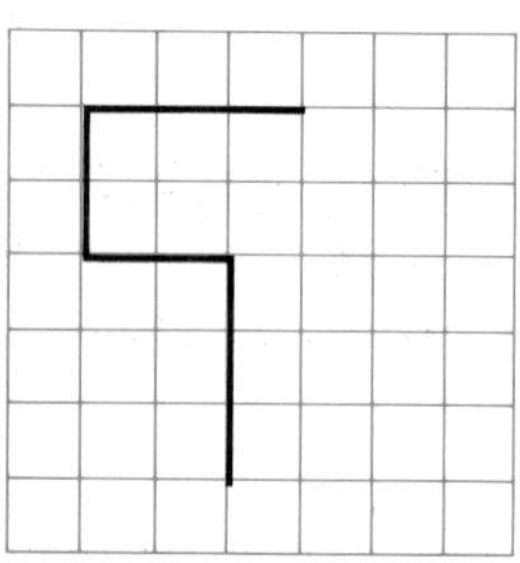

Fig. 13:8

6 (a) Make a three times enlargement of the word TUB on 5 mm squared paper.

(b) Find the area of each letter in the same square units as you used in question 4.

7 (a) Compare the scale factors of the enlargement and the subsequent areas in questions 5 and 6. Write down what you notice.

(b) Would you expect to find the same result if you compared the areas of ABCD, $A_1B_1C_1D_1$ and $A_2B_2C_2D_2$ in questions 1 to 3?

8 State the scale factor of the enlargement for each pair of shapes in Figure 13:9.

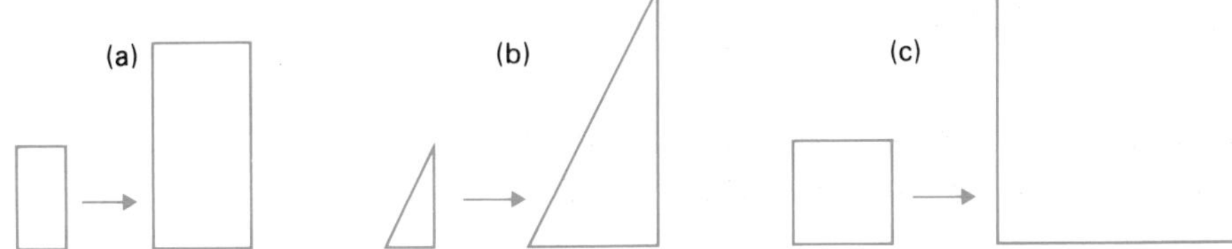

Fig. 13:9

9 On 1 cm squared paper draw x- and y-axes: x from 0 to 15, y from 0 to 10.
Join (6, 0) to (6, 4) and (6, 4) to (0, 4) to make a rectangle.
Using rays from the origin as the centre of enlargement, draw similar rectangles using scale factors of $1\frac{1}{2}$, 2 and $2\frac{1}{2}$.

10 Figure 13:10 shows a pantograph.

When AB = BC = CD = DA the pantograph enlarges by scale factor 2. Try other positions of A, B and C.

Use strips of stiff card, each 15 cm by 2 cm, and 5 drawing pins.

Fig. 13:10

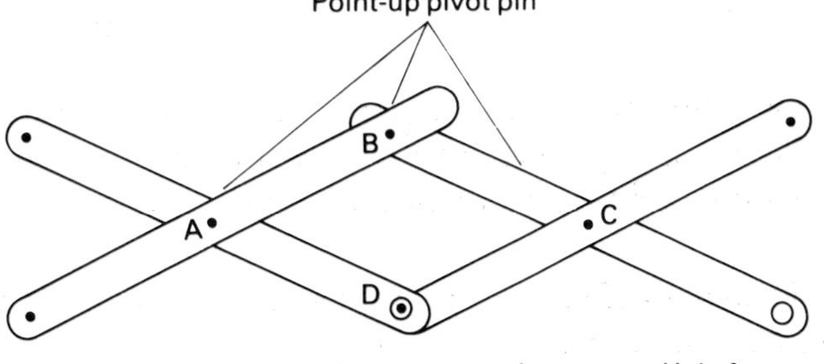

14 Common fractions: add; subtract; multiply

A Addition and subtraction

● To remind you . . .

- $\frac{2}{5}$ — 2 ← numerator, 5 ← denominator

- **Lowest Common Multiple (LCM)**
  The lowest number which is a multiple of each of 2, 3 and 4 is 12. We call 12 the **lowest common multiple** of 2, 3 and 4. This means that 12 is the lowest number that 2, 3 and 4 all divide into exactly.

- **Like fractions** have the same denominators, e.g. $\frac{1}{7}$, $\frac{3}{7}$.

- **Unlike fractions** have different denominators, e.g. $\frac{1}{3}$, $\frac{2}{5}$.

▶ Points to discuss . . .

1 **Adding like fractions**

Example $\frac{3}{9} + \frac{2}{9} + \frac{1}{9} = \frac{6}{9} \rightarrow \frac{2}{3}$

2 **Adding unlike fractions**

Change them into like fractions! The kind of fraction you change them into is the LCM of their denominators.

Example $\frac{1}{4} + \frac{1}{2} + \frac{2}{3}$

The LCM of 2, 3 and 4 is 12. Change the fractions into twelfths.

$\frac{1}{4} \xrightarrow{\text{multiply both by 3}} \frac{3}{12}$

$\frac{1}{2} \xrightarrow{\text{multiply both by 6}} \frac{6}{12}$

$\frac{2}{3} \xrightarrow{\text{multiply both by 4}} \frac{8}{12}$

Then $\frac{3}{12} + \frac{6}{12} + \frac{8}{12} = \frac{17}{12} \rightarrow 1\frac{5}{12}$

3 **Adding mixed numbers**

Add the whole-number parts as usual. Add the fraction parts as above.

Example $3\frac{1}{3} + 4\frac{1}{2} = 7 + \frac{2}{6} + \frac{3}{6} = 7\frac{5}{6}$

Examples (i) $\frac{3}{9} + \frac{2}{9} + \frac{1}{9} = \frac{6}{9} = \frac{2}{3}$

(ii) $\frac{1}{4} + \frac{1}{2} + \frac{1}{3} = \frac{3}{12} + \frac{6}{12} + \frac{4}{12} = \frac{13}{12} = 1\frac{1}{12}$

(iii) $3\frac{1}{3} + 2\frac{1}{2} = 3\frac{2}{6} + 2\frac{3}{6} = 5\frac{5}{6}$

(iv) $2\frac{3}{4} - \frac{3}{8} = 2\frac{6}{8} - \frac{3}{8} = 2\frac{3}{8}$

(v) $4\frac{1}{6} - \frac{2}{3} = 4\frac{1}{6} - \frac{4}{6}$

To take $\frac{4}{6}$ from $\frac{1}{6}$ we can change one of the 4 whole ones into 6 sixths, so $4\frac{1}{6}$ becomes $3\frac{7}{6}$. Then $3\frac{7}{6} - \frac{4}{6} = 3\frac{3}{6} = 3\frac{1}{2}$.

1 Link each part with its correct answer in Figure 14:1.

(a) The three fractions in example (i) above are . . . fractions.

(b) 6 and 9 in $\frac{6}{9}$ have been divided by . . . to give $\frac{2}{3}$.

(c) The process in part (b) is called . . .

(d) The LCM of 4, 3 and 2 is . . .

(e) In example (ii) above the unlike fractions have been turned into . . . fractions, namely . . .

(f) The LCM of 3 and 2 is . . .

(g) In example (iii) above $\frac{1}{3}$ and $\frac{1}{2}$ have been changed into . . .

(h) The LCM of 4 and 8 is . . .

(i) In example (iv) above the unlike fractions $\frac{3}{4}$ and $\frac{3}{8}$ are changed so that both are . . .

(j) In example (v) above the $\frac{3}{6}$ has been cancelled to . . .

A 12	B like twelfths		
C sixths		D 8	
E 3	F eighths		
G a half		H like	
I 6	J cancelling		

Fig. 14:1

2 Find the lowest common multiple of:

(a) 2 and 5 (b) 3 and 6 (c) 3 and 4

(d) 5 and 10 (e) 3 and 5 (f) 5 and 8

(g) 2, 3 and 4 (h) 4, 6 and 9

3 Copy the following, replacing the * by the correct number.

(a) $\frac{*}{8} = \frac{1}{2}$ (b) $\frac{*}{12} = \frac{1}{3}$ (c) $\frac{4}{*} = \frac{1}{3}$ (d) $\frac{4}{*} = \frac{1}{5}$

(e) $\frac{2}{3} = \frac{*}{12}$ (f) $\frac{3}{4} = \frac{*}{12}$ (g) $\frac{2}{5} = \frac{8}{*}$ (h) $\frac{3}{5} = \frac{*}{30}$

4 $\frac{15}{6} = 2\frac{3}{6} = 2\frac{1}{2}$ ($2\frac{3}{6}$ and $2\frac{1}{2}$ are both mixed numbers).

Write each of these as a whole number or as a mixed number, cancelling where necessary.

(a) $\frac{9}{9}$ (b) $\frac{18}{6}$ (c) $\frac{21}{6}$ (d) $\frac{15}{9}$

(e) $\frac{40}{5}$ (f) $\frac{14}{8}$ (g) $\frac{36}{24}$ (h) $\frac{42}{24}$

5 Evaluate the following, cancelling if possible.

(a) $\frac{3}{4} + \frac{1}{4}$ (b) $\frac{3}{4} - \frac{1}{4}$ (c) $\frac{1}{2} + \frac{1}{3}$ (d) $\frac{1}{2} - \frac{1}{3}$

(e) $\frac{3}{4} + \frac{2}{3}$ (f) $\frac{3}{4} - \frac{2}{3}$ (g) $1\frac{2}{7} + \frac{2}{3}$ (h) $1\frac{2}{7} - \frac{2}{3}$

6 The owner of a garden centre divided her growing area into 24 equal parts. Her plan is on the right.

What fraction of the growing area is taken up by:

(a) tulips (b) roses

(c) shrubs (d) ferns

(e) alpines (f) fruit bushes?

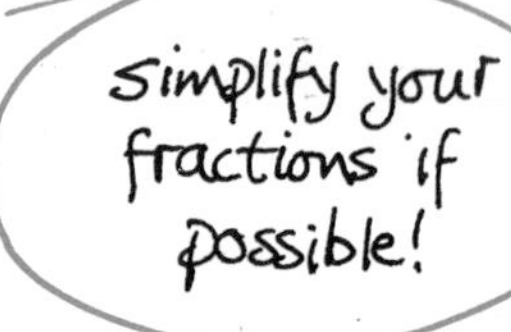

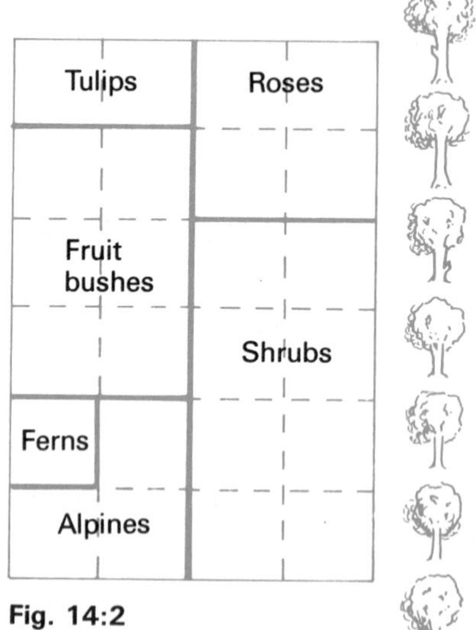

Fig. 14:2

7 Put the following fractions in ascending order of magnitude. (Start with the smallest and go up.)

$\frac{1}{3}$, $\frac{5}{6}$, $\frac{1}{2}$, $\frac{2}{3}$, $\frac{1}{4}$, $\frac{1}{6}$, $\frac{3}{4}$

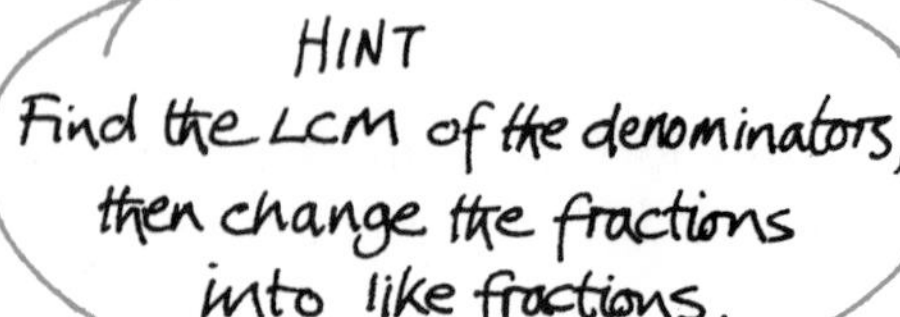

8 (a) Find the sum of $2\frac{5}{9}$ and $3\frac{3}{4}$.

(b) Find the difference between $5\frac{1}{3}$ and $7\frac{2}{15}$. (Subtract the whole numbers first.)

9 In a survey 25 000 people were asked which television channel they liked best. 10 000 chose ITV. What fraction of the people asked is this? Give your answer in the lowest terms. (SEG)

10 $P = 4(1 - \frac{1}{3} + \frac{1}{5} - \frac{1}{7} + \ldots)$

(a) Copy the series printed above. The fractions go on for ever. What do you think the next four fractions are?

(b) Use a scientific calculator to find what number P is when the series stops at $\frac{1}{7}$. Do it like this:

4 [×] [(] 1 [−] 1 [÷] 3 [+] 1 [÷] 5 [−] 1 [÷] 7 [)] [=]

(c) Now work out P when the next fraction ($\frac{1}{9}$) is included, like this:

4 [×] [(] 1 [−] 1 [÷] 3 [+] 1 [÷] 5 [−] 1 [÷] 7 [+] 1 [÷] 9 [)] [=]

(d) What will P be when you include the next fraction $(-\frac{1}{11})$?

(e) If you keep on long enough (a long way!) you will find that P gets nearer and nearer to π (3·141 . . .)
Here is a computer program that will do this for you.

```
10  LET C = 0
20  FOR N = 1 TO 9999 STEP 4
30  LET A = 1/N
40  LET B = 1/(N+2)
50  LET C = C+A-B
60  PRINT "P = "; 4*C
70  NEXT N
```

B Multiplication

To multiply two fractions we multiply the top numbers together and we multiply the bottom numbers together.

Note If possible, cancel the fraction numbers before you multiply, but this is not essential. You can always cancel the answer fraction instead.

Example $\frac{5}{9} \times \frac{3}{10}$

Cancelling first:

$$\frac{{}^{1}\cancel{5}}{{}_{3}\cancel{9}} \times \frac{\cancel{3}^{1}}{\cancel{10}_{2}} = \frac{1}{6}$$

(5 has been cancelled with 10 and 3 has been cancelled with 9.)

Multiplying then cancelling:

$$\frac{5}{9} \times \frac{3}{10} = \frac{15}{90} \xrightarrow{\text{divide 15 and 90 by 5}} \frac{3}{18} \xrightarrow{\text{divide 3 and 18 by 3}} \frac{1}{6}$$

(We could also have divided 15 and 90 by 15 to get $\frac{1}{6}$.)

If you are multiplying mixed numbers, make them into top-heavy fractions first.

Example $\frac{5}{9} \times 1\frac{4}{5}$

Change the mixed number $1\frac{4}{5}$ to $\frac{9}{5}$.

$$\frac{{}^{1}\cancel{5}}{{}_{1}\cancel{9}} \times \frac{\cancel{9}^{1}}{\cancel{5}_{1}} = \frac{1}{1} = 1$$

Or, multiplying then cancelling:

$$\frac{5}{9} \times \frac{9}{5} = \frac{45}{45} = 1$$

1 Multiply:

(a) $\frac{1}{3} \times \frac{2}{3}$ (b) $\frac{1}{4} \times \frac{1}{2}$ (c) $\frac{2}{3}$ of $\frac{1}{2}$ (d) $\frac{1}{8}$ of $\frac{3}{5}$

2 Multiply:

(a) $1\frac{1}{2} \times \frac{1}{2}$ (b) $1\frac{1}{4} \times \frac{1}{3}$ (c) $2\frac{1}{2} \times 6$

(d) $\frac{3}{4} \times 8$ (e) $\frac{2}{3} \times 5$ (f) $2\frac{1}{3} \times \frac{1}{7}$

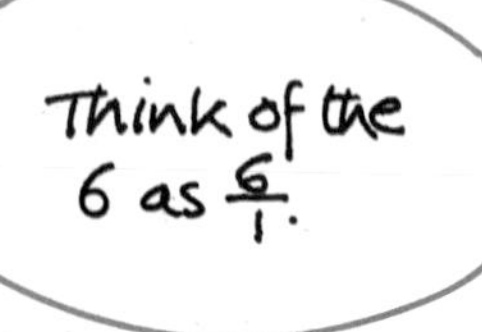

3 Multiply:

(a) $\frac{5}{9}$ by $\frac{2}{5}$ (b) $1\frac{2}{3} \times 3\frac{1}{5}$ (c) $1\frac{1}{3}$ of $1\frac{4}{5}$

4 What must I multiply $\frac{3}{4}$ by to get a whole one?

5 What must I multiply $\frac{2}{3}$ by to get a whole one?

6 How many $\frac{4}{5}$s make a whole one?

7 A bag of grass fertiliser has a mass (weight) of 28 kg. Mr Evergreen estimates that he will need $1\frac{3}{4}$ times this amount to feed his lawn. How much fertiliser will be need?

Fig. 14:3

8 Figure 14:3 is a plan of a patio made up of square concrete slabs. The shaded ones are cracked.

(a) What fraction of the total number of slabs are cracked?

(b) Each slab measures $\frac{1}{2}$ m × $\frac{1}{2}$ m. What is the perimeter of the patio?

(c) If new slabs costs 95p each, how much will it cost to replace all the cracked slabs?

(d) If it is decided to cement over the cracked slabs what area needs to be cemented? (SEG)

9 $\frac{2}{7}$ of a class do not take French.
20 pupils do take French.
How many pupils are there in the class?

10 About $\frac{13}{20}$ of the weight of the average adult is composed of the water in his or her body. If a woman weighs 50 kilograms, what is the approximate weight of the water in her body?

11 How much did I have at the beginning if:

(a) I spent $\frac{1}{2}$ and had £20 left

(b) I spent $\frac{1}{4}$ and had £12 left

(c) I spent $\frac{1}{3}$ and had £20 left

(d) I spent $\frac{3}{4}$ and had £25 left?

12 Evaluate:

(a) $2\frac{1}{2} \times 4\frac{1}{2}$ (b) $3\frac{1}{3} \times 75$p (c) $4\frac{2}{3} \times 180$ metres

13 Mrs Brown spent $\frac{1}{2}$ of her housekeeping money on food and $\frac{5}{12}$ on two bills. She then had £5 left in her purse.

(a) Express her total spending as one fraction.

(b) What fraction is represented by the £5 she had left?

(c) How much did she spend on:
(i) the two bills (ii) food?

(d) How much money did she have at the beginning?

15 Scales

To remind you . . .

- **Map scales**

The map in Figure 15:1 is drawn to a scale of 6 miles to 1 inch. This means that 1 inch on the map represents a true distance of 6 miles.

The kilometres scale for the same map is 1 cm to 4 km. So 5 cm on the map would be a true distance of
5×4 km = 20 km.
25 km would be represented on the map by
$(25 \div 4)$ cm = 6·25 cm.

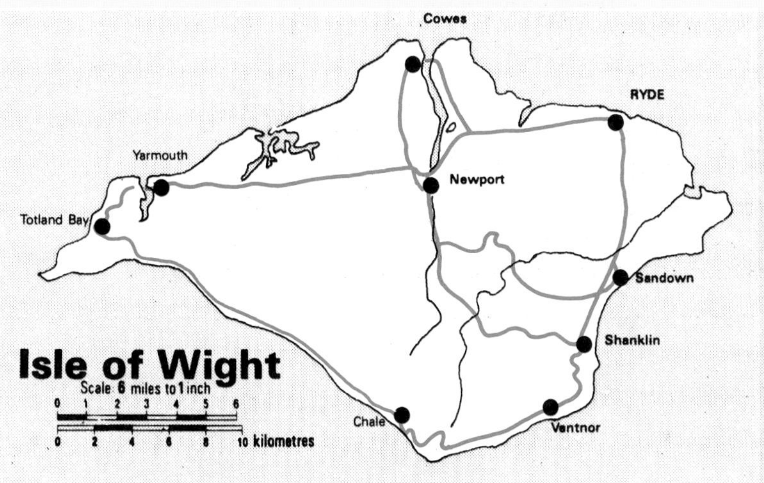

Fig. 15:1

- **Scale models**

A model maker might use a scale of one to a hundred (1 : 100) for a model of the QE II. The ship is 960 feet long. The scaled-down model would be $(960 \div 100)$ = 9·6 feet long.

Many plastic model kits use a scale of 1 : 72. Other scales used include 1 : 24 and 1 : 160 (for N gauge model railways).

- **Representative fraction**

A scale of $\frac{1}{10}$ means the model is a tenth of the true size. So 1 cm on the model represents 10 cm on the real thing. And 1 mm on the model represents 10 mm on the real thing. And 1 inch on the model represents 10 inches on the real thing.

$\frac{1}{10}$ is called the **representative fraction.**

For a map, the representative fraction might be $\frac{1}{1\,000\,000}$, or 1 cm represents 1 000 000 cm.

1 000 000 cm = 10 000 m = 10 km,

so in this scale 1 cm represents 10 km.

'Representative fraction' is often shortened to RF and is written as a ratio, for example 1 : 1 000 000.

▶ Points to discuss . . .

1 In Figure 15:1 (page 77, the scale is 1 cm represents 4 km. Approximately how far is it by road from Cowes to Ryde?

2 About how long would you expect a model Vauxhall Astra to be, made to the following scales:

(a) 1 : 24 (b) 1 : 72 (c) 1 : 160?

This Astra is just over 4 metres long

1 The answers to this question are given in Figure 15:2. Link up each part with its answer.

A 94 cm	B representative fraction	C 1 : 25
D 4·7 cm = 47 mm	E 670 cm	F 10 times longer
G 6·7 cm	H 15 times smaller	I 67 cm

Fig. 15:2

(a) If a figure is drawn to a scale of 1 : 10 then the real distances will be . . .

(b) If a model is made with a scale of 1 : 15 then the measurements of the model compared to the real thing will be . . .

(c) The line AB measures . . .

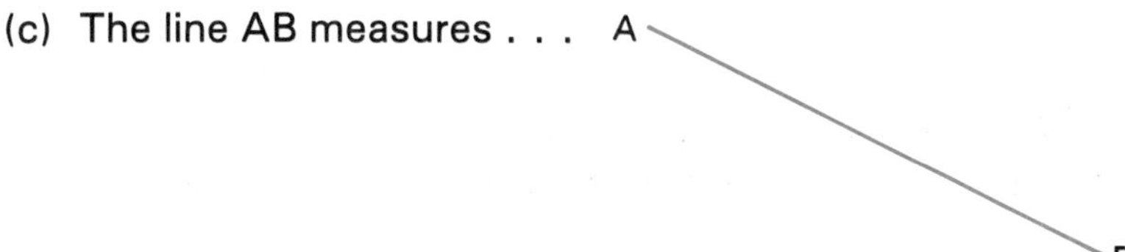

(d) If line AB was drawn to a scale of 1 : 20 then the real measurement of AB is . . .

(e) A scale can be given as a . . .

(f) A scale of $\frac{1}{25}$ is the same as writing . . .

(g) 6·7 cm × 10 = . . .

(h) 6·7 cm × 100 = . . .

(i) 670 cm ÷ 100 = . . .

2 Rectangle A of Figure 15:3 on page 80 has sides measuring 5 cm and 3 cm. It is drawn to a scale of 1 : 10, so the real measurements of the rectangle are 10 × 5 cm = 50 cm long and 10 × 3 cm = 30 cm wide.

(a) Measure rectangles B, C, D and E accurately, giving your answer in centimetres, e.g. 6 cm or 6·5 cm.

(b) Find the true measurements of rectangles B, C, D and E, using the scales given inside the scale drawings.

A

Scale 1 : 10

B

Scale 1 : 10

C

Scale 1 : 10

D

Scale 1 : 20

E

Scale 1 : 25

Fig. 15:3

3 Example A wall is represented on a plan by a line 10 cm long. The plan is to a scale of 1 : 100. What is the length of the wall?

The wall is 100 times longer than the line that represents it on the plan, so it is

100×10 cm $=$ 1000 cm $=$ 10 m long.

Copy and complete the tables below.

Plan length	Scale	Real length
12 cm	1 : 100	100×12 cm $=$ 1200 cm $=$ 12 m
15 cm	1 : 100	
30 cm	1 : 100	
50 cm	1 : 100	

Real length	Scale	Plan length
12 m	1 : 100	$\frac{1200}{100}$ cm $=$ 12 cm
17 m	1 : 100	
14·5 m	1 : 100	

4 Figure 15:4 shows a plan of a bungalow drawn to a scale of 1 : 100.

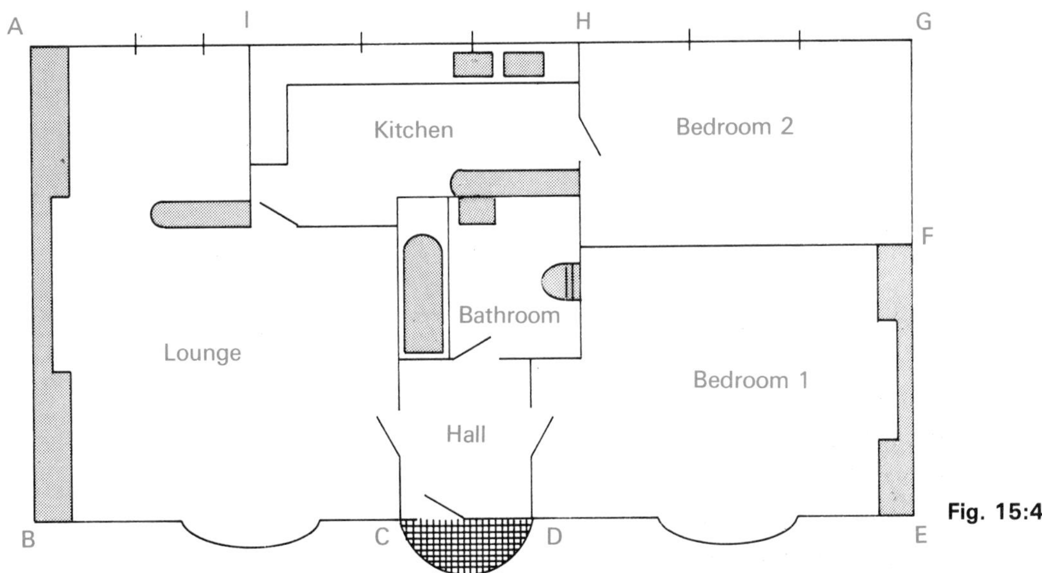

Fig. 15:4

(a) What do these symbols represent?

(i) (ii) (iii)

(b) Copy and complete this table.

Plan length	Real length
GH = 4·5 cm	100 × 4·5 cm = 450 cm = 4 m 50 cm
AB	
BC	
CD	
EF	
AG	

5 Solve these clues to the word puzzle in Figure 15:5 and write down the answers.

(a) 1 to 20 and 1 : 10 are examples.

(b) The actual or the . . . length.

(c) Figure 15:4 is scaled . . .

(d) Millimetres in one centimetre.

(e) 1 : 20 can be shown as a representative . . .

(f) 100 cm equals this.

(g) To simplify $\frac{400}{900}$ we can . . . the noughts.

(h) 1000 m equals one of these.

(i) Number of millimetres in ten centimetres.

(j) Often made to scale.

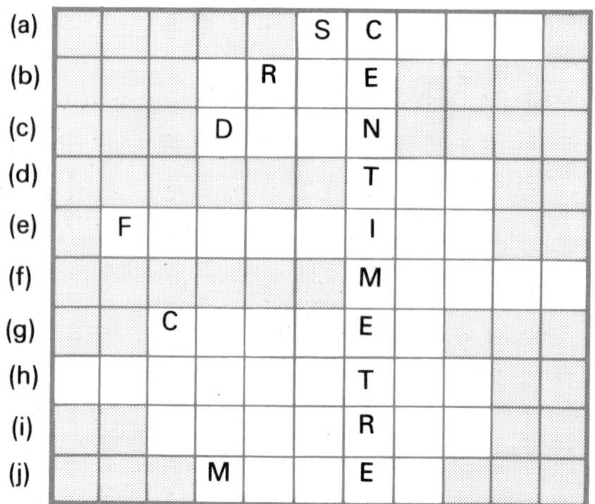

Fig. 15:5

6 A model boat is built to a scale of 1 to 20.

(a) Calculate the length of the model, in centimetres, if the actual length of the boat is 6 metres.

(b) Calculate the length of the actual mast in metres, given that the length of the mast on the model is 45 centimetres. (LEAG)

7 Ahmed wants to make a model of the supersonic airliner Concorde, using a scale of 1 : 100. He has this information.

Length	5624 cm
Wingspan	2556 cm
Height	1108 cm
Max. speed	2140 km/h
Max. altitude	17 680 m
Passengers	100

(a) What is the meaning of:
(i) supersonic (ii) wingspan?

(b) What size, to the nearest cm, should he make the model's:
(i) length (ii) wingspan (iii) height?

Worksheets 15A and 15B may be used here.

8 100 cm = 1 metre and 1000 metres = 1 kilometre.
So 1 km = 1000 × 100 cm = 100 000 cm.

Some Ordnance Survey maps are drawn to a scale of 2 cm to 1 km or 2 : 100 000. This simplifies to 1 : 50 000.

Copy and complete the tables.

Actual distance	Scale	Map length in cm
5 km	1 : 50 000	$\frac{100\,000 \times 5}{50\,000} = \frac{50}{5} =$ **10 cm**
7 km	1 : 50 000	
12·5 km	1 : 50 000	

Map length	Scale	Actual distance in km
3 cm	1 : 50 000	$\frac{50\,000 \times 3\text{ cm}}{100\,000} = \frac{15}{10} =$ **1·5 km**
5 cm	1 : 50 000	
8·5 cm	1 : 50 000	

9 Figure 15:6 on page 84 shows part of Scotland and England drawn to a scale of 1 : 1 000 000 (one to one million).

As a straight-line distance it is approximately 4·65 cm on the map from Dumfries to Carlisle.
The approximate true distance, in kilometres, will be:

$$\frac{4{\cdot}65 \times 1\,000\,000}{100\,000}\text{ km} = 46{\cdot}5\text{ km}.$$

Find as accurately as you can the true straight-line distances in kilometres between Dumfries and

(a) Keswick (b) Kirkcudbright

(c) Whitehaven (d) Cairnryan

Measure from the MIDDLE of a dot.

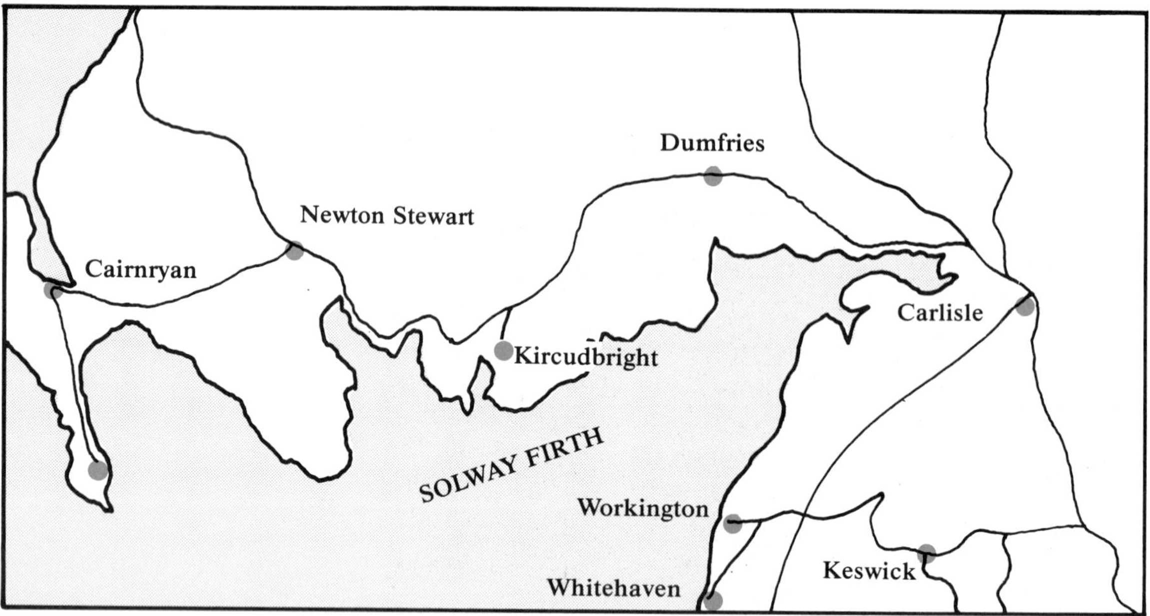

Fig. 15:6

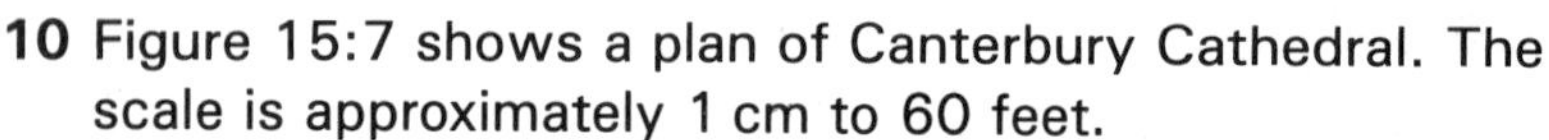

10 Figure 15:7 shows a plan of Canterbury Cathedral. The scale is approximately 1 cm to 60 feet.

(a) Find the approximate true length of:
  (i) the inside of the nave
  (ii) the inside of the choir
  (iii) the perimeter of the inside square of the cloisters.

(b) If you took a rectangular path around the outside of the cathedral, approximately how far would you have to walk in
  (i) feet   (ii) yards?

3 feet = 1 yard

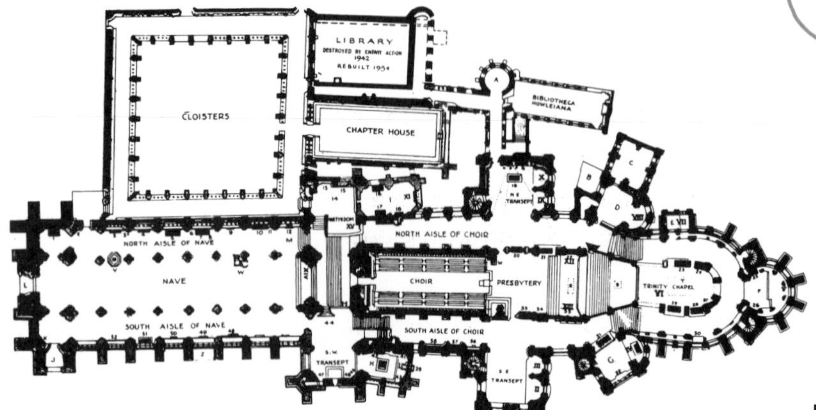

Fig. 15:7

Assignment 1

▶ Points to discuss . . .

How would you approach the problem of improving the design of the kitchen shown in Figure A1:1?

Fig. A1:1

You could do it like this.

1. **Understand the problem.** What are you being asked to do?
2. **Plan your approach.** What information and equipment do you need? What method should you use?
3. **Carry out the task,** through measuring, reasoning, modelling, surveying, calculating, exploring, extending, . . .
4. **Communicate the results,** through talking, writing, drawing, . . .

A

Here are two assignment examples for you to try.

Links

	How many straight lines can you draw to join these two dots?
	How many straight lines can you draw to join any two of these three dots?
	How many straight lines can you draw to join any two of these four dots?
	How many straight lines can you draw to join any two of these five dots?
Six dots? Seven? Eight? . . .	

Figure A1:2 shows the lines joining 5 dots. Four pairs of dots can be joined from point A. Then, counting clockwise, 3 more pairs, 2 more pairs, and so on.

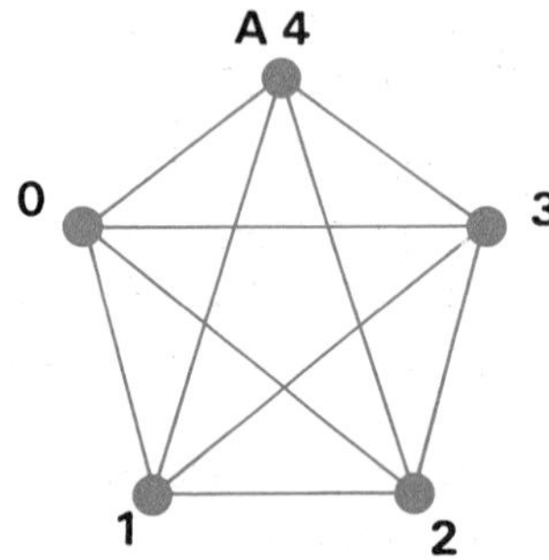

Fig. A1:2

Total: $4 + 3 + 2 + 1 + 0 = 10$

Find the rule:

$$0 + 1 + 2 + 3 = 4 \times 3 \div 2$$
$$0 + 1 + 2 + 3 + 4 = 5 \times 4 \div 2$$
$$0 + 1 + 2 + 3 + 4 + 5 = 6 \times 5 \div 2$$

How many straight lines can you draw to join any two out of a hundred dots? 1000 dots?

What has this to do with teams playing each other in a football league?

5 Divide 3·6 tonnes in the ratio 2 : 3 : 4 : 9.

REMEMBER! 1 tonne is 1000 kg.

6 A general-purpose mix for concrete is 1 part cement, $2\frac{1}{2}$ parts sand and 4 parts gravel. I need 5 cubic metres of mix (before the water is added). How many cubic metres of cement, sand and gravel do I need, correct to 2 decimal places?

7 Faizal, Ken and Bill staked £8 on the football pools. Faizal paid £2, Ken £2·50 and Bill £3·50. They won £864 which they shared in the same proportion as they contributed to the stake money. How much should each receive?

8 To start a business, Emma Penny invested £15 000 and Helen Pound invested £10 000. At the end of a year they shared the profits in the same proportion as their investments.

(a) What total amount did they invest?

(b) Find the fraction, in its lowest terms, of the profits received at the end of the year by Emma Penny.

(c) The profits amounted to £8000. How much did each woman receive?

17 Travel graphs

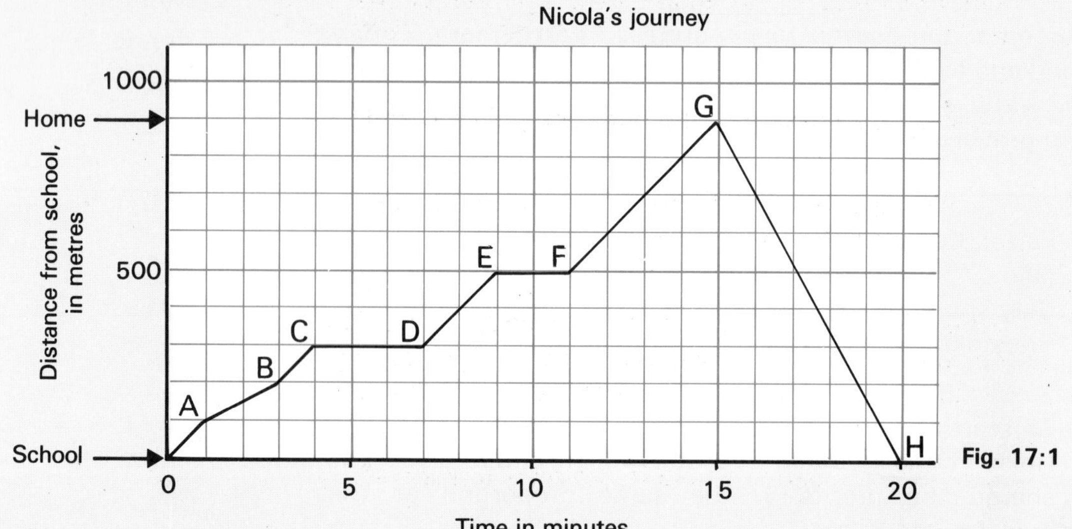

Fig. 17:1

This travel graph shows Nicola's journey home from school – and her hasty return to school.

The black line represents Nicola's journey. Point A, for example, is at the intersection of the 100 metres grid-line and the 1 minute grid-line. This shows that Nicola covered 100 metres in one minute.

NOTE
The graph does NOT show Nicola climbing and falling down a mountain!

▶ Points to discuss . . .

1 What does point B represent in time and distance?

2 How long a time did Nicola take from A to B?

3 What distance did Nicola cover between A and B?

4 When was Nicola walking faster, from A to B or from school to A?

5 What do you notice about the steepness of the journey line when Nicola walks faster?

6 Nicola stops for three minutes to look in a shop window. Which part of the line shows this?

7 What distance does Nicola cover between points D and E?

8 How long does Nicola take between points D and E?

9 Nicola stops for two minutes to talk to a friend. Which part of the line shows this?

10 When Nicola reaches home at G she finds she has left her homework at school. She runs back to school. Which part of the line shows her return to school?

11 How long does Nicola take to get back to school?

12 How long does Nicola take for the complete return journey, that is, from school to home and then back to school?

Average speed

Average speed may be found by the formula

$$\text{Average speed} = \frac{\text{Total distance}}{\text{Total time}}$$

Example Mrs Stewart has to drive 180 miles in 4 hours. She calculates that she needs to average $(180 \div 4)$ m.p.h.

Example If I travel 50 kilometres in one hour and then 70 kilometres in another two hours my average speed is
$(50 \text{ km} + 70 \text{ km}) \div (1 \text{ h} + 2 \text{ h})$
$= 120 \text{ km} \div 3 \text{ h} = 40 \text{ km/h}$.

1 Figure 17:2 on page 92 shows journeys by bus and by motorbike. The bus journey is shown by a continuous line, and the motorbike's journey by a dashed line.

Write down the letter of the correct answer. For example, (a) B.

(a) The time 1400 is the same as
A 4 p.m. B 2 p.m. C 7 a.m.

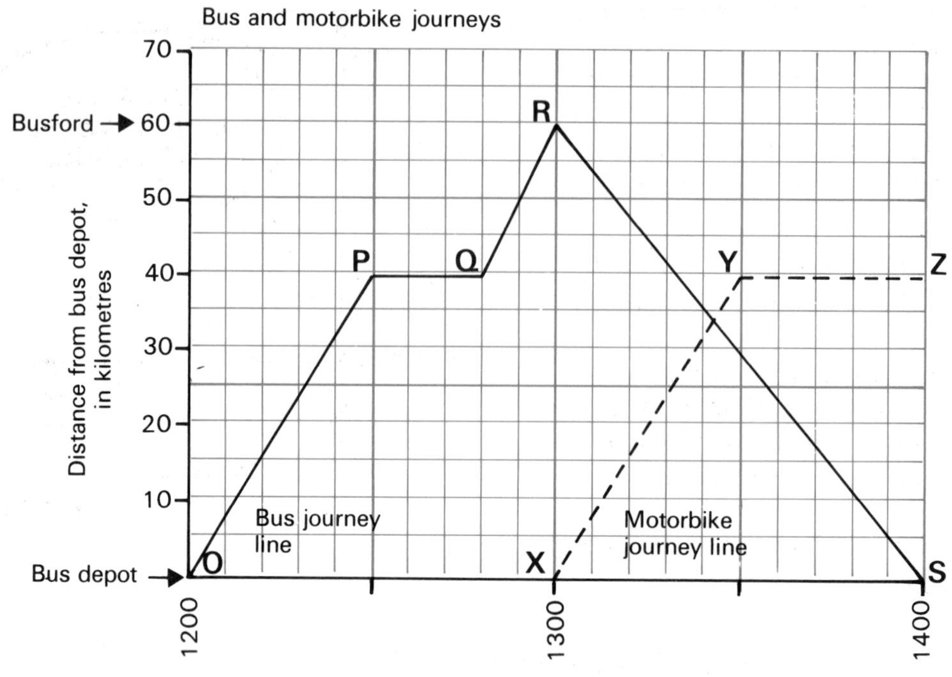

Fig. 17:2

(b) The times are given on the
A vertical axis B horizontal axis C either axis

(c) Each hour is divided into 10 smaller parts. Each smaller part represents
A 5 minutes B 6 minutes C 10 minutes

(d) Each 10 km is divided into smaller parts. Each smaller part represents
A 3 km B 4 km C 5 km

(e) The coach stopped between
A O and P B P and Q C Q and R

(f) The distance from the depot to Busford is
A 60 km B 50 km C 40 km

(g) The motorbike broke down at
A 1300 B 1330 C 1400

(h) The bus and the motorbike passed each other at approximately
A 1315 B 1325 C 1330

(i) At 1400 the coach was
A back at the depot B nowhere in particular
C in London

2 Draw a travel graph for Jim's cycle ride.
Use these scales:
Horizontal: Time, 2 cm to 1 hour from 1000 to 1500
Vertical: Distance from Herne Bay, 2 cm to 5 miles from 0 miles to 30 miles

Jim sets out from Herne Bay at 1000 hours. After 30 minutes he is 5 miles away.
He then covers the next $7\frac{1}{2}$ miles in 30 minutes before taking a 30 minute rest.
Going on again he travels 10 miles in the next hour, then takes another 30 minutes rest.
Finally he returns to Herne Bay in 2 hours without stopping.

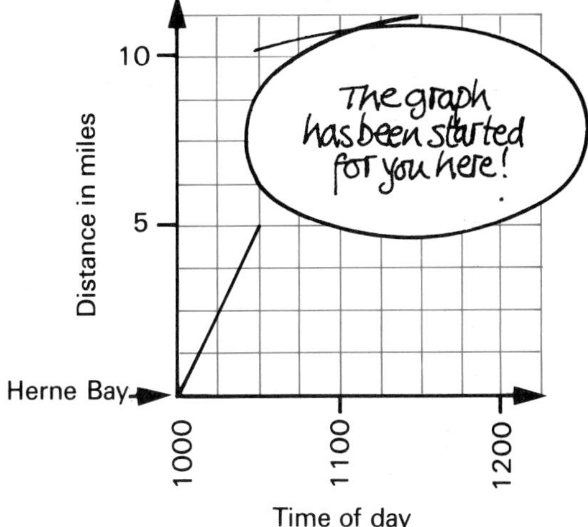

Fig. 17:3

3 These questions refer to the graph you drew for question 2.

(a) How far did Jim cycle in the first two hours?

(b) How far did he cycle altogether?

(c) At what time did Jim start his second rest?

(d) At what time did Jim get back to Herne Bay?

4 Copy and complete this table.

Distance	Time	Average speed
100 km	4 hours	
140 miles	4 hours	
83 · 2 km	8 hours	
	3 hours	20 m.p.h.
	4 hours	3 · 5 km/h
	6 · 5 hours	21 · 4 km/h
120 km		30 km/h
130 km		32 · 5 km/h
41 · 5 miles		8 · 3 m.p.h.

5 The graph in Figure 17:4 shows the distance from home of a motorist during a journey of one hour.

(a) Find his maximum distance from home.

(b) Find the total distance he travelled.

(c) Find his average speed in m.p.h. for the whole journey.

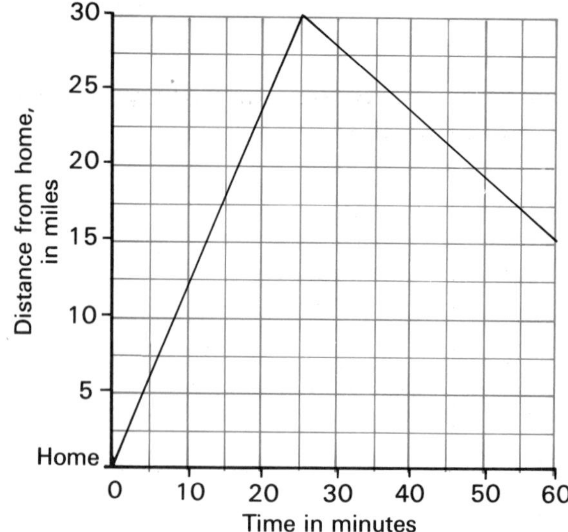

Fig. 17:4

6 Find the average speed for each journey shown below.

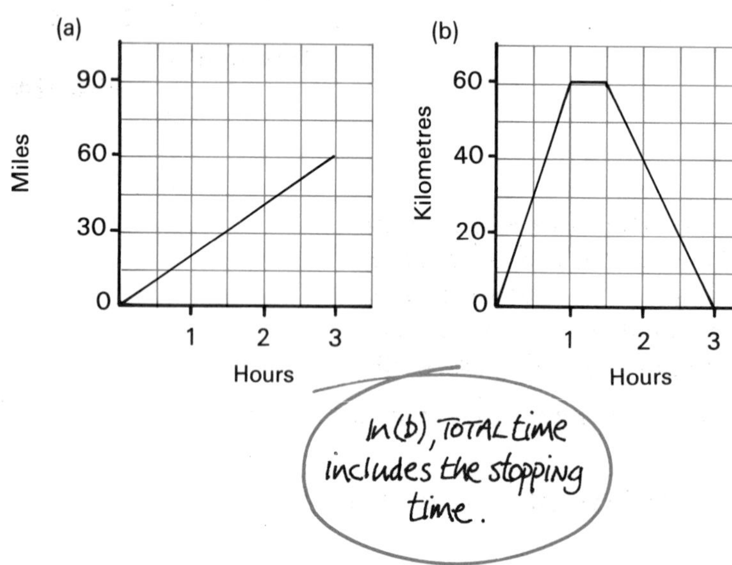

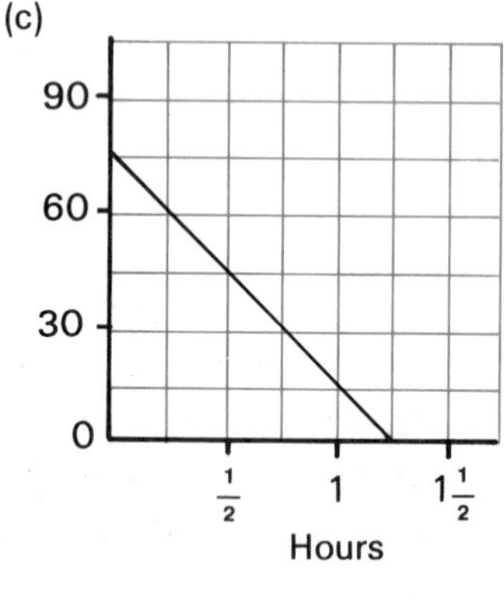

Fig. 17:5

7 Example Find the average speed in km/h for a journey of 40 km which takes 25 minutes.

40 km in 25 minutes is $\frac{40}{25}$ km in 1 minute.
In 1 hour one would go 60 times further, giving the speed as $\frac{40}{25} \times 60$ km/h $= 96$ km/h.

Find answers (a) to (d) in the table.

Distance	Time	Average speed
30 km	20 min	(a)
45 miles	15 min	(b)
20 km	25 min	(c)
1 mile	$2\frac{1}{2}$ min	(d)

Worksheet 17A may be used here.

8 Describe in full the journeys represented by the travel graphs below.

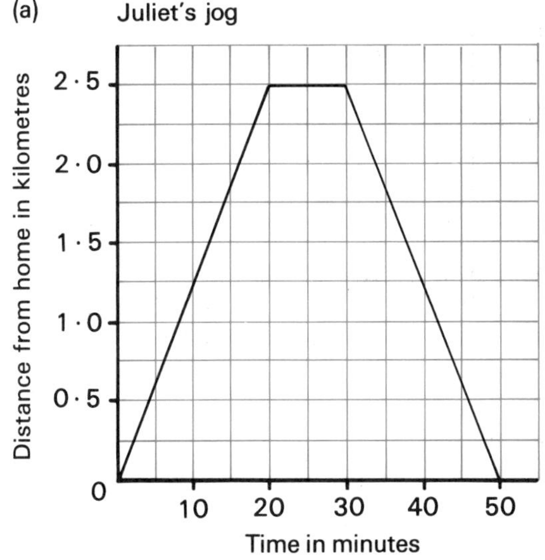

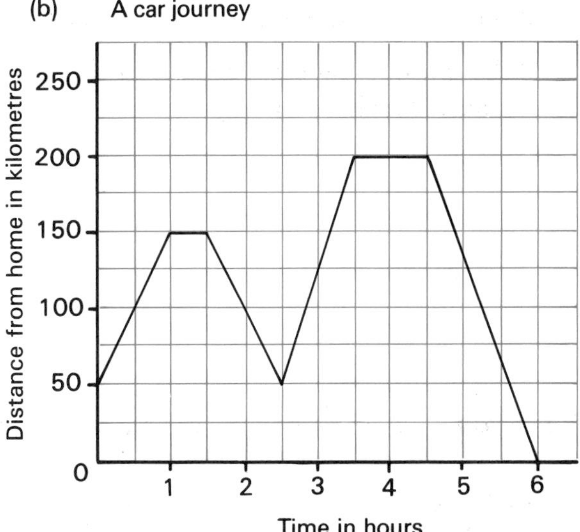

Fig. 17:6

Worksheet 17B may be used here.

9 Figure 17:7 on the next page shows Mrs Parr's journey from her home in Winchester to Bournemouth, a distance of 60 km. Mrs Parr left home at 0900 and travelled towards Bournemouth for 40 km. She stopped at a garage to fill up with petrol before continuing her journey to Bournemouth.

Copy the graph on to 2 mm graph paper and then answer the questions.

(a) What was the time when Mrs Parr stopped at the garage?

(b) For how long did Mrs Parr stop at the garage?

(c) (i) After leaving the garage, how long did it take Mrs Parr to reach Bournemouth?

(ii) What was Mrs Parr's speed, in kilometres per hour, during this stage of her journey?

Mrs Parr stayed at Bournemouth for 3 hours before starting her return journey to Winchester.

(d) (i) At what time did she leave Bournemouth?

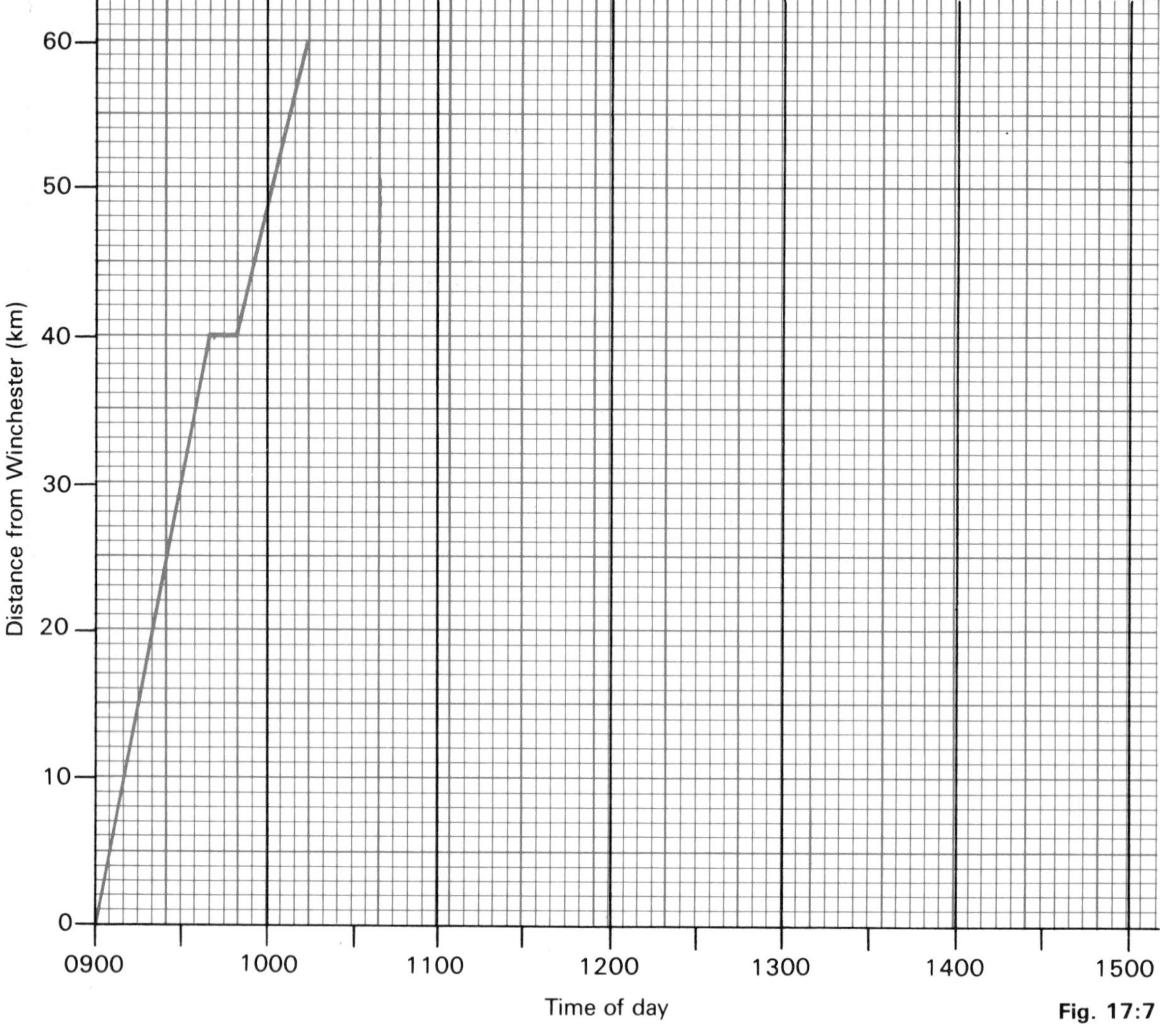

Fig. 17:7

(ii) Draw a line on your travel graph to represent her stay in Bournemouth.

(e) Mrs Parr began driving home at an average speed of 60 kilometres per hour, but 15 minutes after starting her journey she punctured a tyre and had to stop. She took 18 minutes to change the wheel and then continued at the same average speed.

(i) Complete your travel graph to show Mrs Parr's return journey.

(ii) At what time did Mrs Parr arrive home? (SEG)

10 Draw axes:
Horizontal: Time, 4 cm to 5 minutes, from 0 to 15 minutes
Vertical: Distance, 1 cm to 100 metres, from 0 to 1000 metres.

A donkey and a mule set out on a 1000 metre race. The donkey runs at 20 km/h (how many minutes to cover 1 km?), but every 400 metres it stops for 5 minutes to eat a carrot. The mule keeps on going at 5 km/h.

(a) Record the race on your graph.

(b) Who wins and by how many seconds?

(c) At what time does the donkey pass the mule?

(d) At what time does the mule pass the donkey?

18 Proportional changes; scatter graphs

A Proportional changes

Direct proportion

If two quantities decrease or increase at the same rate, they are said to be in direct proportion.

Example A recipe for a pizza serves 8 people. To make a pizza for 4 people (half as many people) we need to halve the ingredients.

Indirect or inverse proportion

If one quantity increases in the same proportion as another decreases, they are said to be in inverse proportion.

$\frac{1}{2}$ is the reciprocal of 2. The reciprocal of a number is $\frac{1}{\text{number}}$.

Example If a train **doubles** its average speed it will take **half** as long to cover the same distance.

Example If 5 bricklayers take 12 days to build a wall, then 15 bricklayers (3 times as many) working at the same rate should take $\frac{1}{3}$ of the time, which is 4 days.

The unitary method

Example 7 pens cost £1·40. What would 9 identical pens cost?

7 pens cost £1·40
1 pen costs £1·40 ÷ 7 = 20p
9 pens cost 9 × 20p = £1·80

1 The ingredients needed to make a Lemon Delicious pudding for 4 people are listed on the right.

Write out the ingredients needed to make enough pudding for:

(a) 8 people (b) 2 people

Lemon Delicious serves 4
4 eggs
120 g sugar
300 ml milk
15 ml self-raising flour
2 small lemons
15 ml castor sugar
pinch of salt

Fig. 18:1

2 Are (a) and (b) good examples of direct proportion? If your answer is 'No', give your reasons.

(a) Harry jogged for 15 minutes, which raised his heart-beat from 65 to 130 beats a minute. Harry refused to jog for a further 15 minutes as he believed his heart-beat would then reach 260 beats a minute.

(b) Glow-white toothpaste is sold in three different size tubes: 25 g, 50 g and 100 g. The 25 g tube costs 40p. Therefore the 50 g tube must cost 80p and the 100 g tube must cost £1·60.

3 It takes 15 women four days to pick the apples in an orchard. Working at the same rate, how long should it take:

(a) 5 women (b) 3 women (c) 30 women?

4 Six men can paint a school in 46 days. Working at the same rate, how long should it take:

(a) 12 men (b) 3 men (c) 1 man (d) 8 men?

5 10 square metres of carpet cost £30. How much would 25 square metres of the same carpet cost?

6 A car travels 150 miles on 20 litres of petrol. How much petrol is needed for 225 miles?

7 Solve these clues to the word puzzle in Figure 18:2 and write down the answers.

(a) 5 : 1 is an example.

(b) The . . . method can be used to find different proportions.

(c) Speed doubles, time halves is an example of . . . proportion.

(d) Halve the recipe, halve the people is an example of . . . proportion.

(e) Another word instead of inverse.

(f) £36 = 9 parts. Find one part by . . .

(g) Do this to 12 : 36 and you obtain 1 : 3

Fig. 18:2

8 In a certain town, 32 500 people watch ITV. How many watch BBC?

ITV : BBC
5 : 4

Fig. 18:3

9 15 500 people attend a football match.

(a) How many police should be on duty at the match?

(b) It costs the club £18·50 to hire one police officer. How much does the club pay for the police on duty?

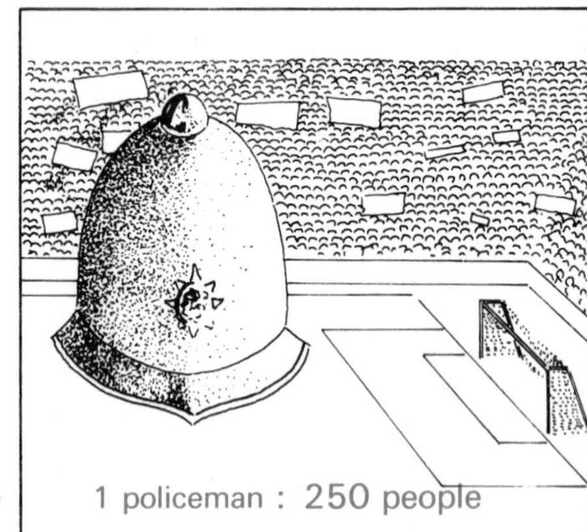

Fig. 18:4

10 A zoo has 105 snakes. How many wolves and monkeys does the zoo have?

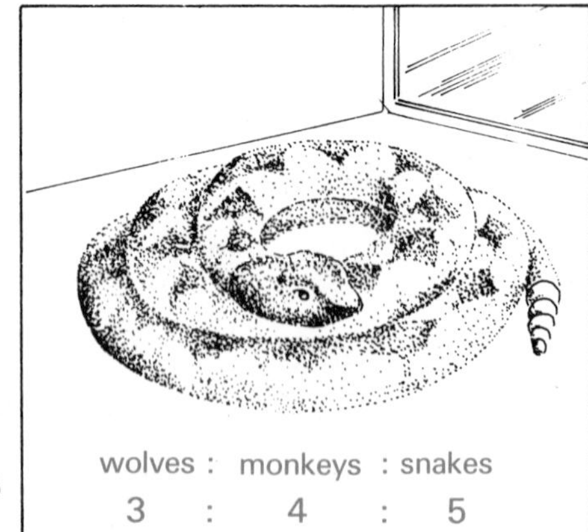

Fig. 18:5

11 An American tourist received 60p for 1 dollar. How many dollars would he need to obtain £30?

12 A manufacturer charged £108 for making 450 identical toys. At the same rate what would be the charge for making 750 of these toys? (LEAG)

13 (a) How many currant cakes could be made using a 0·6 kg bag of currants?

(b) How many **whole** cakes could be made using two 250 g packets of butter?

Currant cake

110 g flour
120 g butter
110 g castor sugar
2 eggs
150 g currants

Fig. 18:6

14 A bicycle has three gears. The ratios of the distance travelled for one turn of the pedals are:

1st gear : 2nd gear = 1 : 2
1st gear : 3rd gear = 2 : 5

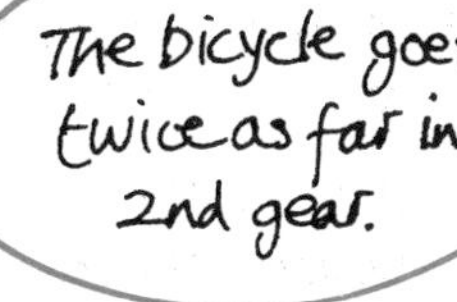

In 1st gear, one turn of the pedals moves the cycle 1 metre.

(a) How far will one turn of the pedals move the bicycle in:
(i) 2nd gear (ii) 3rd gear?

(b) How many turns of the pedals are needed to go 1 km in:
(i) 1st gear (ii) 2nd gear (iii) 3rd gear?

15 To increase £20 in the ratio 5 : 4 you can multiply £20 by $\frac{5}{4}$, giving

$$\frac{\pounds\cancel{20}^{5}}{1} \times \frac{5}{\cancel{4}_{1}} = \pounds 25.$$

(a) Increase £100 in the ratio 5 : 2.

(b) Increase 10 kg in the ratio 13 : 4.

(c) Decrease £15 in ratio 3 : 10.

(d) Decrease 130 in the ratio 1 : 13.

16 a and b are in inverse proportion. If $a = 10$ when $b = 20$, what is a when $b = 40$? (NEA)

17 x and y are in inverse proportion. If $x = 6$ when $y = 10$, what is x when $y = 30$? (NEA)

B Scatter graphs

Scatter graphs are used to find out if there is a link, or **correlation**, between two sets of data.

This table shows the heights of 18 boys, to the nearest centimetre.

Age	6	7	8	9	10	11	12	13	14	15	16
Height in centimetres	115	125, 131	129, 138	136	135, 141	147	142, 155	135, 160	161	170, 176	165, 184

Figure 18:7 shows part of a scatter graph which records some of the data in the table.

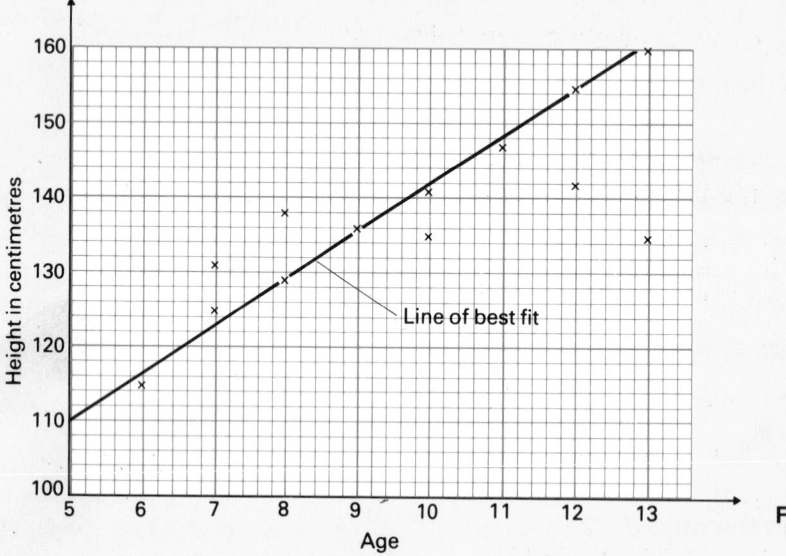

Fig. 18:7

Line of best fit

The crosses are mainly in a band sloping across the graph, showing a link, or correlation, between age and height for this group of boys. The line of best fit, illustrating the link, is drawn so that as many crosses as possible are on or close to the line, and about the same number of crosses are above it as below it.

Examples of correlation

(a)

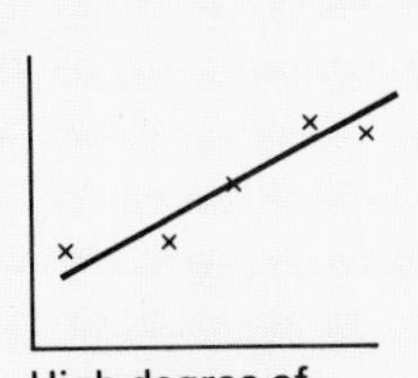

High degree of positive correlation
Example Rate of inflation and pay awards

(b)

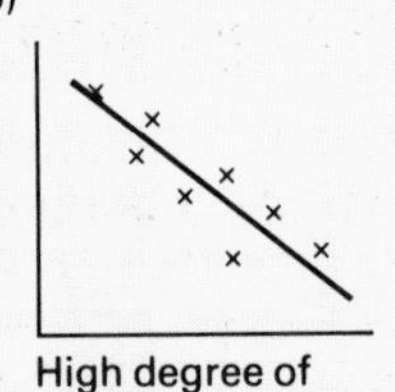

High degree of negative correlation
Example Age of car and value

(c)

Little or no correlation
Example Height and IQ

Fig. 18:8

1 (a) Copy and complete the scatter graph in Figure 18:7. Title your graph and draw your own line of best fit (it will be different from the one shown opposite).

(b) From your graph about what height do you think a boy of five might be?

2 Which of the following do you think would give positive correlation, negative correlation or no correlation?

(a) weight of girls – age of girls

(b) number of cigarettes sold – deaths from lung cancer

(c) worry – bitten nails

(d) a car's engine size – miles per gallon of petrol

(e) value of television – age of television

(f) determination – success

(g) heights of mountains – inches of rainfall

(h) accidents on motorway – number of eagles in the area

3 The results of two tests of a group of children are shown in the table below. A scatter graph recording the data has been started in Figure 18:9.

Name	Maths	Science	Name	Maths	Science
Bill	55	45	Tariq	69	68
Angela	72	60	Alec	32	27
Cicero	63	65	Robina	26	28
Susan	45	47	Allen	87	80
Tom	83	74	Paul	31	25
Kahn	56	65	Iqbal	27	36
Parveen	Absent	54	Sharma	91	84

(a) The point nearest to the vertical axis in Figure 18:9 records Robina's marks (26, 28). Which other three pupils' marks are recorded in Figure 18:9?

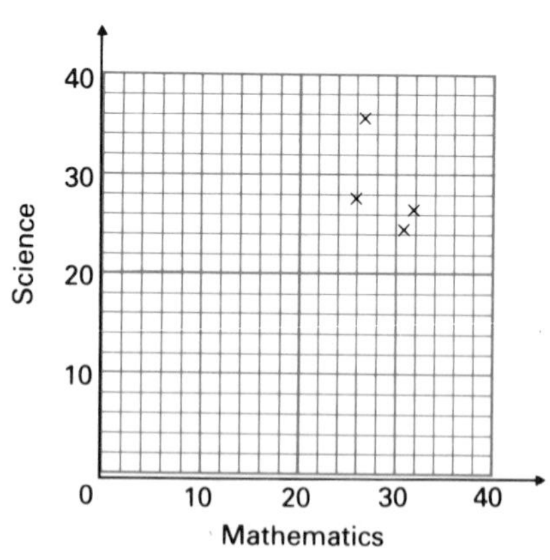

Fig. 18:9

(b) Copy and complete the scatter graph in Figure 18:9. Note that you cannot record Parveen's marks because she was absent for the mathematics test.

(c) If you think there is correlation, draw a line of best fit.

(d) From your line estimate the score Parveen might have got for the mathematics test.

4 A psychologist is investigating the connection, if any, between Intelligence Quotient and the number of books read by a person in a year. He records the following data:

IQ	80	80	85	85	90	90	90	95	95	95	95
No. of books	8	10	4	12	10	16	20	12	15	4	30

100	100	100	100	100	100	100	105	105	105	105
20	25	35	40	26	18	50	40	10	40	45

110	110	110	110	115	115	120	120	125	130
36	40	50	48	30	50	40	50	45	45

Draw up a scatter graph to illustrate the data. If you consider that there is correlation then draw the line of best fit.

5 Conduct your own survey on correlation and draw a suitable scatter graph.

19 Fraction conversions

A Decimal to common fraction

● To remind you . . .

- The fraction line

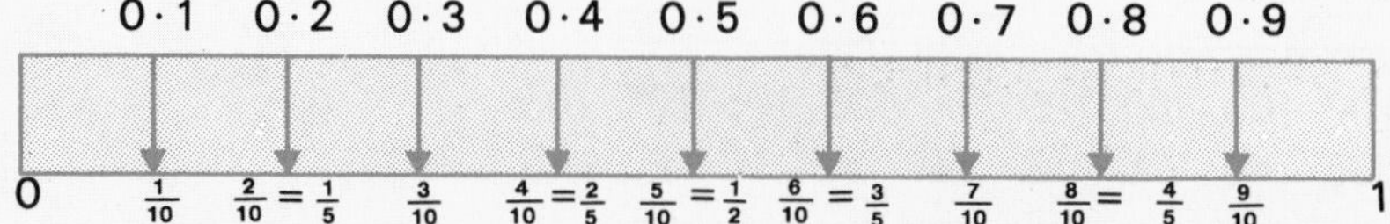

Fig. 19:1

Example In 0·3 the figure 3 is in the tenths column, so 0·3 is $\frac{3}{10}$.

Example In 0·45 the last figure (5) is in the hundredths column, so 0·45 is $\frac{45}{100}$.

We simplify whenever possible. By dividing both 45 and 100 by 5 we can simplify $\frac{45}{100}$ to $\frac{9}{20}$.

1 Write as a common fraction:

(a) 0·7 (b) 0·9 (c) 0·37

(d) 0·371 (e) 0·03

2 **Example** $0{\cdot}84 = \frac{84}{100} = \frac{21}{25}$

84 and 100 have both been divided by 4.

Always cancel to the smallest possible numbers.

Change the following into common fractions. Where possible simplify them by cancelling.

(a) 0·5 (b) 0·8 (c) 0·25 (d) 0·75

(e) 0·12 (f) 0·35 (g) 0·08 (h) 0·05

(i) 0·64 (j) 0·80

3 **Example** The last figure in 0·225 is 5, which is in the *thousandths* column. So 0·225 as a common fraction is $\frac{225}{1000}$.

$\frac{225}{1000}$ as a simplified (cancelled) common fraction is $\frac{9}{40}$. 225 and 1000 have both been divided by 25 to get $\frac{9}{40}$.

We could instead have cancelled first by 5 and then by 5 again.

Write as a simplified common fraction:

(a) 0·125 (b) 0·175 (c) 0·275 (d) 0·350

(e) 0·525 (f) 0·116 (g) 0·128 (h) 0·168

4 Example $1{\cdot}75 = 1\frac{75}{100}$, which simplifies to $1\frac{3}{4}$.
$1\frac{3}{4}$ is a mixed number.

Write as a mixed number as simply as possible:

(a) 3·25 (b) 5·125 (c) 4·075

(d) 6·325 (e) 6·375

5 Can you change decimals into fractions in your head? Write down as many as you can.

6 Can you change fractions into decimals in your head? Write down as many as you can. (You could use the same fractions as in question 5.)

B Common to decimal fraction

To remind you . . .

- **Decimals by division**

When a whole 1 is divided into 4 equal pieces, each piece is 1 out of 4, or $\frac{1}{4}$.

So $\frac{1}{4} \rightarrow 1 \div 4 \rightarrow 0{\cdot}25$

To change a common fraction to a decimal fraction divide the top number by the bottom number.

It is useful to learn decimal equivalents of everyday fractions. For example,

$\frac{1}{4} = 0{\cdot}25$, $\frac{1}{2} = 0{\cdot}5$, $\frac{3}{4} = 0{\cdot}75$, $\frac{1}{10} = 0{\cdot}1$,

$\frac{1}{3} = 0{\cdot}333\ldots$

▶ Points to discuss . . .

Decimal places

1 Divide £200 by 7 on your calculator.

It would be sensible to give the answer correct to the nearest penny, that is, correct to 2 decimal places. We say £200 ÷ 7 is £28·57 correct to 2 d.p.

2 Now divide £300 by 7.

This time we give the answer as £42·86 correct to 2 decimal places. Why?

Rule If the figure after the last decimal place you require is 5 or more, round up.

Examples 2·3497 → 2·3 to 1 decimal place

2·3497 → 2·35 to 2 decimal places

2·3497 → 2·350 to 3 decimal places.

Where did the 0 come from in this example?

1 Write as a decimal fraction:

(a) $\frac{1}{2}$ (b) $\frac{1}{4}$ (c) $\frac{3}{4}$ (d) $\frac{3}{10}$ (e) $\frac{1}{5}$

(f) $\frac{7}{10}$ (g) $\frac{7}{20}$ (h) $\frac{9}{20}$ (i) $\frac{11}{20}$ (j) $\frac{3}{5}$

2 Use the fact that $\frac{1}{40} = 0{\cdot}025$ to change the following common fractions to decimal fractions.

(a) $\frac{3}{40}$ (b) $\frac{4}{40}$ (c) $\frac{5}{40}$ (d) $\frac{7}{40}$ (e) $\frac{9}{40}$

3 Write as a decimal number:

(a) $2\frac{1}{4}$ (b) $3\frac{3}{4}$ (c) $4\frac{1}{10}$ (d) $5\frac{3}{10}$ (e) $6\frac{7}{20}$

4 Use the fact that $\frac{1}{8} = 0{\cdot}125$ to change the following to decimal fractions.

(a) $\frac{2}{8}$ (b) $\frac{4}{8}$ (c) $\frac{5}{8}$ (d) $\frac{6}{8}$ (e) $\frac{7}{8}$

5 Change the following fractions into decimals and then write them in ascending order of magnitude (start with the smallest).

$\frac{1}{4}$, $\frac{1}{5}$, $\frac{7}{8}$, $\frac{4}{5}$, $\frac{9}{20}$, $\frac{13}{40}$, $\frac{5}{8}$, $\frac{1}{10}$, $\frac{7}{10}$, $\frac{27}{50}$, $\frac{5}{10}$, $\frac{9}{40}$

6 Using your calculator change the following to decimals correct to (i) 1 decimal place and (ii) 3 decimal places.

(a) $\frac{1}{7}$ (b) $\frac{2}{7}$ (c) $\frac{5}{7}$ (d) $\frac{4}{9}$

(e) $\frac{5}{11}$ (f) $\frac{7}{11}$ (g) $\frac{1}{3}$ (h) $\frac{2}{3}$

Worksheet 19 may be used here.

A Congruency

If two shapes are **identical in every respect** they are said to be congruent.

Examples

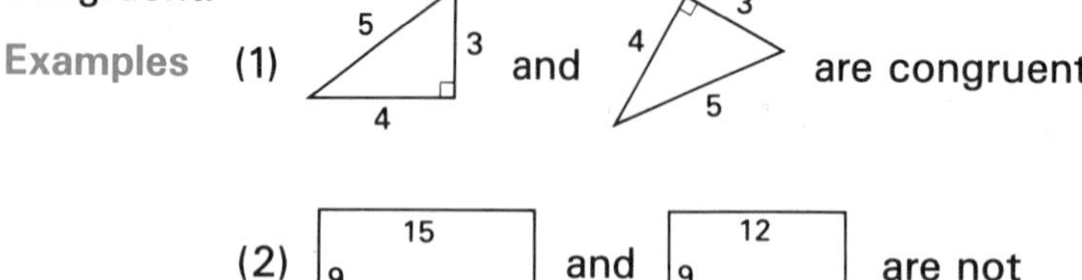

1 Name the pairs of congruent shapes in Figure B3:1. (Don't be misled by some of the drawings.)

Fig. B3:1

2 (a) Draw two congruent triangles, but draw them in different positions.

(b) Measure the angles of the two triangles. What do you notice?

B Perspective

1 Would you say the houses in Figure B3:2 are the same?

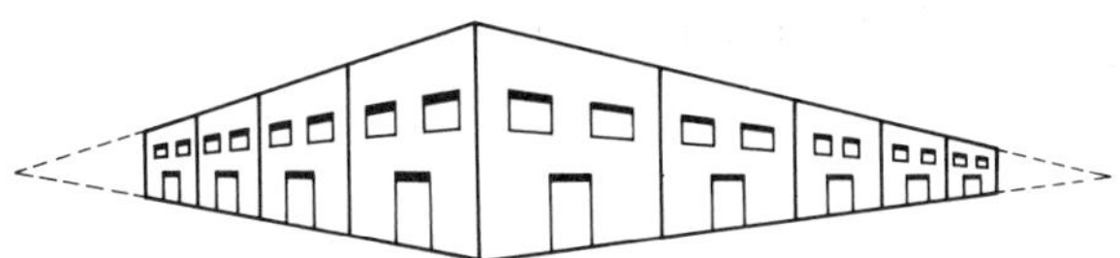

Fig. B3:2

2 Draw your own picture showing perspective. Some ideas are: a line of identical trees; a row of telegraph poles; a length of fence panelling; a long brick wall and so on.

20 Money

A Spending money

This gold coin was issued by King Croesus of Lydia in about 550 BC. It bears the imprint of a lion and a bull.

▶ Points to discuss . . .

1 Before money was invented people used the barter system. What does this mean? Have you ever used this system?

2 Is the metal in a £1 coin worth £1?

3 In 1923 German inflation was so bad that wheelbarrow loads of notes were needed to buy a loaf of bread. What is 'inflation'?

1 The answers to this question are given in Figure 20:1. Link up each part with its correct letter.

(a) Which imaginary animal is shown on the back of some English £1 coins?

(b) The Prince of Wales' . . . are shown on the 2p piece.

(c) Which seated figure is shown on the back of some 50p pieces?

(d) The . . . of Scotland is shown on the 5p piece.

(e) The shape of a 20p piece is called a . . .

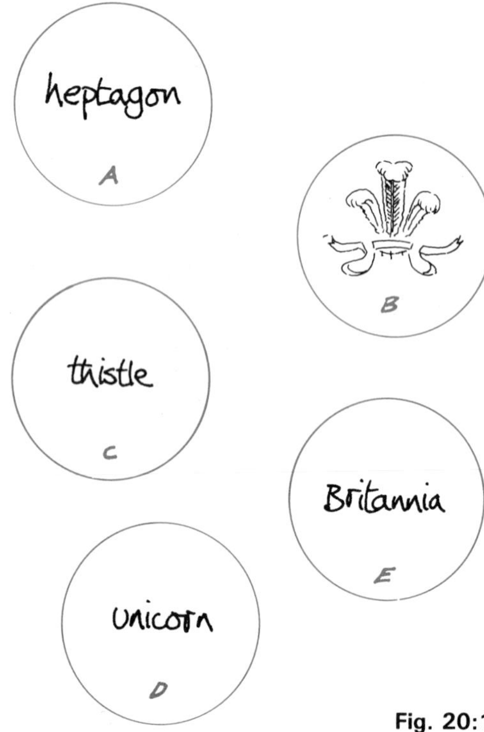

Fig. 20:1

2 Many popular sayings and songs reflect some of our ideas about money. Find the correct ending for each of these.

(a) Take care of the pennies and . . .	**A** she was honest
(b) As safe as the . . .	**B** pound foolish
(c) The man who broke the . . .	**C** there's brass
(d) She was poor but . . .	**D** Croesus
(e) Neither a borrower nor . . .	**E** are soon parted
(f) Where there's muck . . .	**F** a church mouse
(g) She's as poor as . . .	**G** bank at Monte Carlo
(h) Penny wise, . . .	**H** a lender be
(i) A fool and his money . . .	**I** Bank of England
(j) He is as rich as . . .	**J** the pounds will take care of themselves.

3 Give the meanings of sayings (a), (e) and (h) above.

4 Link the countries with their currencies.

Currencies
Lira Pesetas Dollar Rupee Yen Kronor

Countries
Canada Sweden Italy Spain India Japan

5 Mrs Brown has these notes and coins in her purse. List which notes and coins she would need in order to pay the following amounts, using as few notes and coins as possible.

(a) 72p (b) £6·80

(c) £16·67 (d) £17·92

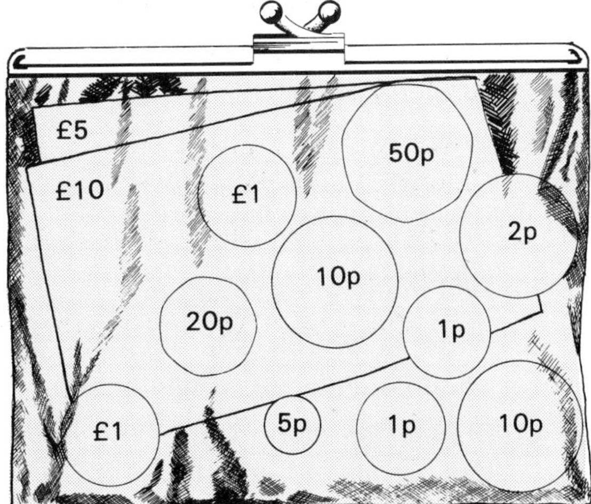

Fig. 20:2

6 Mr and Mrs Green are going on holiday to Paris.

(a) Name the famous landmark in Figure 20:3.

(b) If the rate of exchange is 9·5 French francs to the pound sterling, how many francs will they receive for £100?

(c) At the end of the holiday they have 60 francs left. The rate of exchange is 9 francs to the pound. How much British money will they receive?

Fig. 20:3

7 This table shows approximately how much the British government spent on different things during the financial year 1985–86.

	Amount spent (£ billion)
Social security	41
Health	17
Education	15
Defence	18
Law and order	5
Transport	5
Housing	3
Trade, energy, employment	6

(a) Find the total expenditure.

(b) Write in words the amounts spent on (i) social security, and (ii) education.

(c) Draw a bar-chart to show the information in the table. Use a scale of 5 mm to £2 billion on the vertical axis.

Worksheet 20 may be used here.

B Money calculations

▶ Points to discuss . . .

You have to be careful when using a calculator to answer the following questions. Why?

(a) £16 + 25p (b) £4·65 × 4 (c) £3 ÷ 7

(d) £8·16 × 4·8 (e) £157·81 ÷ 4·3

1 John, Helen and Gary each have a spare-time job. John has a newspaper round, Helen helps in her parents' ice-cream parlour, and Gary works on Saturdays at a small garage. The amounts they earned and spent over ten weeks are shown in the tables below.

John

Week	Income	Spent
1		£2·25
2		£1·57
3		£4·36
4	£7·50	£0·98
5	per	£1·10
6	week	£5·31
7		£7·00
8		£2·19
9		£1·87
10		£0·86

Helen

Week	Income	Spent
1		£3·75
2		£1·15
3		£1·12
4	£9·25	£1·18
5	per	£2·39
6	week	£5·07
7		£1·34
8		£0·40
9		£3·21
10		£2·37

Gary

Week	Income	Spent
1	£8·42	£3·40
2	£12·50	£2·70
3	£14·80	£4·05
4	£9·84	£3·23
5	£10·00	£2·58
6	£15·20	£6·76
7	£13·60	£8·92
8	£9·82	£1·25
9	£12·44	£2·10
10	£12·56	£5·63

(a) What kind of extra income would John expect around Christmas time?

(b) In what season of the year would Helen's family probably make (i) most money, and (ii) least money?

(c) Give two advantages (other than money) that Gary might eventually gain by working at the garage.

(d) Total the ten weeks' income and spending for John, Helen and Gary.

2 Evaluate:

(a) £4·80 ÷ 2 (b) £9·09 ÷ 3 (c) £15·45 ÷ 5

(d) £5·53 ÷ 7 (e) £4·68 ÷ 9 (f) £9·24 ÷ 11

3 A house has to be restored after being badly damaged by fire. The builders estimate they will need the following amounts of materials:

- 9500 bricks at £22·15 per 100 bricks
- $2\frac{1}{2}$ cubic metres of sand at £18·30 a cubic metre
- 12 bags of cement at £4·31 a bag
- 52 metres of 10 cm by 5 cm timber at £1·72 a metre

(a) What is meant by a cubic metre?

(b) How many hundreds is 9500?

(c) Make out a bill for the total estimated cost of the materials.

4 Mr and Mrs Sussex and their two children aged 7 years and 4 years want to go on a Mini-Break holiday. How much will it cost?

Mini-Break Holidays

£53 · 60 for each adult

Half price for children aged 5 – 14

Quarter price for children under 5

Fig. 20:4

5 **Example**

£81·40 × 10 = £814·0 → £814·00

£81·40 × 20 = £81·40 × 2 × 10

= £162·80 × 10

= £1628·00

£81·40 × 100 = £8140· → £8140·00

Copy and complete this table.

×	£4·20	£2·06	£6·30
10		£20·60	
20			£126·00
50			
100			

6 Example 1 kg of apples costs 78p. Find the cost of $4\frac{1}{2}$ kg.

4 kg cost 4×78p $= 312$p
$\frac{1}{2}$ kg costs $\frac{1}{2} \times 78$p $= 39$p
Answer: $4\frac{1}{2}$ kg costs £3·51.

Copy and complete this table.

×	72p	£2·40	£5·40
$2\frac{1}{2}$			
$3\frac{1}{3}$			
$4\frac{1}{4}$			

7 (a) A man earned £171 for a 38-hour basic working week. At what rate per hour was he paid?

(b) The cost of printing each of 20 000 copies of a book is £3·75. What was the total cost of printing these books?

(LEAG)

8 Answers in £s need to be given correct to 2 decimal places.

Example £81·70 ÷ 100 = £0·817 → £0·82

Copy and complete the table, giving answers in £s correct to the nearest penny.

Remember to round up if the figure in the third decimal place is 5 or more.

÷	£4·20	£2·05	£6·30
10	£0·42		
20		£0·10	
50			
100		£0·02	

9 A telephone bill is made up of a fixed charge of £16·50 and 389 metered units at 4p a unit. Calculate the total amount of the bill.

10 A club has 185 members, each paying a subscription of £2·75 per year. The hire of a room for each monthly meeting costs £21. Other expenses during the year total £283·47. The club receives a grant of £50 a year from the local council.

(a) How much does the club receive in subscriptions in one year?

(b) What is the total income of the club in one year?

(c) What is the total cost of hiring the room for the twelve meetings in one year?

(d) What are the total expenses of the club in one year?

(e) If the club has £97·31 in the bank at the beginning of the year how much will it have at the end of the year?

(NEA)

11 The cash price of a washing machine was £390·00. Helen bought the machine on a credit agreement involving (i) a deposit of £75, and (ii) 36 monthly payments of £11·25 each.

How much extra did the washing machine cost when bought on credit?

12 Paul earns £600 a calendar month before tax. Sarah earns £525 a calendar month before tax. To help them buy a house a building society will lend them $2\frac{1}{2}$ times their combined total annual income. The repayments will be £9·12 a calendar month for each £1000 borrowed.

(a) How much does Paul earn annually?

(b) How much does Sarah earn annually?

(c) How much will the building society lend them?

(d) What would be a monthly repayment?

21 Fraction division

A Dividing decimals

To remind you . . .

- **Division by powers of ten**

$\frac{8 \cdot 3}{10} \xrightarrow{\text{move 1 place}} 0 \cdot 83$

$\frac{8 \cdot 3}{100} \xrightarrow{\text{move 2 places}} 0 \cdot 083$

$\frac{8 \cdot 3}{1000} \xrightarrow{\text{move 3 places}} 0 \cdot 0083$

- **Division without a calculator**

$22 \cdot 2 \div 6 \rightarrow 6 \,\overline{)\,2\;2\,\cdot{}^{4}2}$ (quotient $3 \cdot 7$) $\rightarrow$ Answer: 3·7

$525 \div 0 \cdot 5 \rightarrow 5250 \div 5 \rightarrow 5 \,\overline{)\,5\;2\;5\;0}$ (quotient 1 0 5 0) $\rightarrow$ Answer: 1050

Note how this example has been changed so that division is by an integer.

1 Evaluate:

(a) 19·6 ÷ 7 (b) 19·67 ÷ 7 (c) 77·4 km ÷ 9

(d) £57·28 ÷ 8 (e) 57·6 cm ÷ 6 (f) 27 ÷ 6

(g) 103 ÷ 4 (h) 246 ÷ 8 (i) 91 ÷ 5

(j) 91 ÷ 4 (k) 93 ÷ 5 (l) 75·5 ÷ 25

2 Evaluate:

(a) 7·2 ÷ 10 (b) 3·6 ÷ 100 (c) 36·5 ÷ 100

(d) 19·7 ÷ 100 (e) 19·7 ÷ 1000 (f) 2·15 ÷ 10

(g) 2·15 ÷ 100 (h) 2·15 ÷ 1000 (i) 0·3 ÷ 100

3 State the value of the letter in each of these.

(a) $9{\cdot}5 \div b = 0{\cdot}95$ (b) $9{\cdot}5 \div c = 0{\cdot}095$

(c) $9{\cdot}5 \div d = 0{\cdot}0095$ (d) $345{\cdot}8 \div e = 3{\cdot}458$

(e) $0{\cdot}1 \div f = 0{\cdot}001$ (f) $0{\cdot}1 \div g = 0{\cdot}0001$

4 Example $9{\cdot}6 \div 30 = (9{\cdot}6 \div 3) \div 10 = 3{\cdot}2 \div 10 = 0{\cdot}32$

In a similar way find the answer to:

(a) $4{\cdot}4 \div 20$ (b) $6{\cdot}6 \div 30$ (c) $8{\cdot}4 \div 40$

(d) $8{\cdot}4 \div 400$ (e) $6{\cdot}6 \div 300$ (f) $55{\cdot}5 \div 50$

5 (a) Alec paid £63 for 10 m^2 of carpet. How much did 1 m^2 cost?

(b) Lisa paid £65·80 for 10 m^2. What was the cost of 1 m^2?

6 Be careful not to miss out zeros when the number you are dividing by 'won't go'.

Example £36·12 ÷ 12 = £3·01, **not** £3·1

Evaluate:

(a) £36·36 ÷ 6 (b) £40·56 ÷ 8 (c) £54·63 ÷ 9

(d) £60·75 ÷ 15 (e) £68·51 ÷ 17

(f) £161·92 ÷ 23

7 Farmer Stubble buys a hectare of land (10 000 m^2) for £8500. How much does he pay for each 1 m^2?

8 The heights of Catherine and Laura are in the ratio 5 : 4. If Catherine is 1 m 75 cm tall, how tall is Laura?

9 Work these out correct to two decimal places.

(a) £50·80 ÷ 100 (b) £35·50 ÷ 100

(c) 901 ÷ 1000

10 Example $0{\cdot}8 = \frac{8}{10}$ and $0{\cdot}4 = \frac{4}{10}$.
So we can think of $0{\cdot}8 \div 0{\cdot}4$ as **8** tenths ÷ **4** tenths, giving an answer of 2.

$0{\cdot}36 = \frac{36}{100}$ and $0{\cdot}12 = \frac{12}{100}$, so $0{\cdot}36 \div 0{\cdot}12$ can be thought of as **36** hundredths ÷ **12** hundredths = 3 (see Figure 21:1).

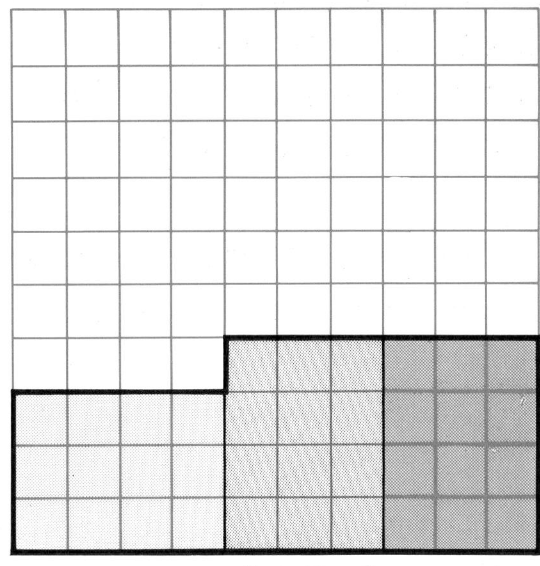

Fig. 21:1

$\frac{36}{100} \div \frac{12}{100} = 3$

Work these out in your head in a similar manner.

(a) $0{\cdot}9 \div 0{\cdot}3$ (b) $0{\cdot}6 \div 0{\cdot}3$ (c) $0{\cdot}8 \div 0{\cdot}2$

(d) $0{\cdot}8 \div 0{\cdot}1$ (e) $0{\cdot}36 \div 0{\cdot}12$ (f) $0{\cdot}48 \div 0{\cdot}12$

(g) $0{\cdot}60 \div 0{\cdot}12$ (h) $0{\cdot}45 \div 0{\cdot}15$

(i) $0{\cdot}84 \div 0{\cdot}12$

11 Shell and Esso produce 7·5 million therms of gas a day from the North Sea. This is equivalent to burning 27 384 tonnes of coal or 127 326 barrels of oil.

(a) What is the production of gas in a year?

(b) What is the equivalent to this in (i) coal, and (ii) oil?

Assume the rigs work all the time.

B Dividing common fractions

● To remind you . . .

● **Division by a fraction**

To divide by a fraction, multiply by the fraction turned upside down.

Example $3\frac{1}{2} \div \frac{3}{8} \rightarrow \frac{7}{\cancel{2}_1} \times \frac{\cancel{8}^4}{3} \rightarrow \frac{28}{3} \rightarrow 9\frac{1}{3}$

Note Change mixed numbers, like $3\frac{1}{2}$, into top-heavy fractions first.

Note As with multiplication of fractions, you can cancel the fractions first, or cancel the answer.

● **Division by an integer**

Place the integer over 1.

Example $5\frac{1}{2} \div 6 \rightarrow \frac{11}{2} \div \frac{6}{1} \rightarrow \frac{11}{2} \times \frac{1}{6} \rightarrow \frac{11}{12}$

● **Using a calculator**

Unless your calculator is programmed to handle common fractions you must

either use brackets round the fractions
or change the fractions to decimals first.

Example $4 \div \frac{3}{4}$

Either 4 [÷] [(] 3 [÷] 4 [)] [=]

or, as $\frac{3}{4}$ is $3 \div 4$ which equals 0·75, key in

4 [÷] 0·75 [=]

Note The correct answer to this example on a calculator is 5·333 333 3. This is the nearest a calculator can get to showing $5\frac{1}{3}$, so the answer is $5\frac{1}{3}$. (See exercise 19A for changing decimal to common fractions.)

▶ Point to discuss . . .

If you key in 4 [÷] 3 [÷] 4 [=] to do $4 \div \frac{3}{4}$ you will get the wrong answer 0·333 333 3. Why is this?

1 Example A farmer wishes to sell off a $3\frac{1}{2}$ acre field in $\frac{1}{4}$ acre plots. How many plots will he sell?

The problem is 'How many $\frac{1}{4}$s in $3\frac{1}{2}$?' or $3\frac{1}{2} \div \frac{1}{4}$.
Figure 21:2 shows that he can sell $3\frac{1}{2}$ rows each containing 4 plots, a total of 14 plots.

Fig. 21:2

Figure 21:2 shows $3\frac{1}{2} \div \frac{1}{4} = 14$. Draw a diagram on squared paper to illustrate:

(a) $2\frac{1}{2} \div \frac{1}{2} = 5$ (b) $1\frac{1}{4} \div \frac{1}{4} = 5$
(c) $\frac{2}{3} \div \frac{1}{3} = 2$

2 Find:

(a) $4 \div \frac{3}{4}$ (b) $6 \div 1\frac{1}{5}$ (c) $\frac{2}{3} \div 1\frac{1}{4}$

(d) $6\frac{2}{5} \div 4$ (e) $\frac{4}{9} \div \frac{2}{3}$ (f) $3\frac{3}{4} \div 7\frac{1}{2}$

3 Use a calculator to evaluate:

(a) $\frac{3}{4} \times 2 - \frac{3}{4}$ (b) $\frac{1}{8} \div \frac{1}{2} + \frac{1}{4}$ (c) $\frac{1}{5} + \frac{1}{2} - \frac{3}{8}$

4 1 km $\approx \frac{5}{8}$ mile, 1 mile $\approx 1\frac{3}{5}$ km.

(a) Approximately how many km are there in
 (i) 2 miles (ii) $2\frac{1}{2}$ miles?

(b) Approximately how many miles are there in
 (i) 10 km (ii) 25 km?

5 If $1\frac{3}{5}$ kg of flour makes 28 cakes, how many cakes can be made from 8 kg of flour?

6 How many $\frac{3}{16}$ litre glasses can be filled from a $5\frac{1}{2}$ litre container?

7 A ferry crosses a stretch of water in approximately $\frac{5}{6}$ of an hour. How many complete crossings could it make in 10 hours?

Worksheet 21 may be used here.

Assignment 2

● To remind you . . .

- **Approaching assignments**

  (a) Understand – what are you being asked to do?
  (b) Plan – how are you going to do it?
  (c) Carry out – reasoning, calculating, exploring, discussing, . . .
  (d) Communicate – talking, writing, drawing, modelling, . . .

Who lied?

The village of Portsea has a sub-post-office that contains a safe. A light is left on over the office door during closing hours. Any unlawful entry into the sub-post-office will turn off the light.

Four people are involved in the story:

Miss Gold, aged 67, has an arthritic hip.
Mr Copper, aged 42, is a salesman and is colour blind.
Mrs Silver, aged 36, suffers from acrophobia (fear of heights).
PC Hutch, aged 32, is the village policeman.

The sub-post-office is broken into. Figure A2:1 (on the next page) sets the scene.

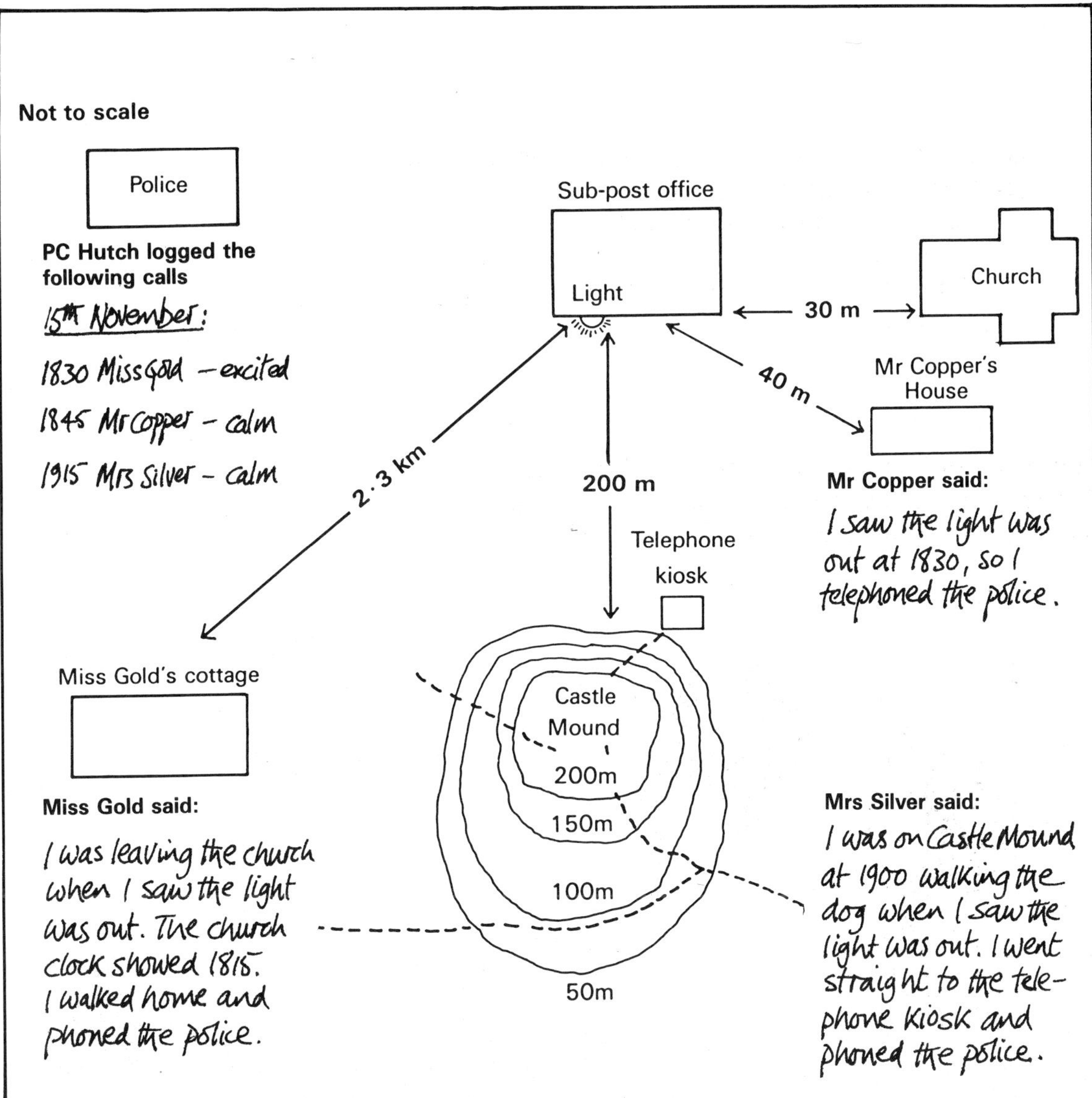

Fig. A2:1

The policeman is telling the truth, but two of the other people told lies. You have to find out which two.

(a) Write down anything you may have to find out before you can begin your investigation.

(b) Which two people lied? Give full reasons for your answers.

Nets

1 (a) Use compasses to draw the three constructions described in Figure A2:2. Draw part (iii) with a radius of 5 cm.

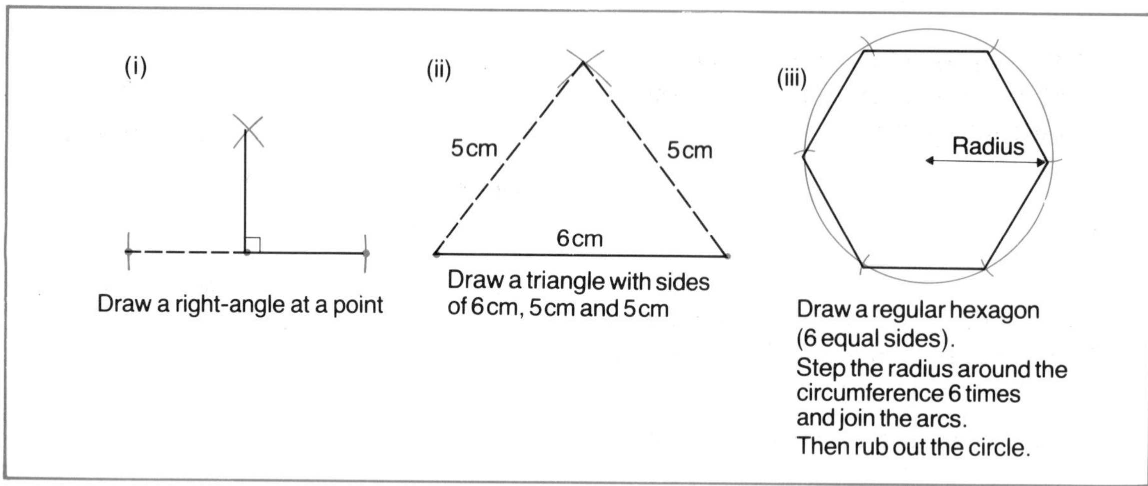

Fig. A2:2

(b) Describe another way of constructing a right-angle.

2

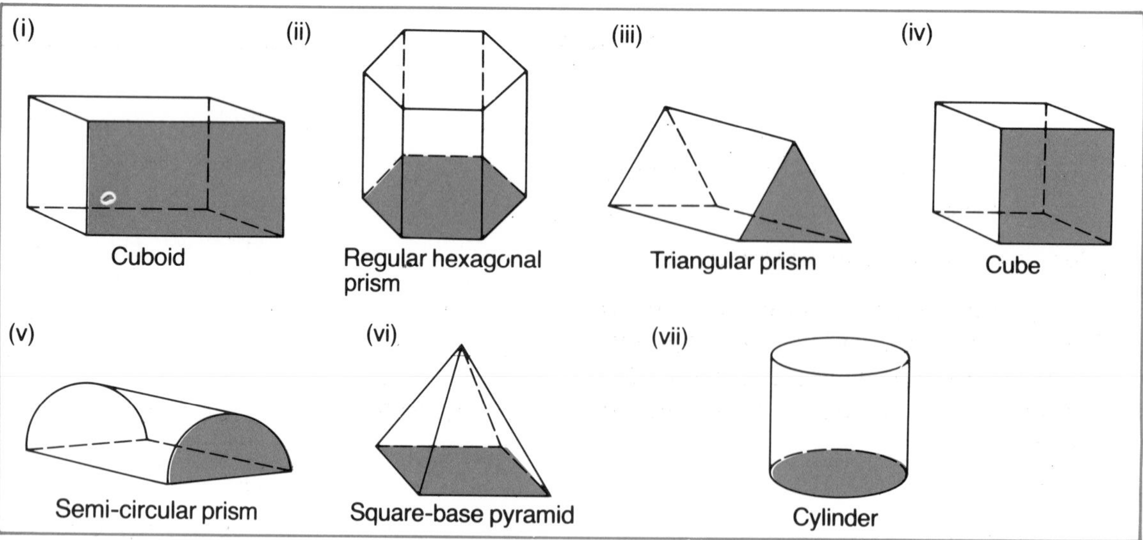

Fig. A2:3

(a) Describe an everyday use for each of the shapes illustrated in Figure A2:3.

(b) Which shapes in Figure A2:3 are prisms? (See the Glossary.)

3 One possible construction net for the cube is shown in Figure A2:4.

(a) Draw two more arrangements of six squares which will make a net for a cube.

(b) Make a cube from one of your nets. Make sure that you have suitable tabs for gluing.

Tabs for gluing

Fig. A2:4

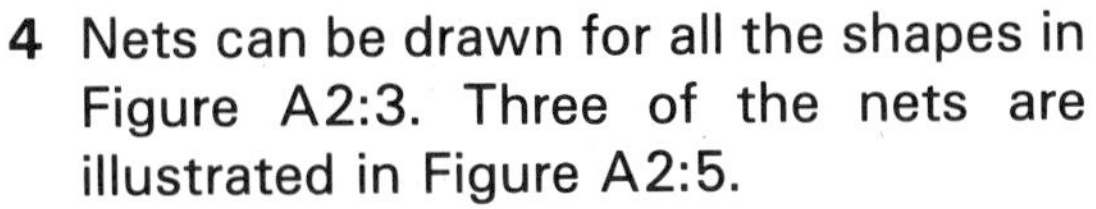

4 Nets can be drawn for all the shapes in Figure A2:3. Three of the nets are illustrated in Figure A2:5.

(a) Which solid does each net make?

Draw a net for:

(b) a cuboid

(c) a regular hexagonal prism.

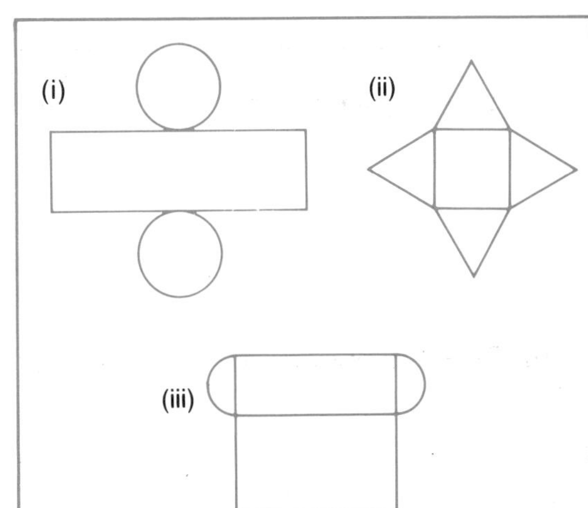

Fig. A2:5

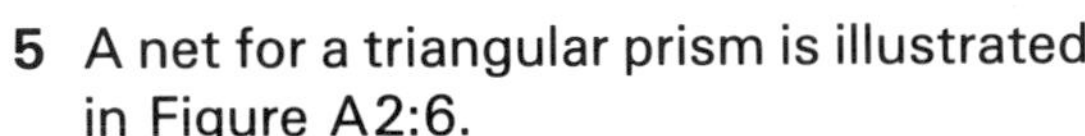

5 A net for a triangular prism is illustrated in Figure A2:6.

Measurements are in centimetres.

Using the measurements shown in Figure A2:6 draw the net, placing construction tabs in suitable places. Cut out your net and make the triangular prism.

4 4 4 4 4 6 6 6 6

Fig. A2:6

Put a tab on every other edge.

Worksheets A2A, A2B and A2C may be used here.

6 Write a report on what you have found out in this assignment. List the main difficulties you encountered.

22 Percentages

A Out of a hundred

● To remind you . . .

- **Out of 100**
  A percentage is a fraction with a denominator of 100.
  Per cent, or %, means 'out of 100'.

▶ Points to discuss . . .

1 What uses of percentages are shown in Figure 22:1?

(a)

Approximately 75% of the world's fresh water is frozen in ice fields.

(b)

In the UK, a minimum 25% solution of antifreeze should be used.

(c)

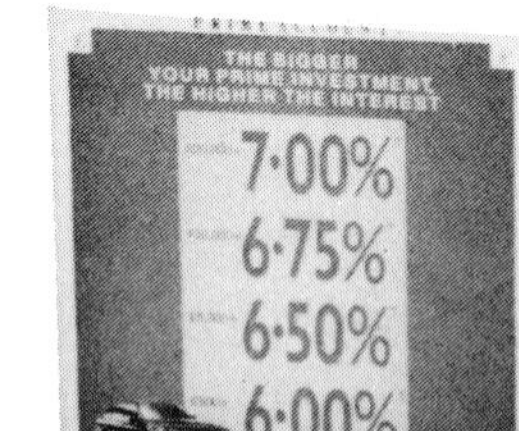

£1000 invested at 6% p.a. grows to £3207.14 in 20 years.

Fig. 22:1

2 Where else do you meet percentages out of mathematics lessons?

3 What do the following mean?

(a) 10% deposit (b) VAT

(c) 25% basic rate of tax (d) Invest at 8%

4 75% of Cheet School take GCSE English, and 80% take GCSE mathematics. The headteacher tells parents that 155% of the pupils take English and mathematics. Is he right?

1 The scales in Figure 22:2 show some equivalent percentages, decimals and fractions.

Note 5% as a decimal is 0·05.
0·10, 0·20 and 0·50 can be simplified to 0·1, 0·2 and 0·5.

Copy Figure 22:2 on cm squared paper. Make it twice as large.

Put the correct percentage, decimal fraction and common fraction against each of the unlabelled marks on the scales.

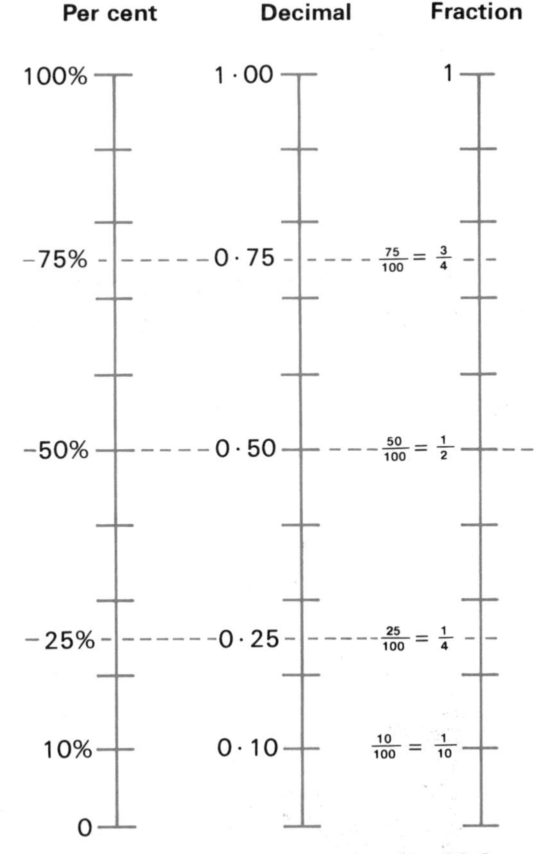

Fig. 22:2

2 Figure 22:3 shows a percentage scale and glasses of squash.

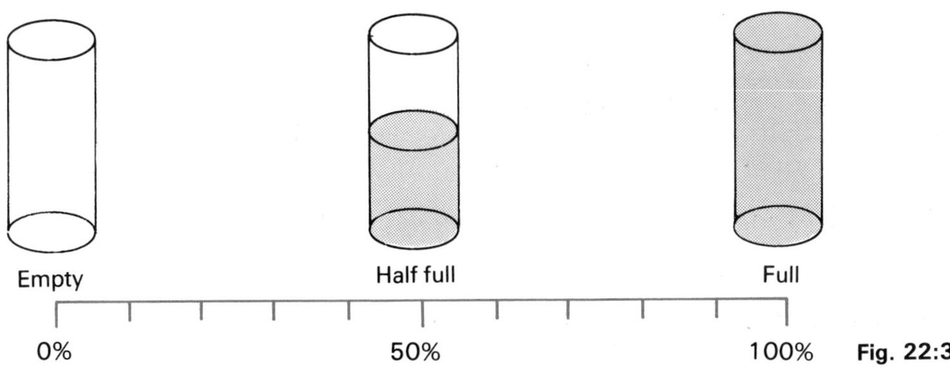

Fig. 22:3

Draw a glass of squash about:

(a) 25% full (b) 75% full

3 Example 12% is the same fraction as 0·12.

Write the equivalent decimal fraction for:

(a) 15% (b) 6% (c) $12\frac{1}{2}$% (d) $62\frac{1}{2}$%

(e) 4·5%

4 (a) 100% of the 600 pupils in Nordern school are boys. How many are girls?

(b) 50% of the Nordern pupils passed an examination. How many was this?

5 (a) 12% of part (i) in Figure 22:4 is shaded. What percentages are shaded in parts (ii), (iii) and (iv)?

(b) What percentages are unshaded in parts (i), (ii), (iii) and (iv)?

(c) Give the answers to part (b) as simplified common fractions.

(i)

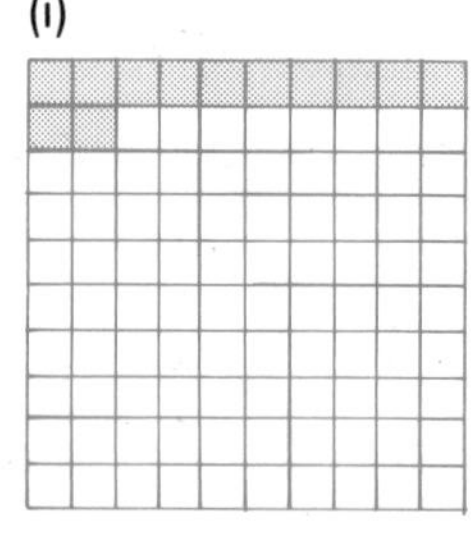

(ii)

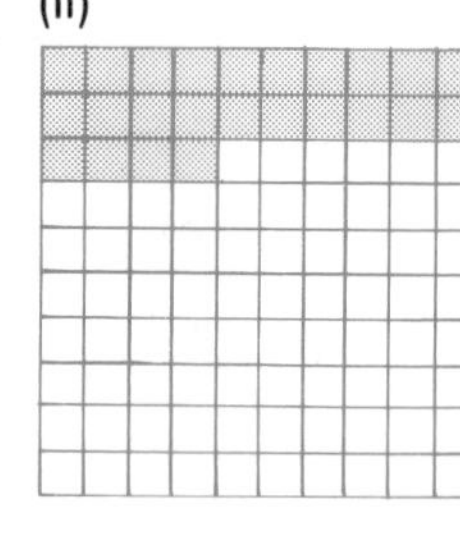

(iii)

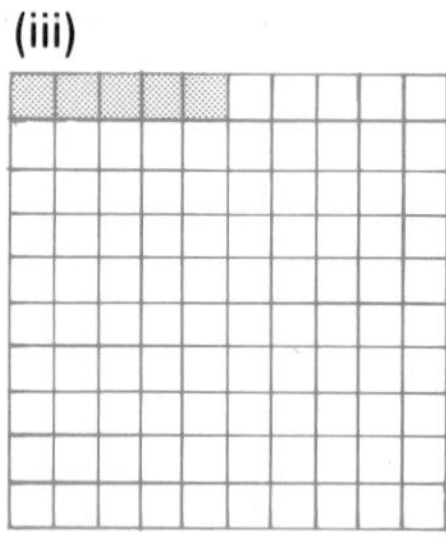

(iv)

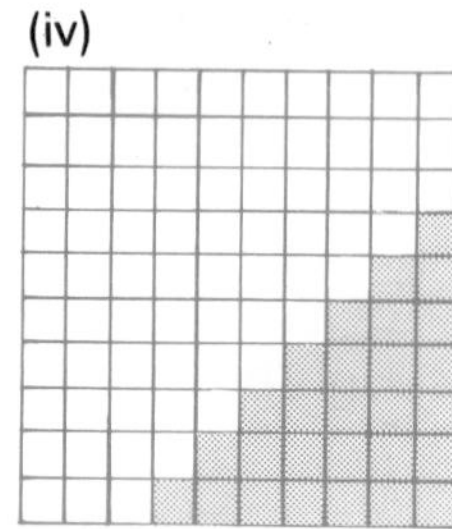

Fig. 22:4

6 Three possible answers are given for each question. Choose the most likely answer.

(a) . . . of the school were away on Monday.
A 90% B 0·8 C $\frac{1}{10}$

(b) Last year prices rose by . . .
A 3% B $\frac{1}{2}$ C 0·30

(c) The baby's height increased in one year by . . .
A $\frac{1}{5}$ B 75% C 0·6

(d) The class did well. . . . passed the examination.
A 0·15 B $\frac{7}{20}$ C 80%

7 Example $45\% = \frac{45}{100} = \frac{9}{20}$. By dividing 5 into 45 and 100, $\frac{45}{100}$ has been simplified to $\frac{9}{20}$.

Example $12\frac{1}{2}\% = \frac{12\frac{1}{2}}{100} = \frac{25}{200} = \frac{1}{8}$.

Simplify:

(a) 75% (b) 25% (c) 35% (d) 40%

(e) 5% (f) $37\frac{1}{2}\%$ (g) $2\frac{1}{2}\%$ (h) $7\frac{1}{2}\%$

8 Example 0·20 is smaller than $\frac{27}{100}$ which is smaller than 30%. Using the symbol $<$, which stands for 'is smaller than', we can write
$0{\cdot}20 < \frac{27}{100} < 30\%$.

Write the following in the correct order using $<$.

(a) 20% $\frac{1}{4}$ 0·45 (b) 0·05 10% $\frac{1}{2}$

(c) $12\frac{1}{2}\%$ 0·21 $\frac{2}{5}$ (d) $\frac{9}{10}$ 0·87 80%

(e) 0·05 $\frac{1}{10}$ 11% (f) $2\frac{1}{2}\%$ $\frac{1}{100}$ 0·07

B Percentage of an amount

● To remind you . . .

- **Percentage of a pound**
  1% of £1 is 1p.
  17% of £1 is 17p.
  17% of £5 is 5 × 17p = 85p.

- **Using a calculator [%] key**
  17% of £5 → 5 [×] 17 [%] **or** 5 [×] 17 [%] [=]

  Note If you have no [%] key, use the fact that 17% = 0·17 and work out 5 × 0·17

▶ Points to discuss . . .

Link each part of Figure 22:5 (on the next page) with a word and its meaning from the lists below.

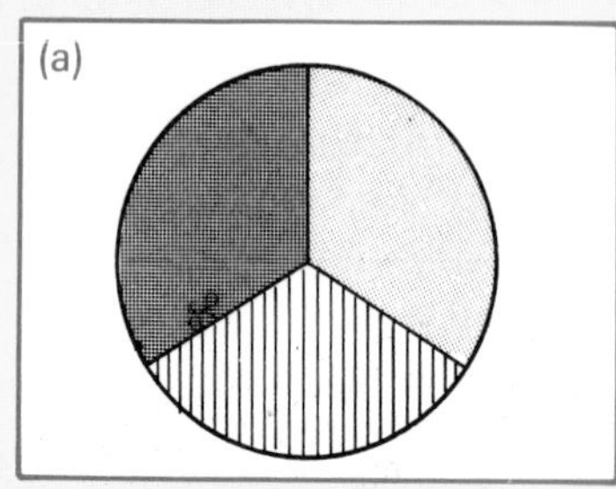

Fig. 22:5

Words	Meanings
VAT	Loses value
Discount	Money down (rest usually paid by HP)
Depreciation	Make a close examination
Deposit	Usually money off for cash
Survey	A way of showing information
Pie-chart	Value Added Tax

1 Copy and complete the table.

Percentage	Fraction	Decimal
17%	?	?
?	$\frac{25}{100} = \frac{1}{4}$	?
?	?	0·75
60%	$\frac{60}{100} = ?$	?
?	? = ?	0·24
?	? = ?	0·125

2 How many pence is each of these?

(a) 5% of £1 (b) 16% of £1 (c) 35% of £1

(d) 5% of £4 (e) 16% of £7 (f) 35% of £9

(g) 1% of £5 (h) 60% of £2 (i) $12\frac{1}{2}$% of £4

3 Figure 22:6 shows the monthly interest rates charged by different credit card companies. Which company charges the highest rate of interest?

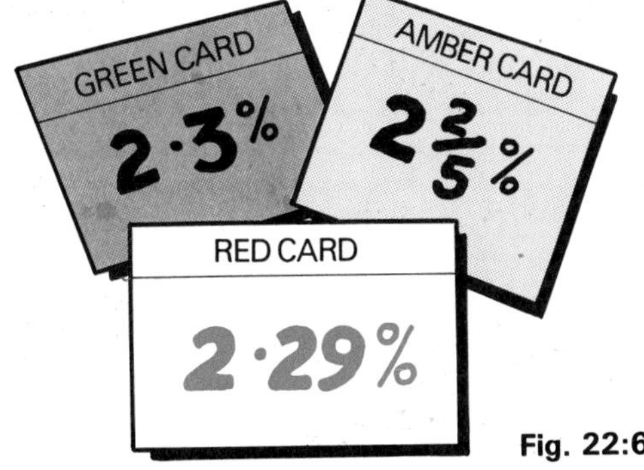

Fig. 22:6

4 Find:

(a) 20% of £4·20 (b) 30% of £4·20

(c) 5% of £4·20 (d) $2\frac{1}{2}$% of £4·20

(e) 10% of £12·60 (f) 5% of £12·60

(g) 40% of £12·60

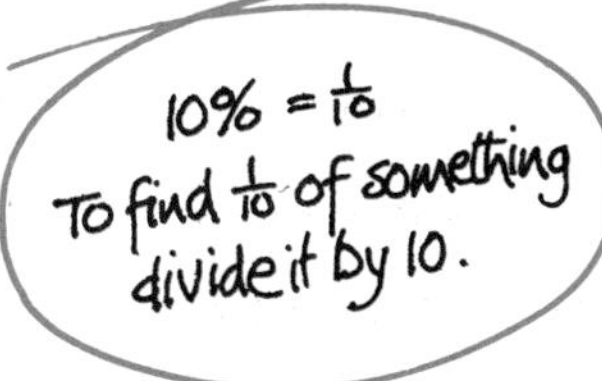

5 VAT is a government tax ('Value Added Tax') on certain goods and services. In 1987 VAT was charged at 15%.

Example Imran bought a chicken curry and some gulabjamun from a Tandoori takeaway. He was charged £4 plus VAT.
The VAT was 15% of £4 = 60p.
The total cost was £4·60.

For each of the items in Figure 22:7 find:

(i) the VAT at 15% (ii) the total price.

Fig. 22:7

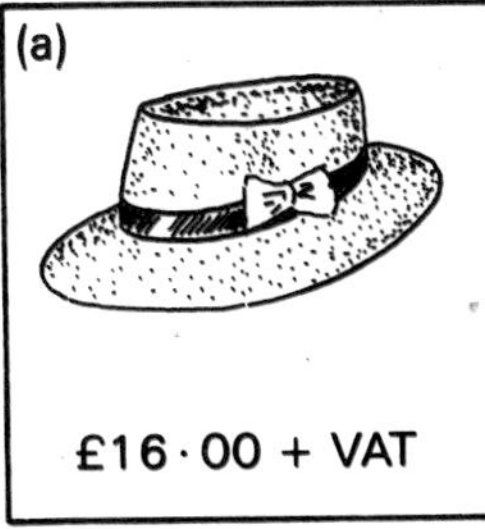

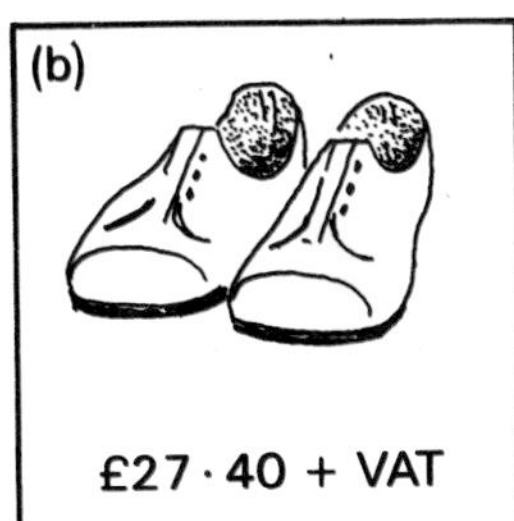

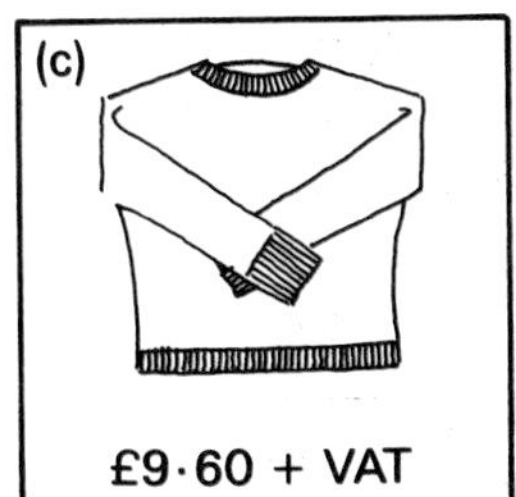

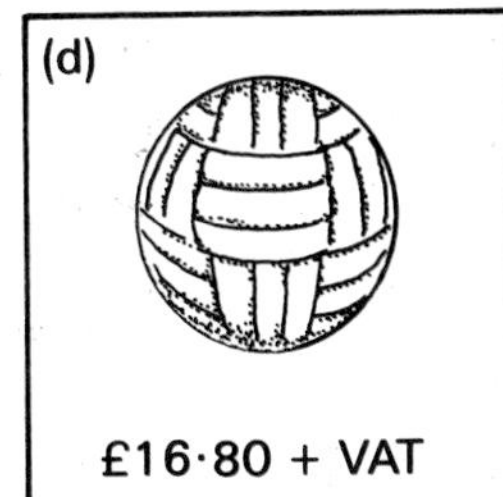

6 Work out the discounts (money off for cash) in Figure 22:8.

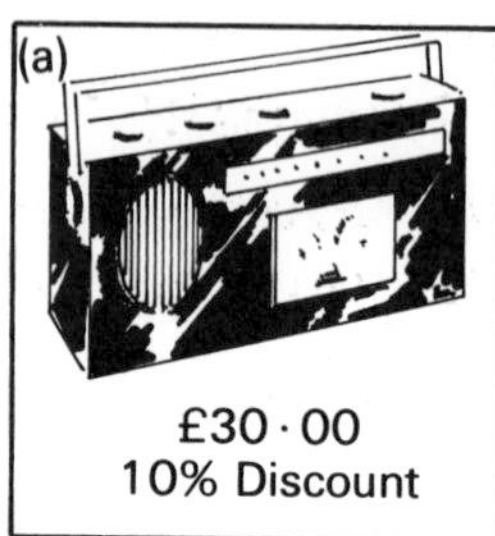
(a) £30·00 10% Discount

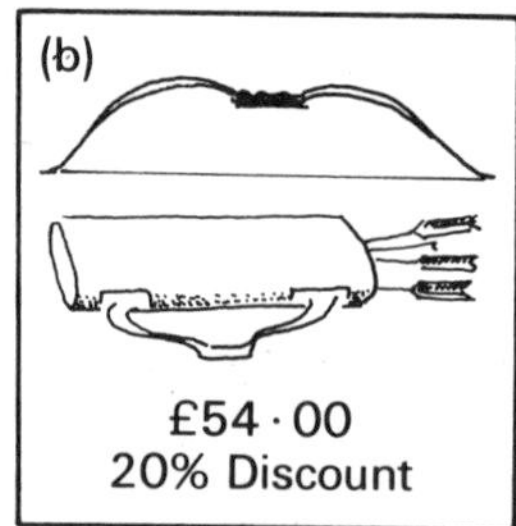
(b) £54·00 20% Discount

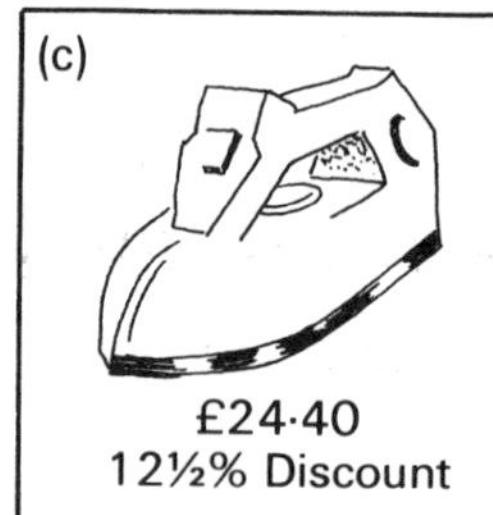
(c) £24·40 12½% Discount

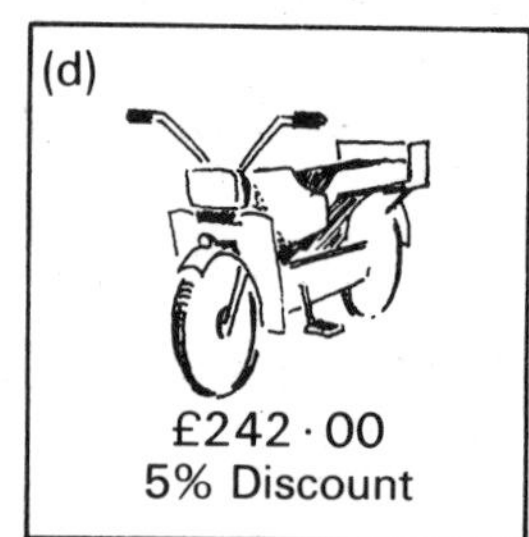
(d) £242·00 5% Discount

Fig. 22:8

7 Cars depreciate (lose value) as they get older. The depreciation can be shown as an annual (yearly) percentage loss.

Copy and complete the following.

Price on 1.1.87	Annual depreciation	Price on 1.1.88
(a) £7000	10% = £700	£7000 − £700 = £6300
(b) £7000	20%	
(c) £8400	20%	
(d) £8400	25%	
(e) £8400	$12\frac{1}{2}$%	
(f) £7230	$33\frac{1}{3}$%	

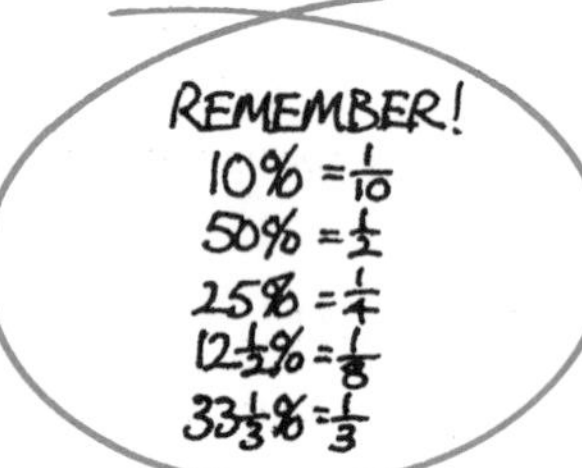

8 3000 homes were surveyed to find which kind of heating was used. The results are shown as a pie-chart in Figure 22:9.

(a) What percentage should be shown for electricity?

(b) How many homes were heated by (i) coal, (ii) gas, (iii) oil, (iv) electricity?

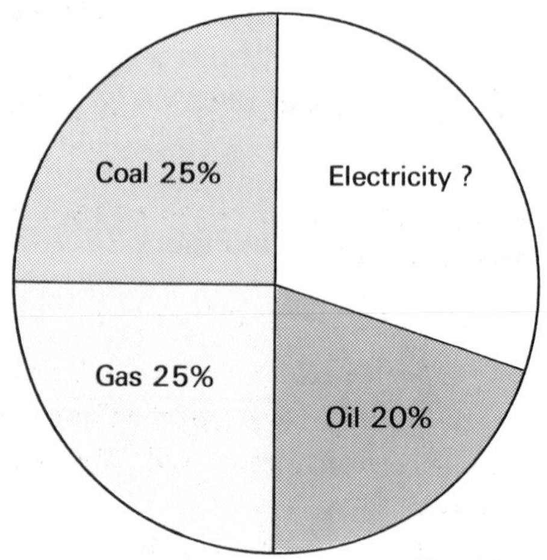

Fig. 22:9

9 In Figure 22:9 the sector showing coal represents 25%. The angle at the centre for this sector is

$$\frac{\cancel{25}^{1}}{\cancel{100}_{4}} \times \frac{360°}{1} = 90°$$

(or, as 25% $= \frac{1}{4}$, we could divide 360° by 4).

What are the angles at the centre for the other three sectors?

10 Refer to the pie-chart in Figure 22:10.

(a) What percentage should be shown for oils and fats?

(b) Which foods contain the greatest amount of fat?

(c) What angle at the centre is needed to draw the sector representing cakes (pastries and biscuits)? (SEG)

11 Evaluate:

(a) 7·5% of £200

(b) 12·75% of £300

(c) 5·345% of £400

(d) 17·25% of £500

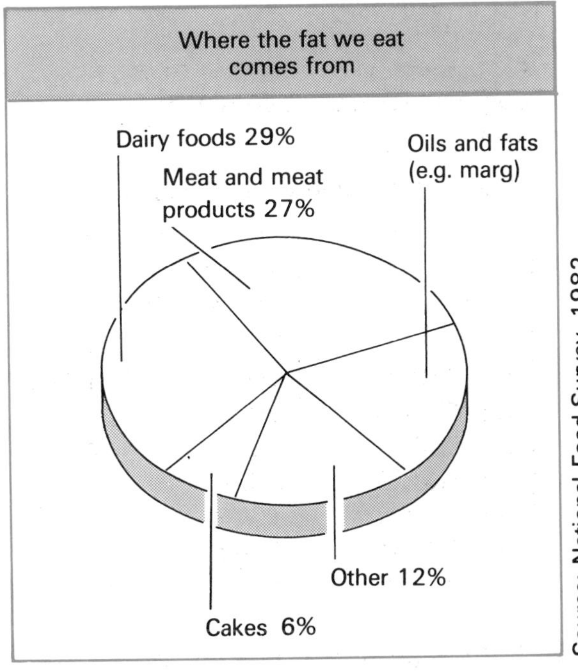

Fig. 22:10

12 Miss Murphy invests £2400 in a Four-Step Account on 1st January 1989.

(a) What percentage interest rate will she receive?

(b) What does 'net p.a.' mean?

(c) Miss Murphy withdraws her interest at the end of each year. What **total** amount of interest will she have received after:
(i) 3 years (ii) 5 years?

Worksheet 22A may be used here.

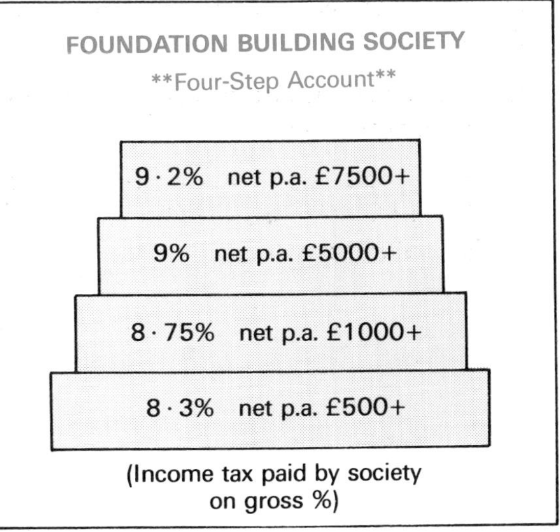

Fig. 22:11

13 Examples $12\frac{1}{2}\% = \frac{12\frac{1}{2}}{100} = \frac{25}{200} = \frac{1}{8}$

$37\frac{1}{2}\% = \frac{3}{8}$

Copy and complete the following.

Percentage	Fraction	Decimal
$17\frac{1}{2}\%$	?	0·175
?	?	0·225
33%	?	?
$7\frac{1}{2}\%$	?	?
?	$\frac{11}{40}$	?
?	$\frac{1}{20}$	?

14 (a) Anne is 13. How much is her membership fee?

(b) Jack is 17 and persuades a friend to join the club. How much is Jack's membership fee?

(c) Joan buys a pair of shorts priced at £7·60 and a pair of track shoes priced at £19·80. How much is Joan's discount?

A–Z Youth Club

Membership: £12·00 annually.

Athletics section: $17\frac{1}{2}\%$ discount on all equipment, including clothing.

20% discount on membership fee if under 14!

$7\frac{1}{2}\%$ discount for you for each new member you get to join!

Worksheet 22B may be used here.

C One number as a percentage of another

Example Michelle scored 32 marks out of 50 in a mathematics test. Show her marks in percentage form.

32 out of 50 can be written in fraction form as $\frac{32}{50}$.

$\frac{32}{50}$ as a percentage is $\frac{32}{\cancel{50}_1} \times \frac{\cancel{100\%}^{2}}{1} = 64\%$.

Profit as a percentage of the cost price

Example It costs £16 to make a shirt, which is sold for £20. What is the profit as a percentage of the cost price?

The profit is £20 − £16 = £4. The cost price is £16.

£4 as a percentage of £16 is

$\frac{\cancel{4}^1}{\cancel{16}_4} \times \frac{100\%}{1} = 25\%$.

1 Figure 22:11 shows part of Michael's school report.

NAME Michael Parkins Autumn Term
CLASS 4/MC

Subject	Mark	Max'm	Comments	
Mathematics	65	100	Good progress	AB
English	34	50	Imaginative Essays	CH
PE	45	75	IMPROVING	RR.
History	71	100	Pleasing Progress	MD
Physics	40	80	A Distinct Improvement	RW
French	41	50	Excellent progress	PS.

Fig. 22:11

(a) What is Michael's percentage mark in each subject?

(b) Arrange his results from best to worst.

2 Write the first amount as a percentage of the second amount. For example, 8 as a percentage of 10 is $\frac{8}{10} \times \frac{100\%}{1} = 80\%$.

(a) 4, 10 (b) 10, 40 (c) 30, 40

(d) 3p, 30p (e) 15 cm, 25 cm (f) 40 cm, 1 m

(g) 600 m, 1 km

3 Copy and complete the table below.

Article	Cost price	Selling price	Profit	Profit as a percentage of the cost price
(a) Blouse	£12	£15	£3	
(b) Hat	£25	£30		
(c) Skirt	£21	£28		
(d) Rugby ball	£16·80	£23·10		

4 Write the first amount as a percentage of the second.

(a) 15, 30 (b) £2, £8 (c) 15 kg, 75 kg

(d) $2\frac{1}{2}$, 20 (e) 100, 500 (f) £12·50, £125

5 A school has 500 pupils. The absence rate in a week was:

Monday, 20; Tuesday, 25; Wednesday, 40;
Thursday, 50; Friday, 60.

Find for each day the percentage of the pupils who were:

(a) absent (b) present

6 Different methods may be used to find the final positions of pupils in a class. Two methods are:

(a) add up the marks in all the subjects and then list the total marks;

(b) add the percentage marks in each subject and then list the total percentage marks.

Investigate these two methods and say what you think about them. Give examples to illustrate your findings.

23 Approximating

You know that there are exactly one hundred pennies in a pound, and that you have exactly one head! But you will never know your exact height or your exact weight, nor be able to tell someone the exact time. Even if you think your watch is accurate, by the time you have told them it will be later!

In our everyday lives we use approximations like 'He is about six feet tall' and 'It's about half a mile down the road'. We say that a new car costs 'about £6000', or that a line is 'six centimetres long'.

● To remind you . . .

- **Rounding**

  £950 is exactly half way between £900 and £1000, but we usually 'round up', and so say £950 is about £1000.

  £951 is more than half way to £1000, so we say it is £1000 to the nearest £100.

  £949 is less than half way to £1000, so we say it is £900 to the nearest £100.

1 Copy and complete these sentences. Choose the missing amounts from the boxes in Figure 23:1.

100 mm²	2·54 cm	30 cm	10 square feet
39 inches	6 feet	12 inches	$2\frac{1}{4}$ lb

Fig. 23:1

(a) A metre is approximately the same length as . . .

(b) A kilogram is approximately the same weight as . . .

(c) One inch is exactly the same length as . . .

(d) A foot is exactly the same length as . . .

(e) A foot is approximately the same length as . . .

(f) Two yards is exactly the same length as . . .

(g) One square centimetre is exactly the same area as . . .

(h) One square metre is approximately the same area as . . .

2 Write the following approximate amounts.

(a) 9·56 to the nearest tenth

(b) 9·566 to the nearest hundredth

(c) 8499 to the nearest thousand

(d) 8499 to the nearest hundred

(e) £83·38 to the nearest 10p

(f) £83·35 to the nearest 50p

(g) £1853·45 to the nearest pound

3 Use a decimal point to make the following statements sensible. Omit any figures you then think are not necessary.

(a) The Highland Terrier weighed about 85 kg.

(b) The Alsatian dog was about 12 metres long.

(c) Mount Everest is about 290·00 feet high.

(d) The garden pond was about 15 metres deep.

(e) The mathematics book cost £3400.

(f) When she was eleven she was nearly 16·0 cm high.

(g) In the deepest places the Atlantic reaches depths of approximately 300·00 feet.

(h) He was a terrific athlete. He could high jump 0·225 m.

(i) The cheetah covered a hundred yards in less than 420 seconds.

(j) The home computer cost her £35 035.

4 Round off to the nearest integer (whole number):

(a) 8·9 (b) 43·6 (c) 9·09 (d) 54·90 (e) $2\frac{1}{3}$

(f) $3\frac{3}{4}$ (g) $7\frac{2}{3}$ (h) $8\frac{1}{3}$ cm (i) $12\frac{2}{5}$ mm (j) $15\frac{4}{7}$ m

5 In the following, (i) write an approximate answer, and (ii) work out the exact answer.

(a) Find the total cost of eleven items at £20·30 each.

(b) Find the total bill for goods costing £11·01, £28·83, £35·36, £59·96 and £0·79.

6 As Jean walks around the supermarket she makes approximations to the nearest 50p, see Figure 23:2.

Item	Approximation £	p	Actual price £	p
Beans	0	50	0	37
Bacon	1	00	1	27
Eggs	1	00	1	06
Meat	2	50	2	79
Tomatoes	1	00	0	80
Bananas	0	50	0	45
Jam	1	00	0	73
Cereal	1	00	0	93
Gateaux	2	00	1	64
	Total:		Total:	

Fig. 23:2

(a) Write down which of Jean's approximations are wrong.

(b) Total the two columns of prices in Figure 23:2.

(c) What do you think of Jean's system? Do you think it is good, or not so good? Give your reasons.

7 Write the following to the accuracy required.

(a) 1315·7 mm correct to the nearest millimetre

(b) 1315·7 mm to the nearest cm

(c) 1315·7 mm to the nearest metre

(d) 29·501 litres to the nearest litre

(e) 8501 ml (millilitres) to the nearest litre

(f) 12·89 to the nearest integer

(g) 3·34 to the nearest tenth

(h) 3·347 to the nearest hundredth

8 Make an estimate first and then evaluate these.

(a) $\frac{18 \times 3{\cdot}2}{9}$ (b) $\frac{18 \times 3{\cdot}2}{0{\cdot}9}$

9 The approximate number of people attending a football match was 25 000 to the nearest 1000.

What was the least number and the greatest number that could have attended to make the approximation correct?

10 The table shows the numbers of people killed or seriously injured in the 15–19 age group on the roads of Great Britain during the years 1975 to 1984.

1975	1976	1977	1978	1979	1980	1981	1982	1983	1984
18 292	20 623	21 330	21 609	20 859	21 501	21 848	21 413	18 456	18 484

(a) Round off each number to the nearest 100.

(b) Represent the rounded off numbers by a bar-chart. Use these scales:
Horizontal: 1 cm to 1 year, from 1975 to 1984
Vertical: 1 cm to every 1000 casualties; begin at 10 000 and go up to 22 000

Worksheet 23 may be used here.

11 The small island in Figure 23:3 is drawn to a scale of 1 cm to 1 km. Each 1 cm square on the map represents a 1 km square.

(a) Estimate the area of the island in square kilometres.

(b) A kilometre is 1000 metres. So the area of one of the small squares in metres is $1000 \times 1000 = 1\,000\,000 \text{ m}^2$. Estimate, as accurately as you can, the area of the island in square metres.

12 Write down six things that we know exactly and six things that we can never find the value of exactly.

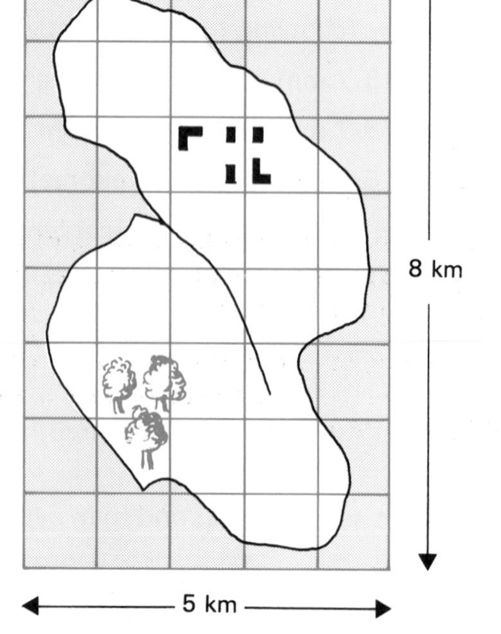

Fig. 23:3

Take a break 4

A Coming and going

Some parts of a train move backwards relative to the train. Which parts?

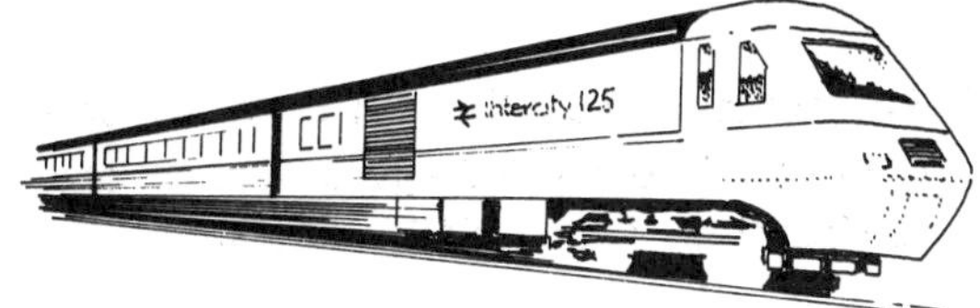

B Topology

In topology you can shrink, enlarge, pull, stretch or twist shapes, but you must *not* tear or break them, nor must you lose any regions or holes. For example, the doughnut shape in Figure B4:1, called a 'torus', can be transformed into a cup.

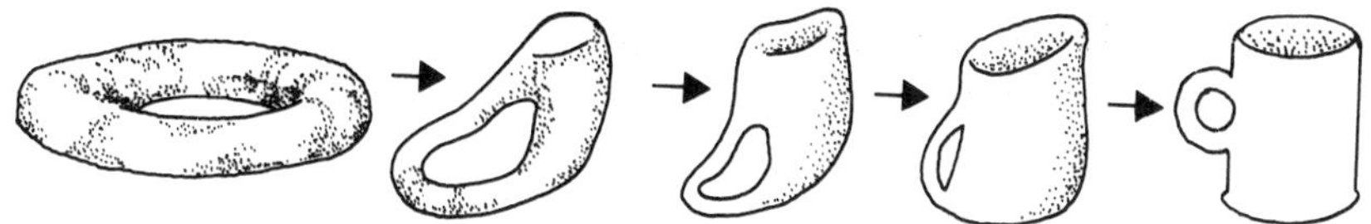

Fig. B4:1

Try, with sketches, to turn a shape into some other shapes. You could start with a hexagon, or a teapot!

C Build a number

Copy Figure B4:2.

The numbers 1 to 16 inclusive are given to two players as 'odds' and 'evens', or they can be selected at random from a face-down pile of numbered cards.

Each player, in turn, writes or places one of their numbers in a cell. The winner is the first to make a row, column, or diagonal add up to 25 or 30.

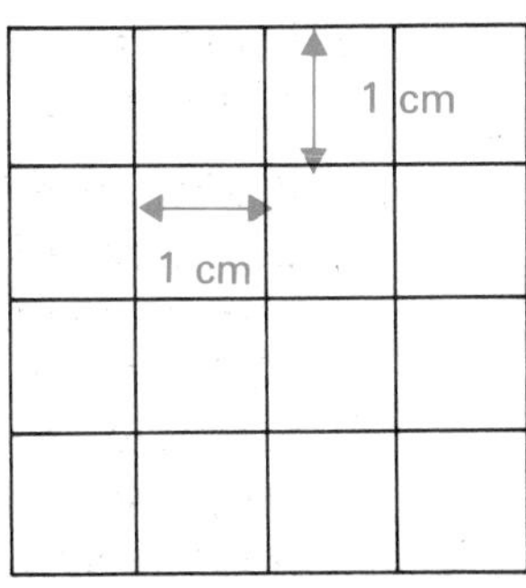

Fig. B4:2

24 Foreign currency

▶ Points to discuss . . .

Six British students go into six shops.

- Cindy pays in pounds and pence.
- John pays in francs and centimes.
- Rose pays in deutschmarks and pfennigs.
- Alan pays in guilders and cents.
- Anne pays in drachmae and lepta.
- Sam pays in dollars and cents.

In which countries were the shops?

Figure 24:1 shows some foreign exchange rates (November 1987). Use these rates to answer questions 1 and 2.

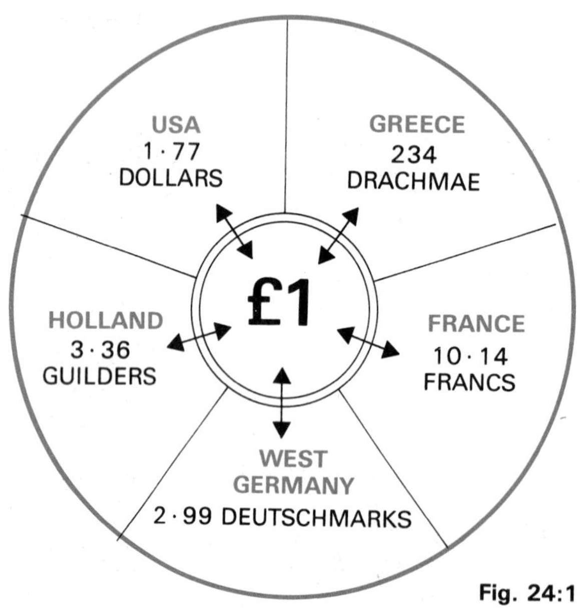

Fig. 24:1

1 Example In France in November 1987, £10 would have been exchanged for 10 × 10·14 francs = 101·40 francs.

How much would £10 have been exchanged for in:
(a) West Germany (b) Holland
(c) Greece (d) USA?

2 Example In France in November 1987, £100 would have been exchanged for 100 × 10·14 francs = 1014 francs.

How much would £100 have been exchanged for in:
(a) West Germany (b) Holland
(c) Greece (d) USA?

3 (a) 1 franc (FF1) = 100 centimes. How many centimes are there in FF0·30?

(b) 1 dollar ($1) = 100 cents. How many cents are worth $100?

4 You are visiting Boulogne on a day trip to France, and have £15 spending money. The exchange rate is FF10 to £1.

(a) How many francs will you receive for your £15?

(b) Using the coin values shown on the right, list the least number of coins you would need to pay for each item in Figure 24:2.

(c) What do items (i) and (ii) cost in pounds and pence?

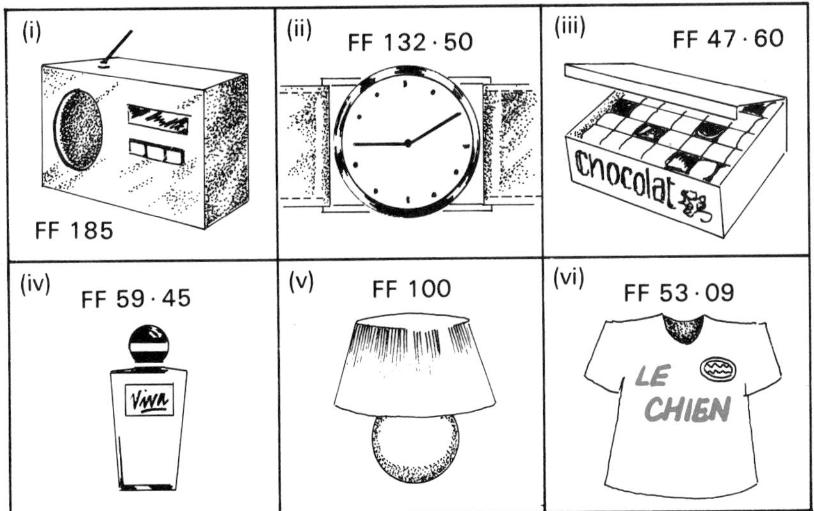

Fig. 24:2

5 An American tourist received 80p for a dollar. How many pounds will he receive for 30 dollars? (SEG)

6 This table (called a 'ready reckoner') shows some approximate exchange rates (November 1987). The values are given to the nearest penny.

Currency units	Country				
	France	W. Germany	Greece	Holland	USA
1	10p	33p	0p	30p	56p
2	20p	67p	0p	60p	£1·13
5	49p	£1·67	2p	£1·49	£2·82
10	99p	£3·34	4p	£2·98	£5·65
50	£4·93	£16·72	21p	£14·88	£28·25
100	£9·86	£33·44	43p	£29·76	£56·50
250	£24·65	£83·61	£1·07	£74·40	£141·24
500	£49·31	£167·22	£2·14	£148·81	£288·49

Examples FF10 → 99p
DM100 → £33·44
500 drachmae → £2·14

The table can be used to work out the approximate cost in pounds and pence of the items in Figure 24:3.

Example (i) 35 guilders = (3 × 10) + 5 guilders
= (3 × £2·98) + £1·49
= £10·43

Work out the cost in pounds and pence of each of the other items in Figure 24:3.

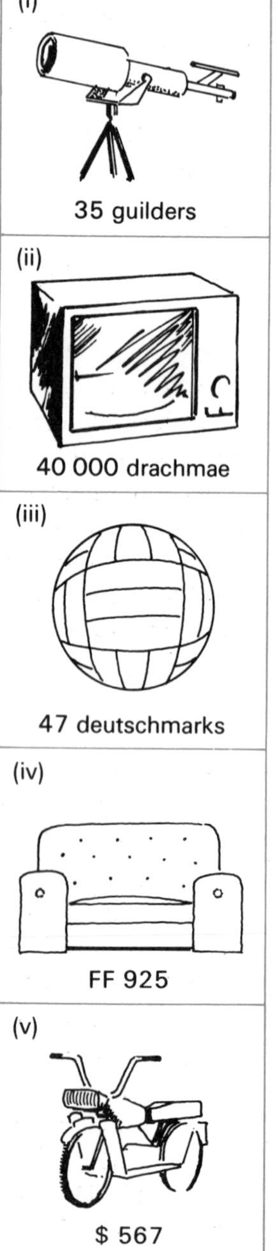

Fig. 24:3

7 When Mr and Mrs Watkins and their two children were on holiday in Spain, they went on a boat trip. The prices are shown in Figure 24:4. (Niños is Spanish for children.)

(a) Calculate the total cost of the trip in pesetas.

(b) The rate of exchange was £1 = 220 pesetas. Find the cost of the boat trip in pounds. (WJEC)

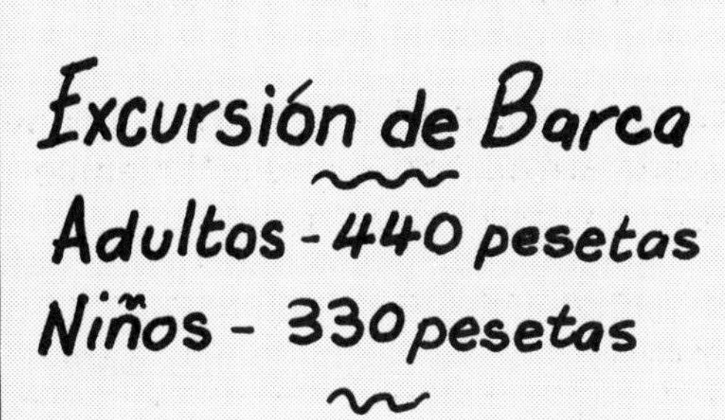

Fig. 24:4

8 The exchange rate for one day in 1986 was 2·15 Canadian dollars to the £.

(a) Find the number of dollars obtained for £500.

(b) Find the value of $258 in pounds sterling. (LEAG)

9 The Deutschmark (DM) is the unit of currency in Germany. A boy went on a three-week skiing holiday to Germany when the exchange rate was DM3·9 to the £1 sterling. He hired skis and ski-boots for three weeks at DM6·15 per week. He paid a total of DM28·45 for skiing lessons and, on average, he spent DM42·65 per week at the ski centre. Find the total amount that the boy spent at the ski centre during his three-week holiday: (a) in DM, (b) in pounds, giving your answer correct to the nearest penny. (WJEC)

Worksheet 24 may be used here.

10 In 1986 £1 could be exchanged for 191 drachmae. Draw a graph with scales of:
Horizontal: 1 cm to £1, from £0 to £10
Vertical: 1 cm to 200 drachmae, from 0 to 2000 drachmae

(a) Plot any two suitable points and draw a line graph.

Use your graph to answer the following accurately.

(b) How many drachmae could be exchanged for:
(i) £3 (ii) £4·50 (iii) £8·70?

(c) How much in pounds and pence could be exchanged for:
(i) 400 drachmae (ii) 1500 drachmae
(iii) 1750 drachmae?

A Rectangle; triangle; parallelogram

London was once surrounded by a defensive wall. Armed men patrolled the perimeter of the city, guarding the citizens who lived in the area inside the walls.

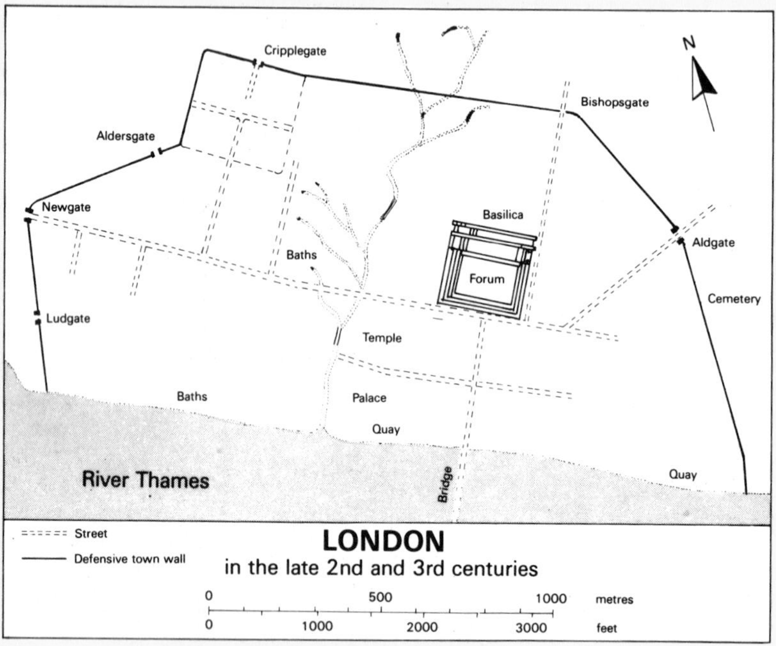

To remind you . . .

- **Plane**
  A plane is a two-dimensional (flat) surface.
- **Perimeter**
  The distance around the outside of a shape is its perimeter.
- **Area**
  The amount of space covered by a shape is its area.
  Areas are measured in square units, like square centimetres (cm^2) and square metres (m^2).
  Note that there must be two lengths in any area formula.
- **Perpendicular**
  A perpendicular forms a right-angle with a base line.

Area of a rectangle, triangle, and parallelogram

For the large rectangle in Figure 25:1, the perimeter is
$2 \times (5\text{ cm} + 3\text{ cm}) = 16\text{ cm}$,
the area is
$5\text{ cm} \times 3\text{ cm} = 15\text{ cm}^2$

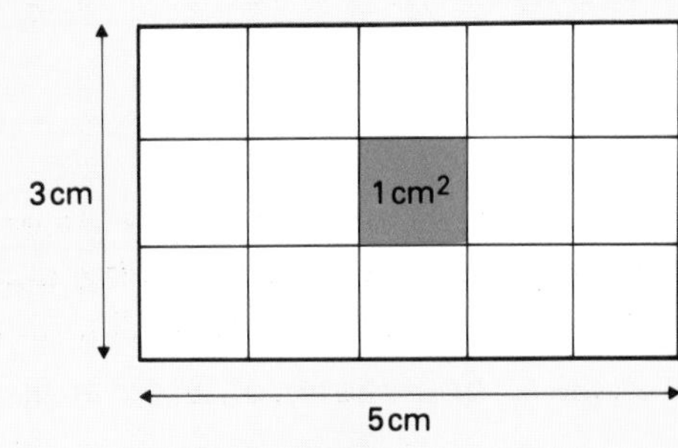

Fig. 25:1

The area of a triangle is half of the rectangle that encloses it, that is, half of its base times its height.

The area of the shaded triangle in Figure 25:2 is half of the large rectangle, that is, $\frac{1}{2}$ of $6\text{ cm} \times 4\text{ cm} = 12\text{ cm}^2$.

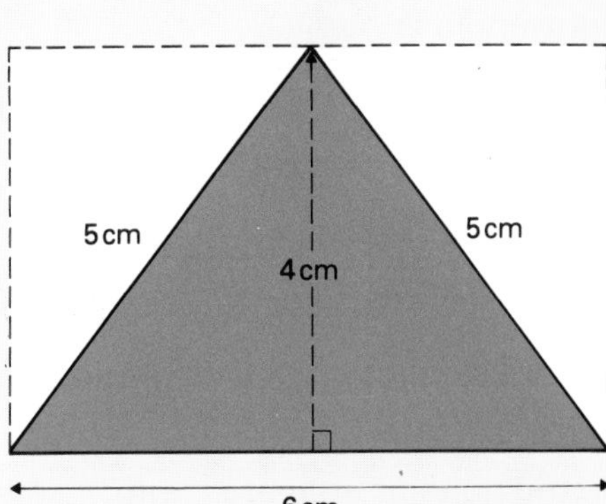

Fig. 25:2

The area of a parallelogram is the same as the area of the rectangle with the same base and height.

The area of the parallelogram PQRS in Figure 25:3 is
$5\text{ cm} \times 3\text{ cm} = 15\text{ cm}^2$.

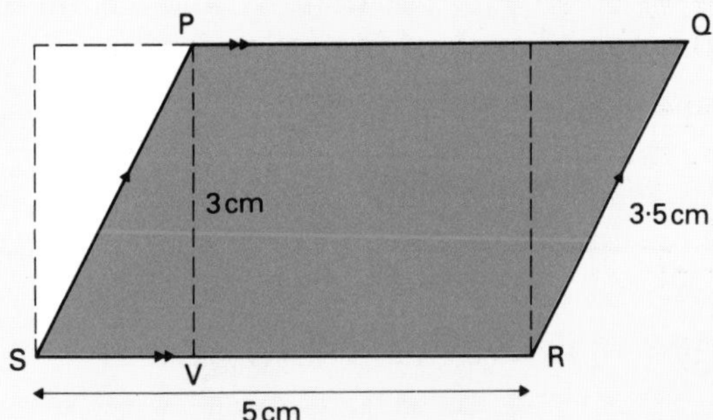

Fig. 25:3

▶ Points to discuss . . .

1. What is the perimeter of the triangle in Figure 25:2?
2. Why are there arrows on the sides of the shape in Figure 25:3?
3. What is the perimeter of the parallelogram in Figure 25:3?
4. How might a DIY enthusiast and a farmer use perimeters and areas? Think of some other people who use them.

1 Copy and complete the following sentences with the contents of one of the boxes in Figure 25:4.

parallel	rectangle	right-angle	area
at right-angles	90°	never meet	perimeter

Fig. 25:4

(a) The shape of this page is a . . .

(b) The angle at one corner of a rectangle is a . . .

(c) A right-angle is . . .

(d) However long they are made, parallel lines . . .

(e) The equal sides of a rectangle are . . .

(f) Perpendicular means . . .

(g) The distance around a rectangle is its . . .

(h) The amount of space inside a rectangle is its . . .

2 Some metric units of area are mm^2, cm^2, m^2, km^2.

Which of these four units would be the best for measuring the area of each of the following?

(a) Ireland (b) a hockey pitch (c) an oak leaf

(d) an insect's wing

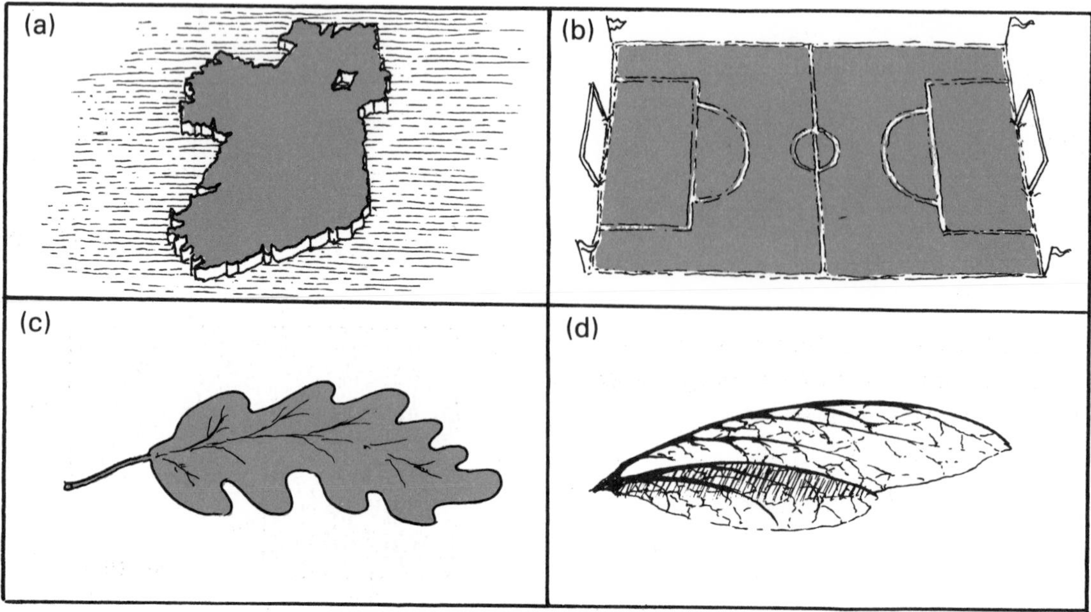

3 Figure 25:5 is a map of the Isle of Wight. Estimate its area by counting the squares inside it. Count only squares with half or more covered by the land.

Remember to multiply your answer by 16.

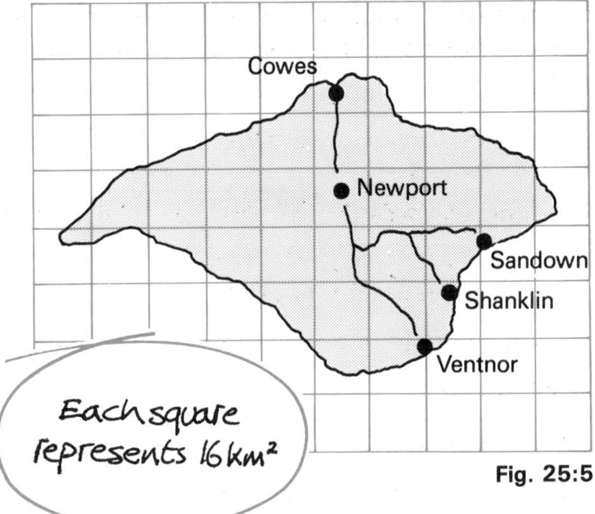

Each square represents 16 km²

Fig. 25:5

4 What is the perimeter of a rectangle with:

(a) length 8 cm, width 3 cm

(b) length 4·5 cm, width 3 cm

(c) length 15 mm, width 10 mm

(d) length 8 m, width 6·5 m?

5 Calculate the area of each rectangle in question 4.

6 In Figure 25:6, it is best to take side EG as the base of triangle EFG. Turn your book round until EG is at the bottom of the triangle. Now FH is the height. Calculate the area of triangle EFG.

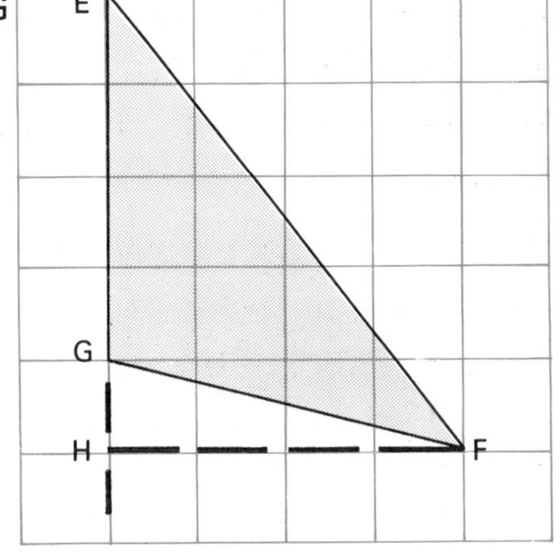

Fig. 25:6

7 Figure 25:7 shows the plan of a room. Find the room's area by adding the areas of rectangles A and B.

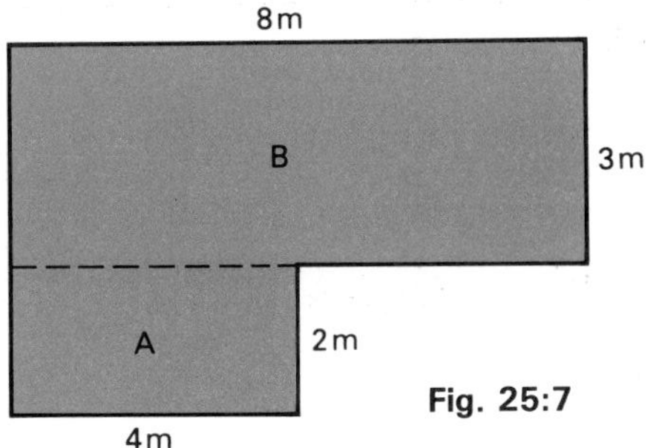

Fig. 25:7

8 Which shapes in Figure 25:8 are:
(i) squares (ii) rectangles (iii) triangles
(iv) parallelograms?

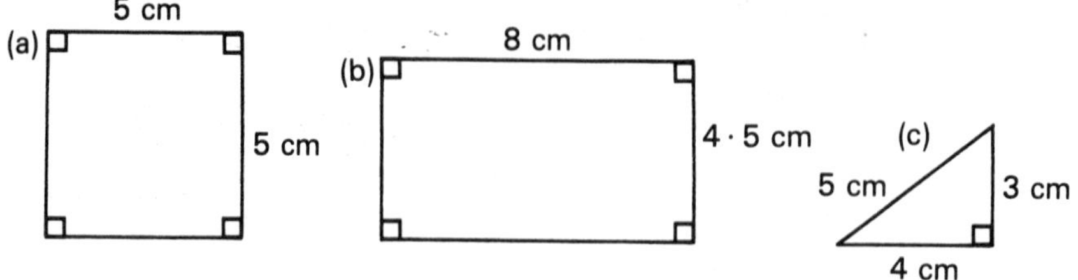

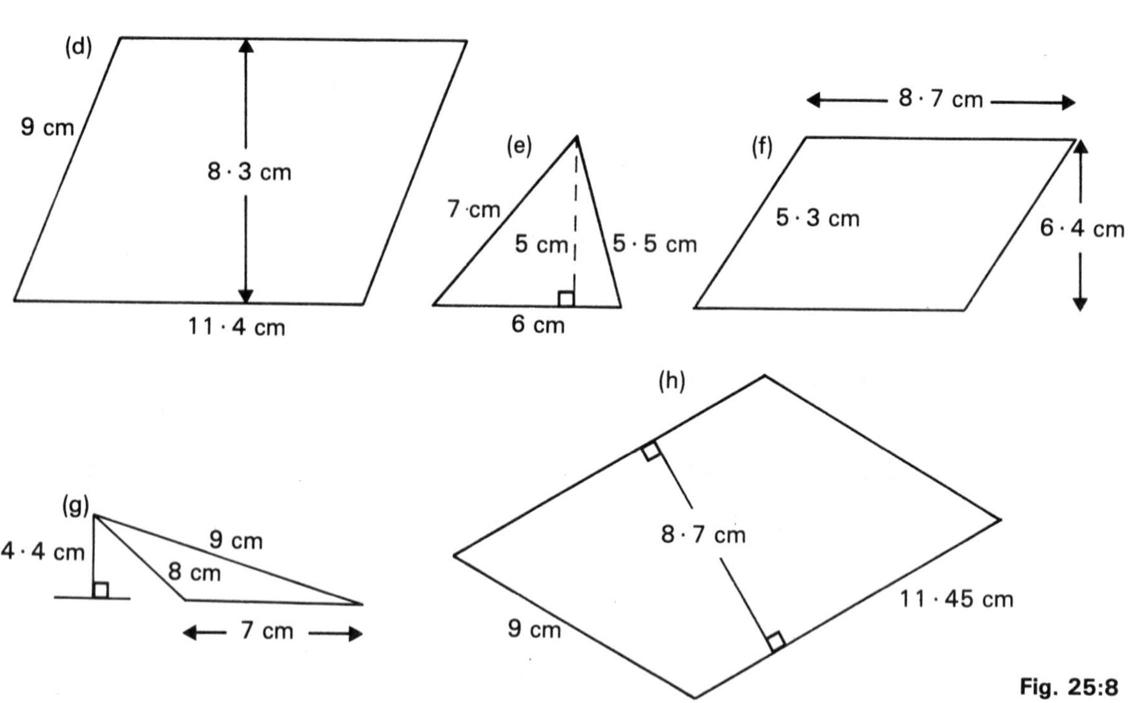

Fig. 25:8

9 Find (i) the perimeter, and (ii) the area of each shape in Figure 25:8. Remember that the perimeter is the whole distance round a shape.

Use these formulas:

Area of rectangle = area of parallelogram = base × height
Area of triangle = half base × height

10 The cost of building this house was estimated to be £950 for every square metre of floor space. Plans of the house are shown in Figure 25:9.

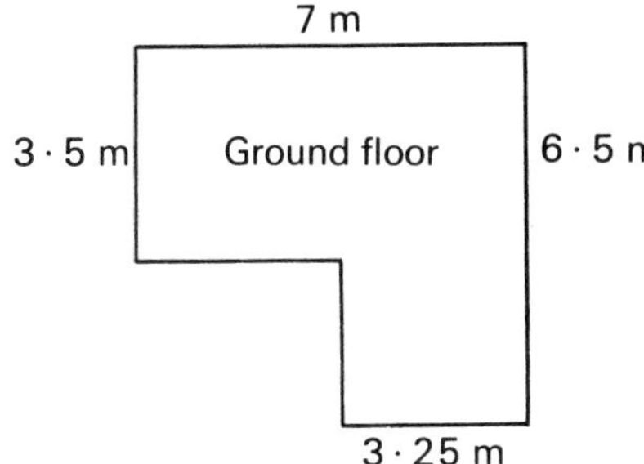

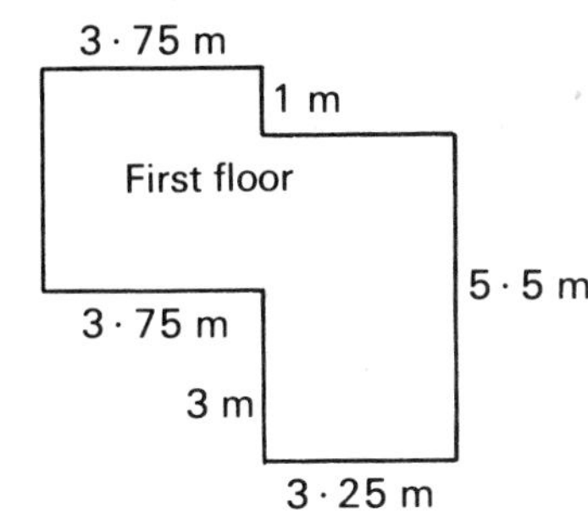

NOT TO SCALE

Fig. 25:9

(a) Copy the plans and write in the missing lengths.

(b) Calculate the perimeter of
(i) the ground floor, and (ii) the first floor

(c) Calculate the area of
(i) the ground floor, and (ii) the first floor

(d) Estimate the cost of building the house.

11 Figure 25:10 shows three rectangular photos.

(a) What is the perimeter of each rectangle?

(b) What is the area of each rectangle?

Worksheet 25A may be used here.

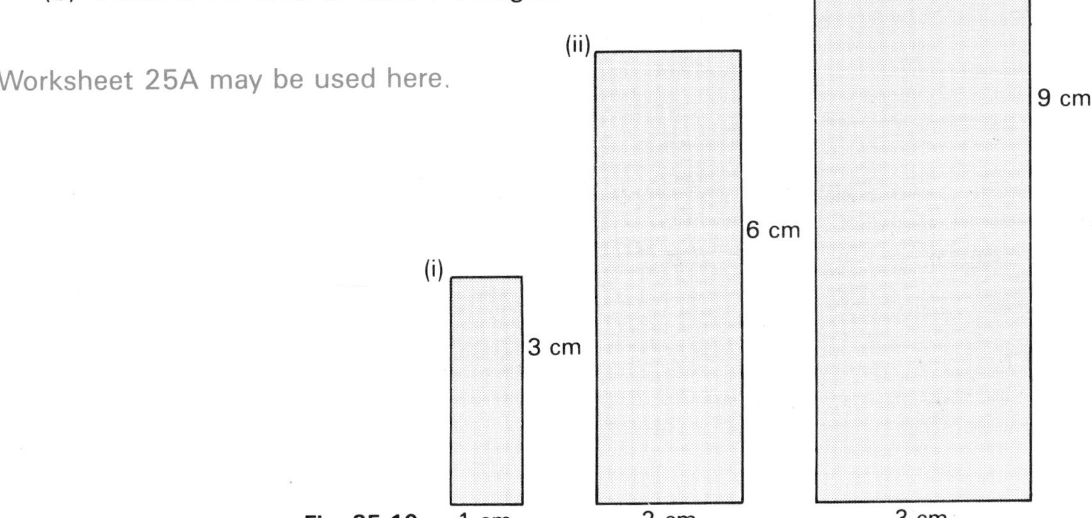

Fig. 25:10

12 Look at Figure 25:10 on page 153.

(a) How many times as long as photo (i) is photo (ii)?

(b) What happens to the perimeter of a rectangle when its length and width double?

(c) What happens to the area of a rectangle when its length and width double?

13 Look at Figure 25:10 on page 153.

(a) How many times as long as photo (i) is photo (iii)?

(b) What happens to the perimeter and the area of the rectangle when its length and width treble (are made 3 times as long)?

14 A farmer wishes to enclose his cattle in a rectangular enclosure, using 300 metres of fencing and the bank of a straight canal. What is the largest area that he can enclose?

15 Investigate the largest area possible in question 14, if the enclosure does not have to be rectangular.

B Volume: cuboid; prism

To remind you . . .

- **Volume** is the amount of space an object occupies. It is measured in cubic units like cm^3 (cubic centimetres). Note that there must be three lengths in any volume formula.
- A **prism** has a regular cross-section; that is, it has the same shape all the way through, like a pencil or a ready-sliced loaf.
- The volume of a prism is found by multiplying the area of its cross-section by its length or height.

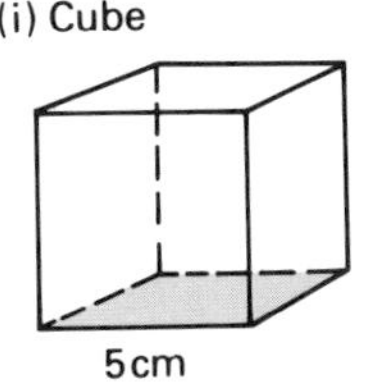

Volume = area of shaded face × height

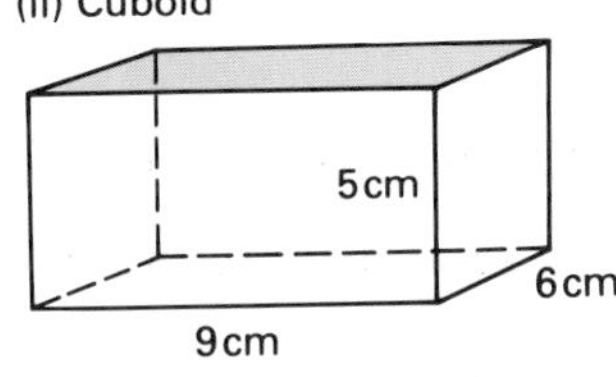

Volume = area of shaded face × depth

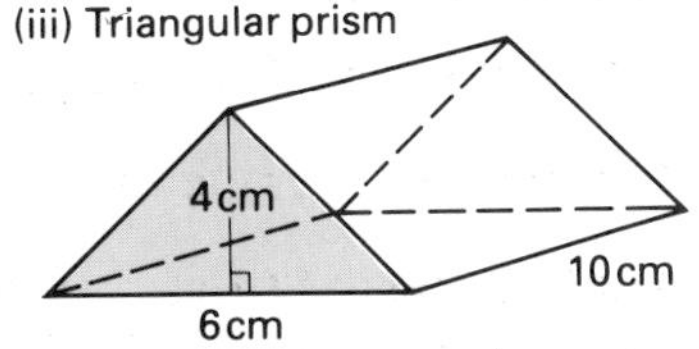

Volume = area of triangular face × length

Fig. 25:11

1 (a) Look at Figure 25:11. Find the area of each shaded face in shapes (i), (ii) and (iii).

(b) Find the volume of each shape.

(c) The volume of the cuboid is given by length × height × depth. Does it matter in which order you multiply the three dimensions? Explain your answer.

2 Give two examples of the use in real life of:

(a) the cuboid (b) the triangular prism.

3 Some metric units of volume are mm^3, cm^3, m^3 and km^3. Which of these units would be the best for measuring the volume of each object in Figure 25:12?

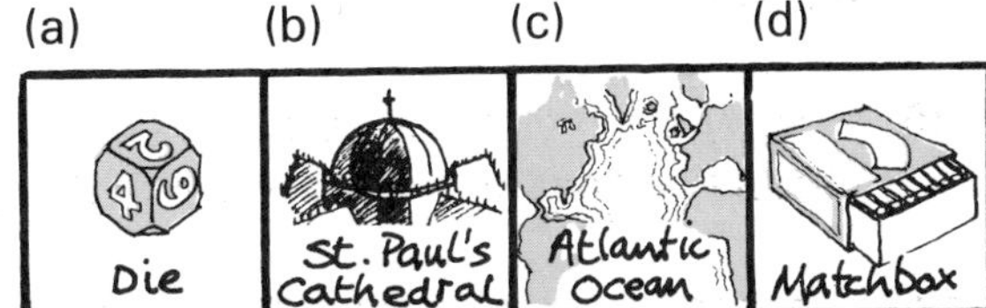

Fig. 25:12

4 Estimate the volume in m^3 of:

(a) your classroom (b) a single-decker bus

(c) a two-person tent (d) a shoe box

5 A hexagonal prism is shown in Figure 25:13.

(a) Why is the hexagonal face not regular?

(b) Find the area of the hexagon by dividing it into a rectangle and two triangles.

(c) Find the volume of the prism.

(d) Give two examples of the real-life use of regular hexagonal prisms.

All sides of the shaded face are 5 cm.

8 cm
11 cm
15 cm
5 cm

Worksheet 25B may be used here.

6 Dave is digging out the footings for an extension to his house (see Figure 25:14). The footings will be 1 m deep and 0·5 m wide.

(a) What will be the total volume of earth removed for the footings?

(b) Ready-mix concrete was £34·50 per cubic metre. How much would it cost to half fill the footings with concrete?

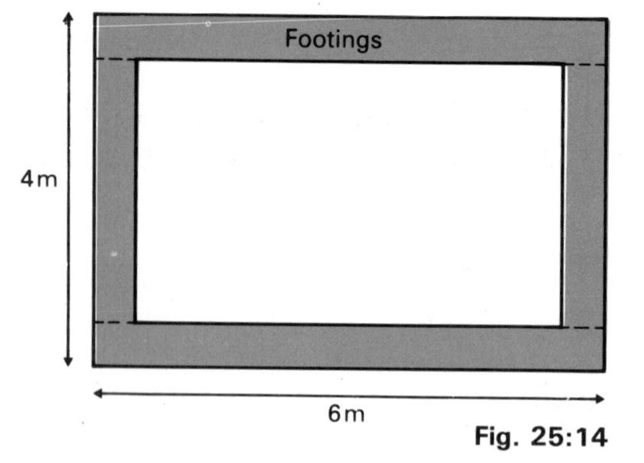

Fig. 25:14

C Circle and cylinder

▶ Points to discuss . . .

1 Give examples of things that make a circle when they move.

2 Why are 20p and 50p coins made the shape they are? Could they be used for wheels?

● Circumference and area of a circle

The formula for the circumference is $C = \pi \times d$, or πd.
The formula for the area is $A = \pi \times r \times r$, or πr^2.

d is the length of the diameter; r is the length of the radius.

π is the Greek letter P (said 'pi'). It is used because no exact number can be given. We usually take π as approximately 3·14.

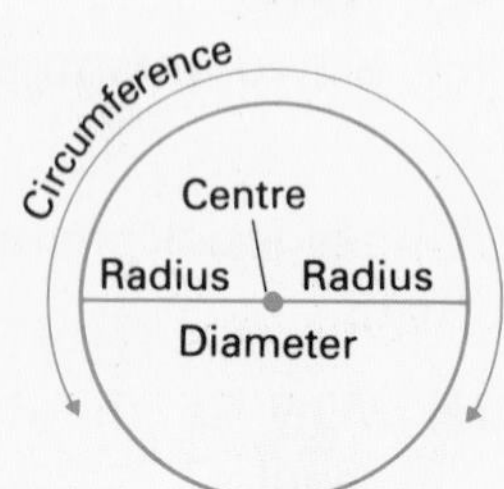

Fig. 25:15

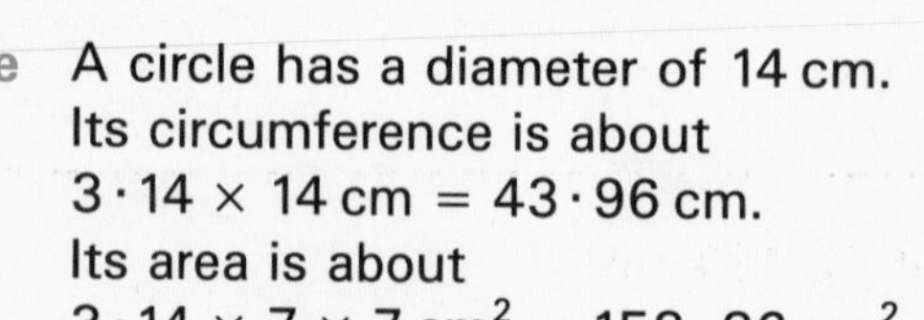

Example A circle has a diameter of 14 cm.
Its circumference is about
$3 \cdot 14 \times 14$ cm $= 43 \cdot 96$ cm.
Its area is about
$3 \cdot 14 \times 7 \times 7$ cm^2 $= 153 \cdot 86$ cm^2.

The $\boxed{x^2}$ key on a calculator may be used to work out 7×7.

Take π as $3 \cdot 14$ in all the following questions, and give answers correct to two decimal places where appropriate.

1 Find the circumference and area of each of the circles whose diameter is shown in Figure 25:16.

(a) 1 m

(b)

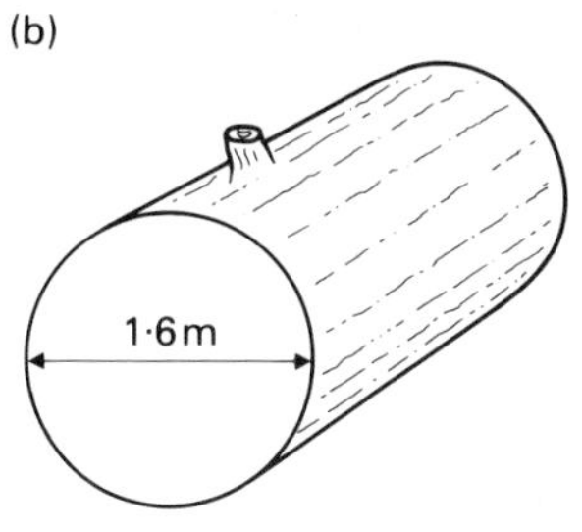

(c)

(d)

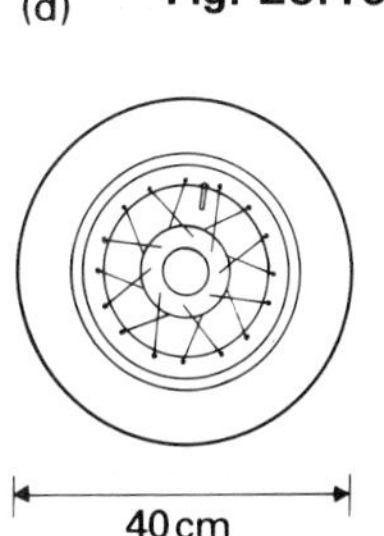

Fig. 25:16

2 A cylinder is a circular prism. The cross-section is a circle, area πr^2. The volume of a prism is the area of the cross-section times the height, so the volume of a cylinder is $\pi r^2 h$, where h is the height.

Example Find the volume of the oil tank in Figure 25:17.

$v = \pi r^2 h \rightarrow 3 \cdot 14 \times 10 \times 10 \times 7\,\text{m}^3 = 2198\,\text{m}^3$.

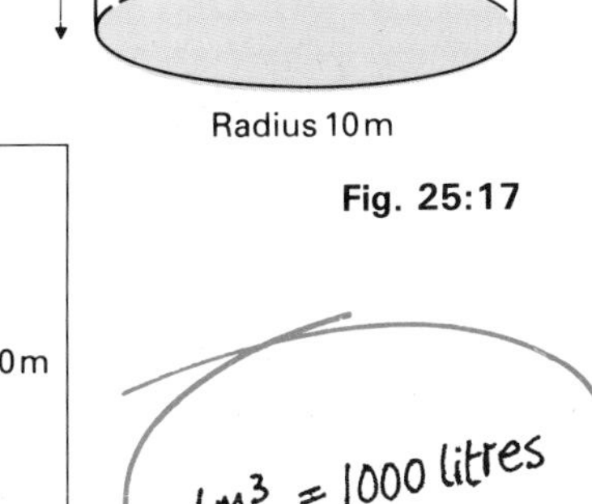

Fig. 25:17

(a) Find the volume of each cylinder in Figure 25:18.

(b) How many litres can each object hold?

(i)

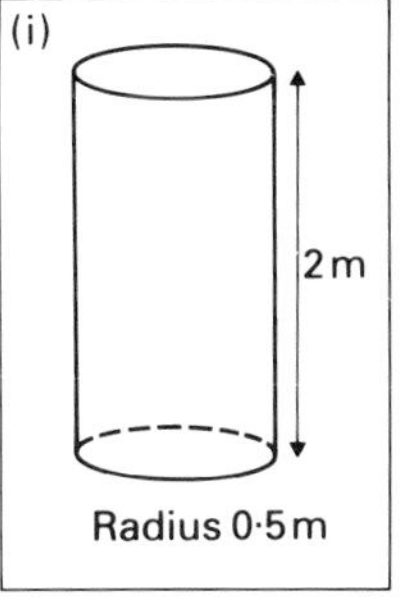

(ii)

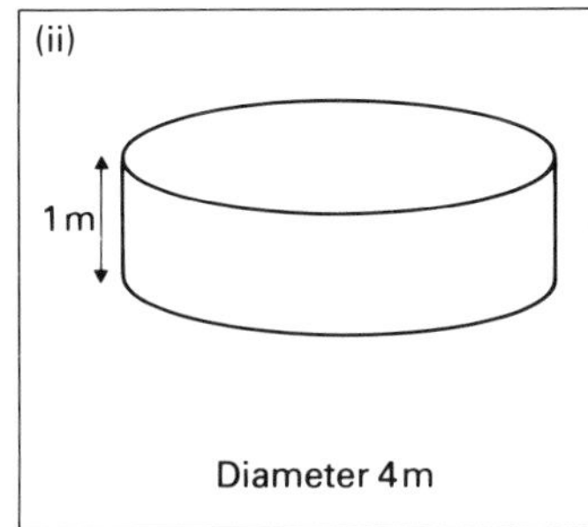

(iii)

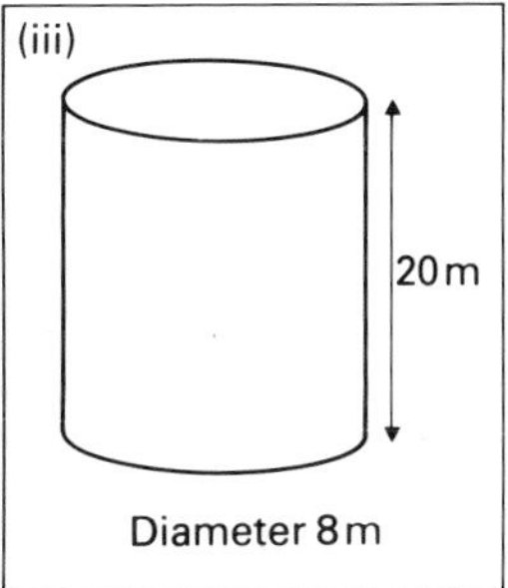

Fig. 25:18

Worksheet 25C may be used here.

3 The diameter of the Earth is about 12 740 km.

(a) Find the length of the equator.

(b) Find the speed of a tree on the equator, correct to the nearest 10 km/h.

26 Best buys

We all want good value when we spend our money. Different people, however, have different wants and needs.

Mrs Pound-Stretcher may buy 'extra large' sizes to feed her family of six.
Her son, John, aged 18, may have his mind fixed on a 500 cc 'Peerless Avenger' motorbike.
Miss Shepherd, aged 70, may prefer to buy a small loaf of bread at 36p rather than the double size at 61p. She knows the larger loaf will go stale before she can eat it all.

Comparing costs

Method A Find the cost of one item.

(a)

35p

(b) VIMO VIMO

65p (two pack)

(c)

90p (three pack)

Fig. 26:1

Example Figure 26:1 shows that one bottle of Vimo costs 35p in drawing (a).

In (b) one bottle costs 65p $\div$ 2 = $32\frac{1}{2}$p.

In (c) one bottle costs 90p $\div$ 3 = 30p.

Pack (c) is the best buy, if you can use that much Vimo.

Method B Find the cost of an easy amount, like 10 g or 25 g or 1 kg.

200 g
50p

500 g
90p

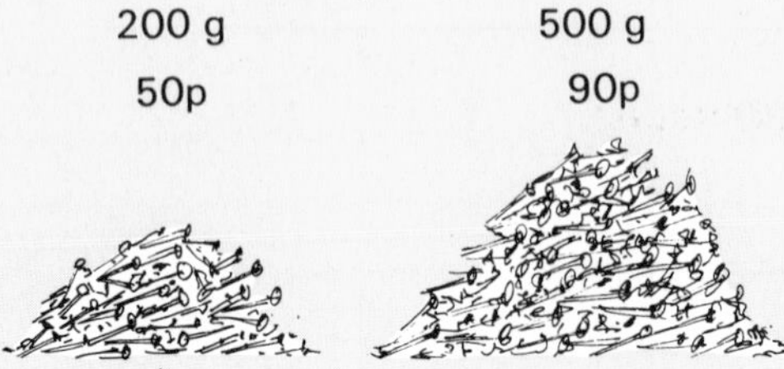

Fig. 26:2

Example Figure 26:2 shows the costs of different amounts of nails. We can easily find what 1 kg would cost at each price.

(a) 1000 g is 5 times 200 g so if 200 g costs 50p, 1000 g will cost 5 × 50p = £2·50.

(b) If 500 g costs 90p then 1000 g will cost 2 × 90p = £1·80.

(c) 1000 g costs £2·00.

We can see that (b) is the best buy.

▶ Points to discuss . . .

1 One day you will probably buy a second-hand car. Decide which of these points about a car are good, and which are bad. Make two lists, headed 'Good points' and 'Bad points'.

(a) Five good tyres.

(b) One careful previous owner.

(c) Rust showing under re-spray.

(d) The car is three years old.

(e) The mileometer records 79 452 miles.

(f) Guarantee covers parts and labour.

(g) Brakes feel 'spongy'.

(h) Exhaust emits blue smoke.

(i) The mileometer records only 18 232 miles, but the pedals show considerable wear.

(j) Car runs well and is clean.

(k) Proof given of regular servicing.

(l) The seller does not like it when you say you would like a mechanic friend to check the car.

(m) The car's manufacturer has a good reputation.

2 Which of the organisations and people in Figure 26:3 might be able to help you if you bought something that proved very unsatisfactory?

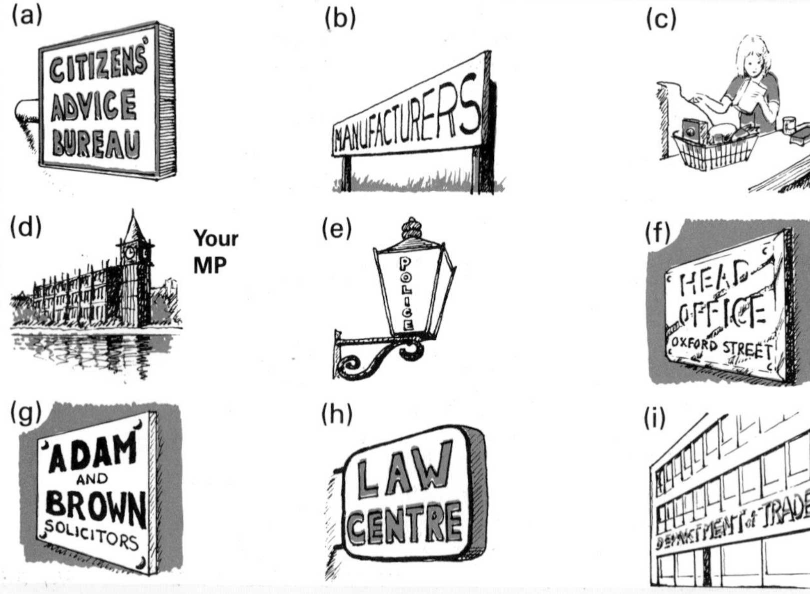

Fig. 26:3

1 Calculate:

(a) 25% (or $\frac{1}{4}$) of £60 (b) 10% (or $\frac{1}{10}$) of £50

(c) 20% of £80 (d) 5% of £110

2 Which jar in Figure 26:4 is the better value? Show your reasons. (LEAG)

Fig. 26:4

3 Which jar of hand-cream in Figure 26:5 is the best value?

(a) £1·25 (b) £2·60

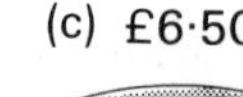

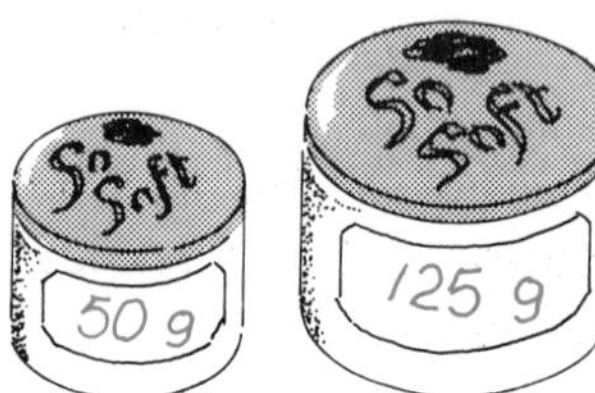

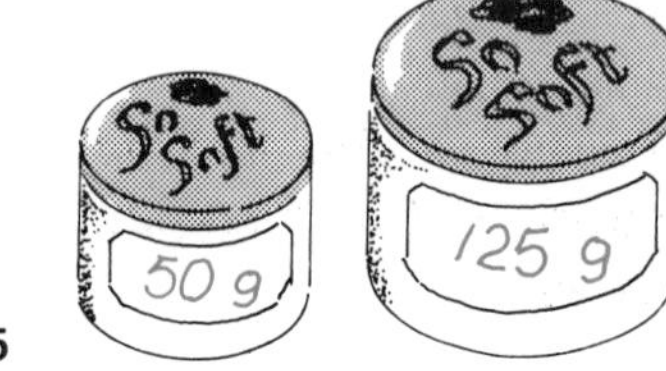

Fig. 26:5

4 Which bottle of wine is the best buy in Figure 26:6?

Fig. 26:6

5 You can buy the fitted kitchen in Figure 26:7 in three different ways. Its cost is £2200.

Method A If you pay cash you are allowed a discount of 10%.

Method B You can take out a bank loan repayable at £88 · 40 a month over three years.

Method C You can pay 25% deposit, with the remainder of the money being repaid over three years at £89 a month.

(a) What is the special name given to method C?

(b) Evaluate the three methods of payment.

(c) How much dearer is the dearest method compared to the cheapest method of purchase?

Fig. 26:7

6 A plywood floor is to be laid in my loft. The floor area will be a rectangle measuring 12 ft by 8 ft.

(a) What is the least number of 8 ft by 4 ft plywood sheets needed?

(b) I am going to buy the plywood from Crumbles. How much will it cost if 9 mm sheets are used?

(c) How much **more** will it cost if 12 mm sheets are used?

(d) After the floor is laid I intend to cover the plywood with Floorstrong tiles. How many tiles will I need?

(e) Is it better for me to buy the tiles I require in packs of 35 tiles or to buy them singly? Give your reasons. (SEG)

CRUMBLES THE BUILDER'S FRIEND
BUILDING MATERIALS

SPECIAL OFFER

Plywood Sheets

8 ft x 4 ft x 4 mm £4.70
8 ft x 4 ft x 6 mm £6.40
8 ft x 4 ft x 9 mm £9.75
8 ft x 4 ft x 12 mm £12.40

SPECIAL TILE OFFER

FLOORSTRONG TILES 12 ins x 12 ins

USUALLY 60p each
NOW ONLY 45p each

OR £14.40 FOR PACKS OF 35 TILES

Worksheet 26 may be used here.

7 Three shops advertised bags of 'Thanet' potatoes.

(a) Evaluate the cost of 1 kg of potatoes from each of the three bags.

(b) A quarter of the potatoes in bag C were found to be bad. What would be the cost, per kilogram, of the edible potatoes?

(c) Mr Evans made a journey of 6 miles in his car to buy two bags of potatoes from shop A. The running costs of the car are 15p for each mile travelled.

(i) Find the total cost to Mr Evans of the two bags.

(ii) Find the cost of 1 kg of potatoes, giving your answer first as a decimal number and then to the nearest penny.

Shop A

Shop B

Shop C

Fig. 26:8

27 Angles

A Measuring angles

● To remind you . . .

- **Degrees and radians**
  Lines BA and CA in Figure 27:1 are called the arms of angle BAC. The angle turned from AB to AC is usually measured in degrees, although in some mathematics radians are also used. (180° is π radians.)

  A complete turn is 360 degrees (360°).

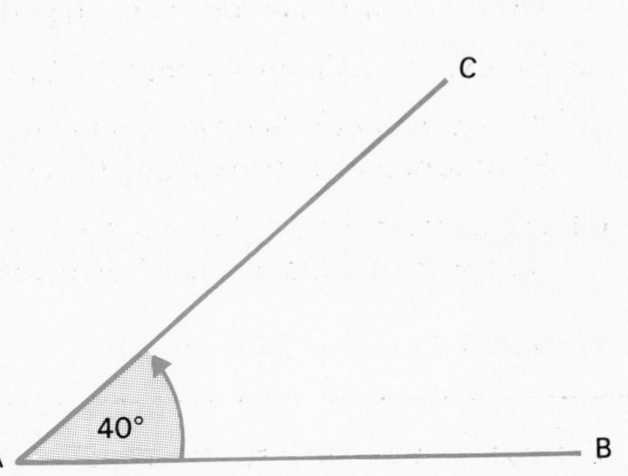

Fig. 27:1

- **Measuring with a protractor**
  To read your protractor correctly, decide first whether the angle you are measuring is more or less than 90° (a right-angle). Then make sure the **0** on the protractor is along one of the arms of the angle.

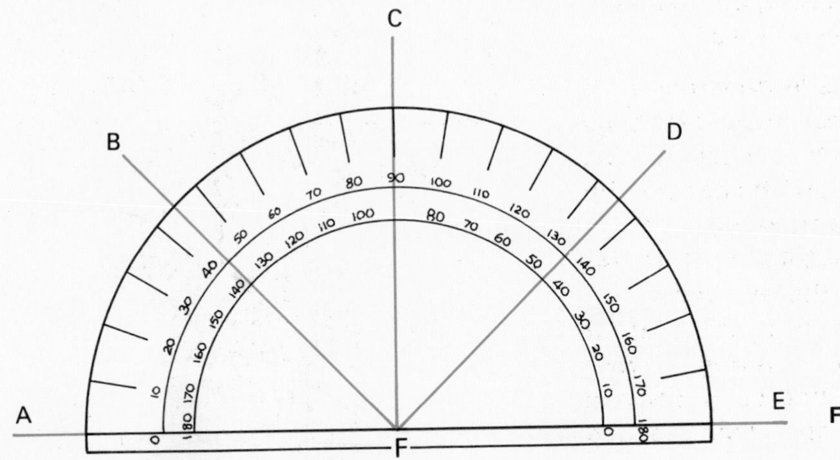

Fig. 27:2

Example Angle DFE in Figure 27:2 is less than a right-angle. So although line DF could be read as 45 or 135, we read angle DFE as 45°, not 135°.

Angle DFA is more than a right-angle, and is 135°.

27

1 What kind of angle makes up each of the four corners of this page?

2 Write five examples of right-angles in your classroom.

3 In this book we use the sign ∠ to stand for the word angle. Measure and write down the sizes of the following angles in Figure 27:2.

(a) ∠CFA (b) ∠AFB (c) ∠EFB (d) ∠EFC

4 In Figure 27:3 say whether the following angles are acute, obtuse or right angled.

(a) ∠HCB (b) ∠GCB (c) ∠FCB (d) ∠ECB

(e) ∠DCB (f) ∠ECH (g) ∠FCD (h) ∠FCE

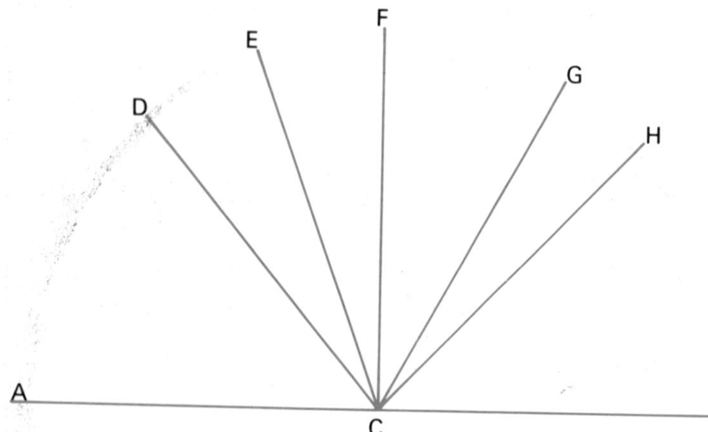

Fig. 27:3

5 Estimate the sizes of the angles (a) to (h) in question 4.

6 Measure the angles (a) to (h) in question 4. Note that sometimes the protractor has to be turned, as in Figure 27:4.

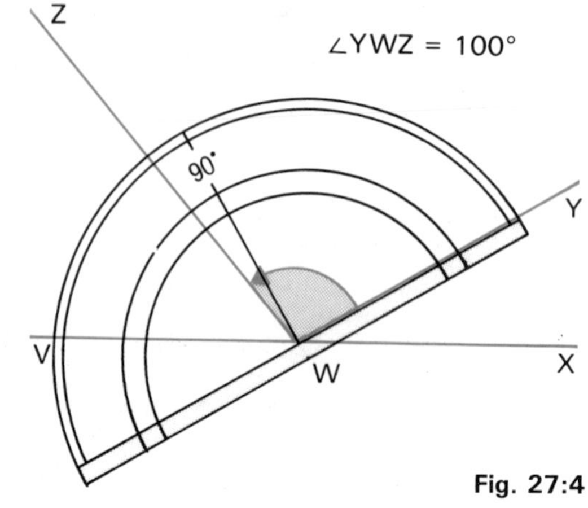

Fig. 27:4

7 Draw an angle of:

(a) 30° (b) 45° (c) 60°

(d) 90° (e) 120°

8 Draw a square with each side 4 cm long. Draw the corners by using a protractor.

9 Solve these clues to the word puzzle in Figure 27:5 and write down the answers.

(a) Between 90° and 180°.

(b) The symbol ° stands for these.

(c) Less than 90°.

(d) The lines that make an angle.

(e) Angles total 180° at a point on this.

(f) Angles total 360° around this.

(g) 90° is a . . . angle.

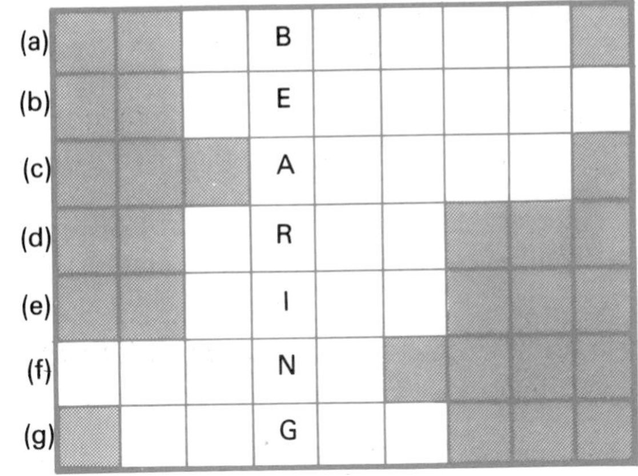

Fig. 27:5

10 In this question, draw the circles using a 360° protractor if you have one. If not, draw the circles using a 180° protractor like this.

- Mark the centre spot.
- Draw the top half of the circle, **from 0° to 180° only**.
- Draw the bottom half.

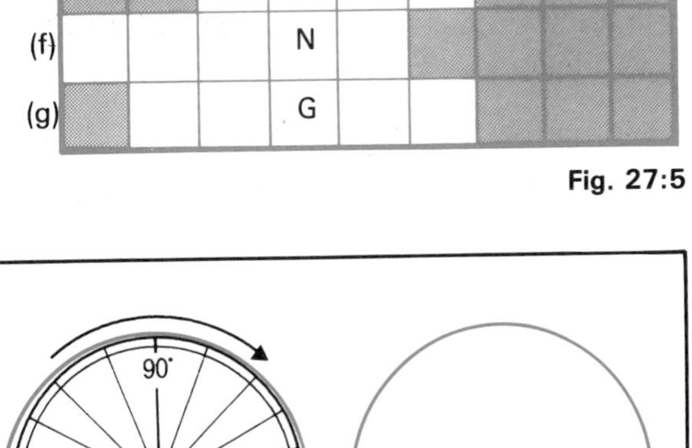

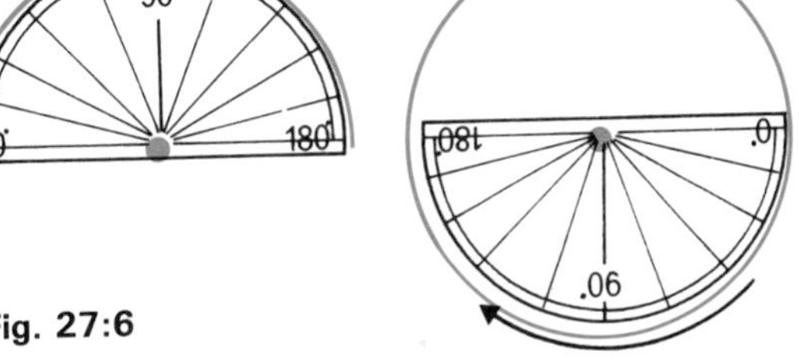

Fig. 27:6

(a) Figure 27:7 shows a regular hexagon. Draw it like this.
- Draw a circle.
- Mark six 60° angles from the centre to the circumference.
- Join A to B, B to C, etc.
- Rub out the circle.

(b) Draw a regular octagon (eight equal sides).

(c) Draw a regular decagon (ten equal sides).

A regular hexagon has six equal sides. Each centre angle is $\frac{360°}{6} = 60°$

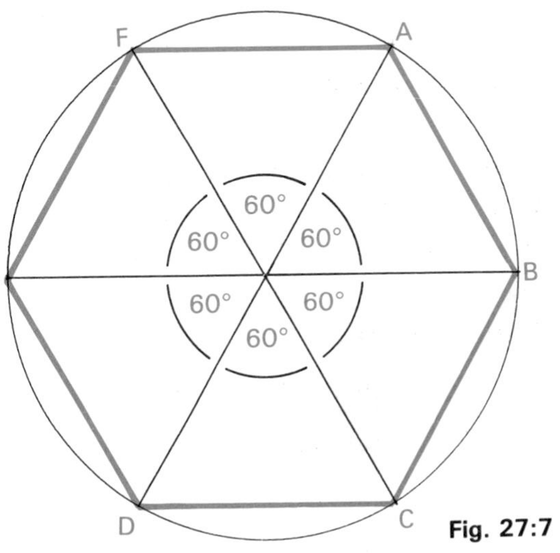

Fig. 27:7

B Angle calculations

To remind you . . .

- Turns and half turns

A complete turn is made up of 360 degrees.
A half turn (a straight line) is made up of 180 degrees.

Example In Figure 27:8, angle a can be calculated by adding 105°, 80° and 100°, then taking the answer from 360°.

$105 + 80 + 100 = 285$

$360 - 285 = 75$, so angle a is 75°.

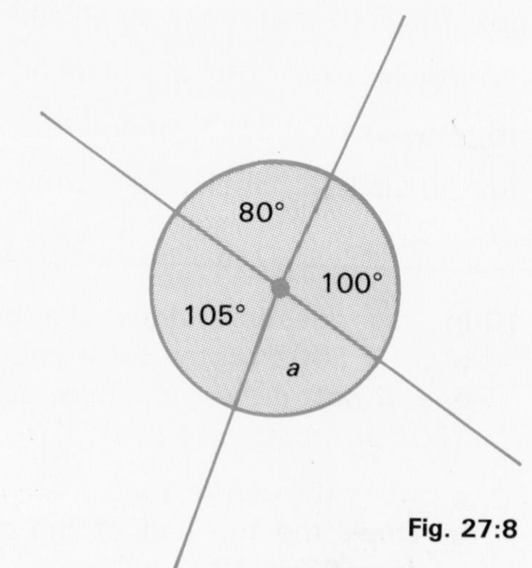

Fig. 27:8

Example In Figure 27:9 each angle is marked x. This means that the five angles are the same size.

$x + x + x + x + x = 5x$

$5x = 360°$,

so $x = 360° \div 5 = 72°$.

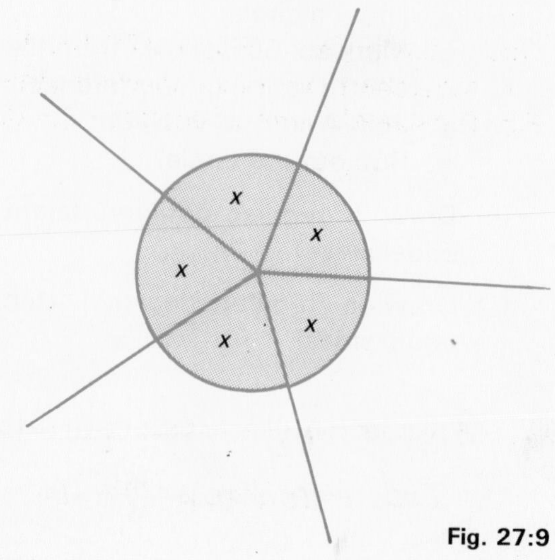

Fig. 27:9

1 Calculate the lettered angles in Figure 27:10.

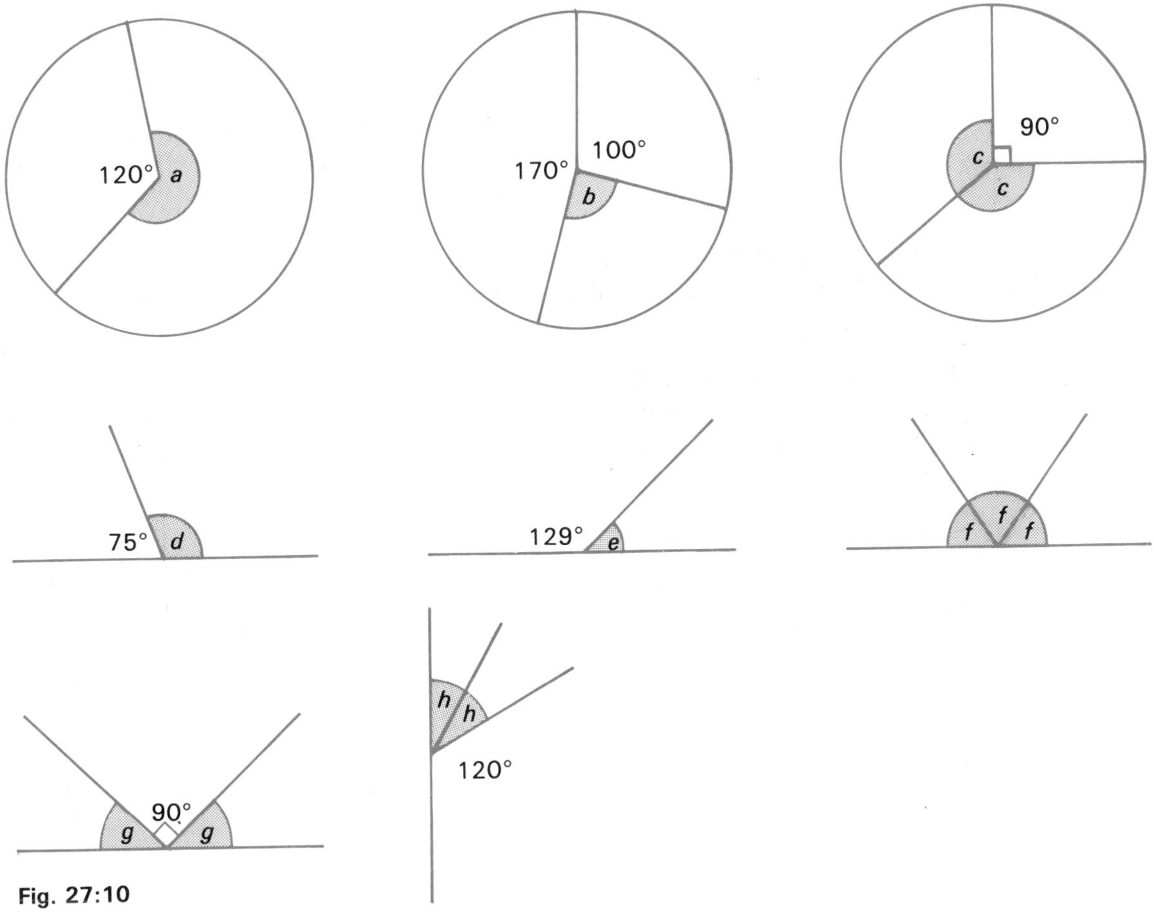

Fig. 27:10

2 One of the angles in Figure 27:11 is 40° and the others are equal to each other. Find the size of the equal angles. (LEAG)

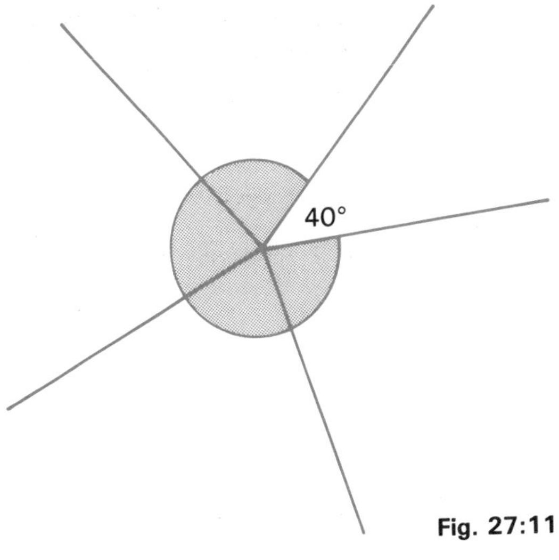

Fig. 27:11

3 Two broken circular frisbees are shown in Figure 27:12. By measuring the centre angles say which parts must be joined to repair the two frisbees.

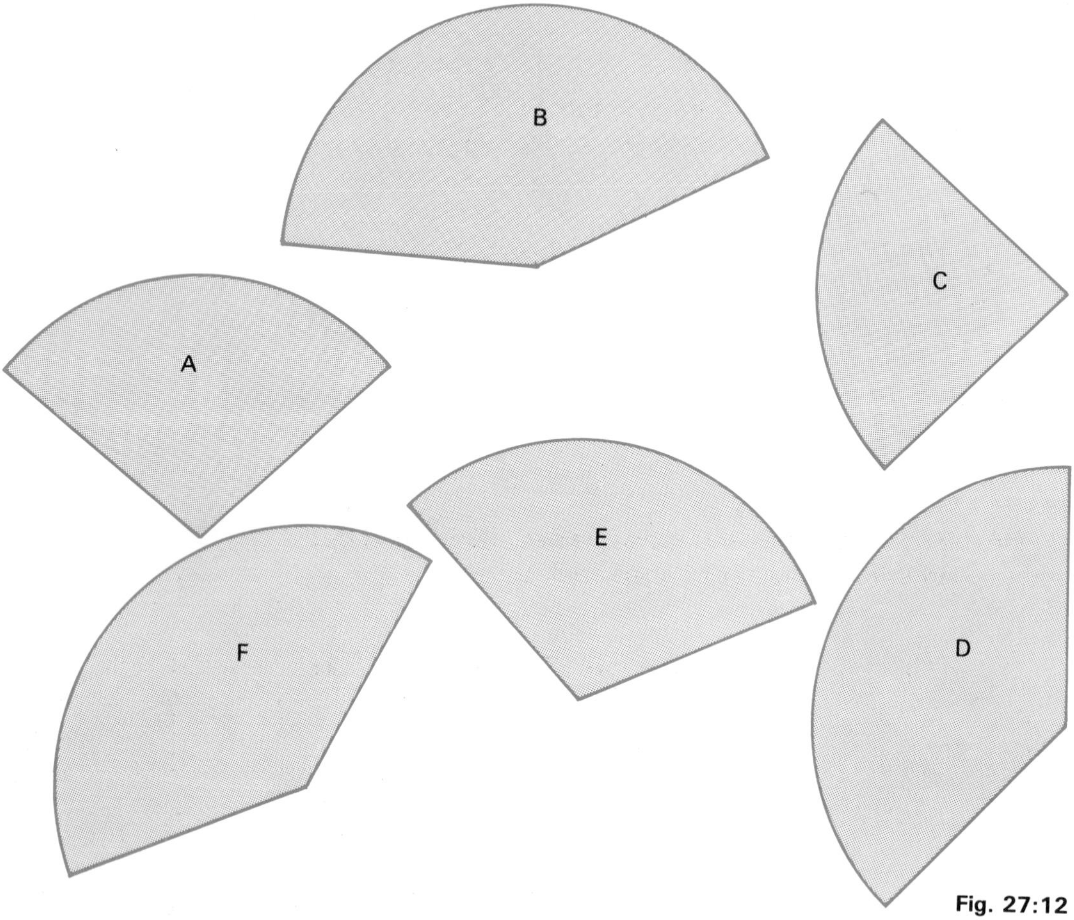

Fig. 27:12

4 Find the angles marked x and $2x$ in Figure 27:13.

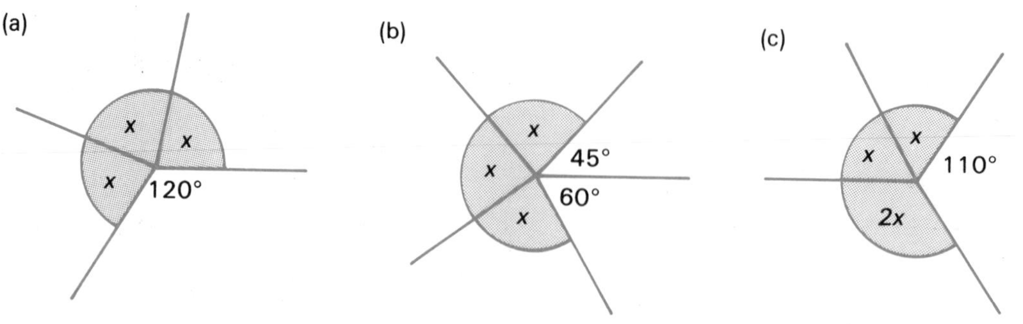

Fig. 27:13

5 Find the sizes of all the unknown angles in Figure 27:14.

(a)

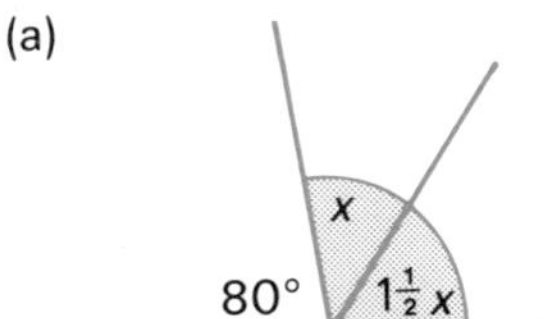

(b)

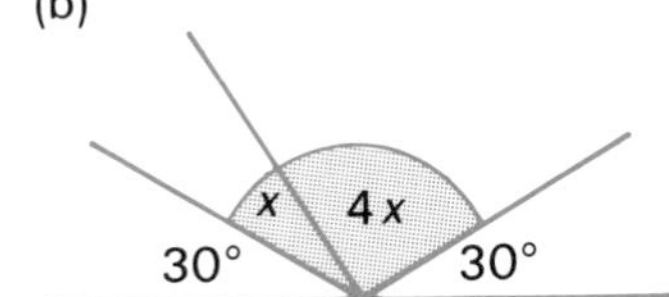

(c)

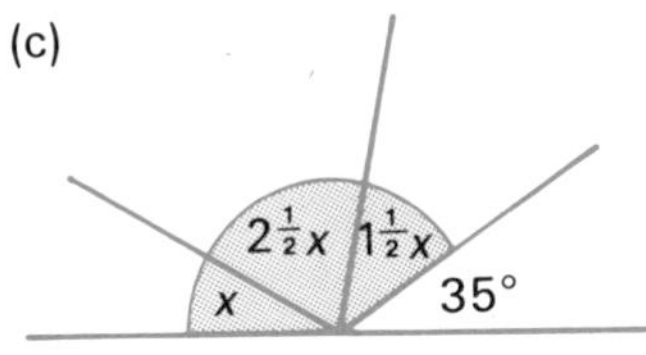

Fig. 27:14

6 Figure 27:15 shows six clock faces. Find without measuring the sizes of the shaded angles.

(a)

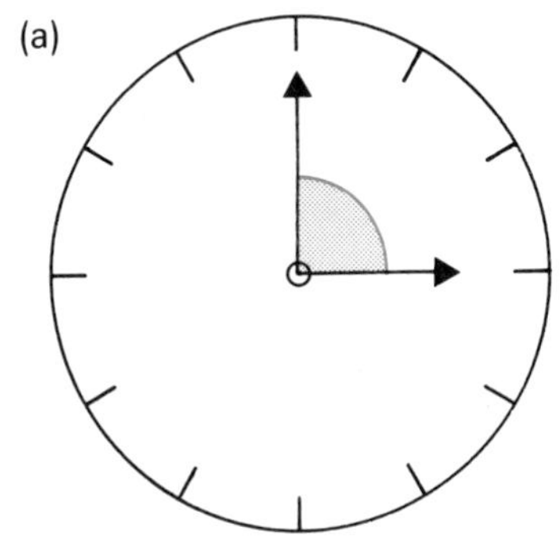

(b)

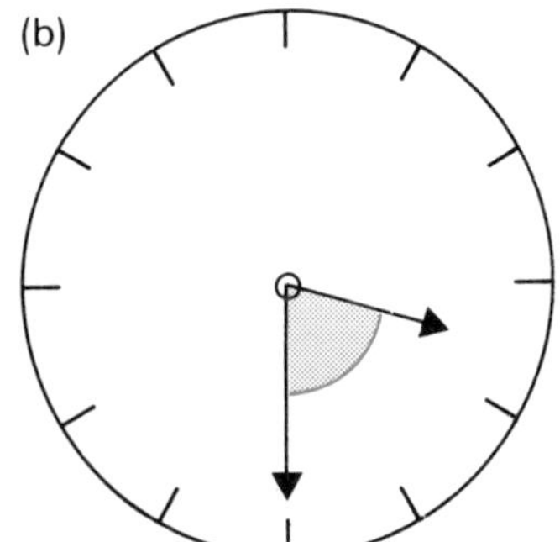

(c)

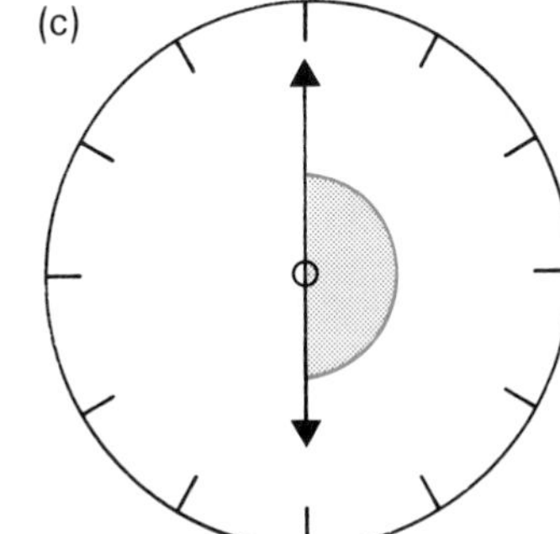

(d)

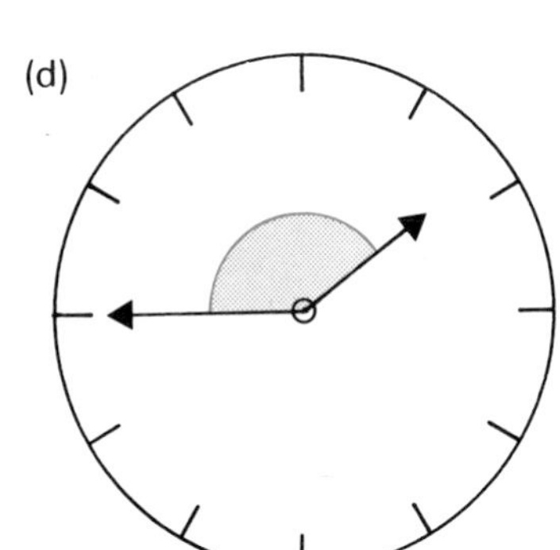

(e)

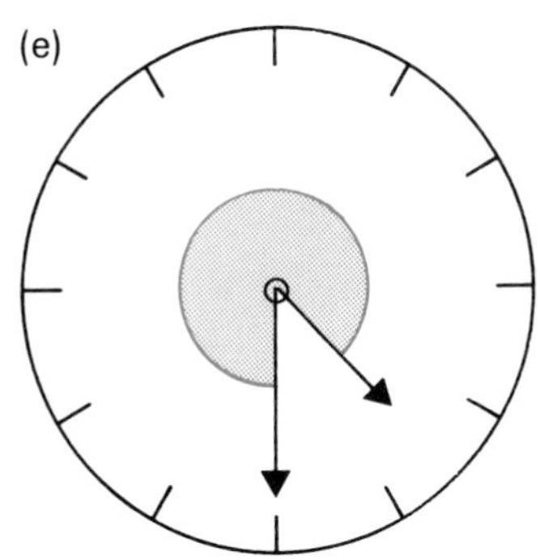

(f)

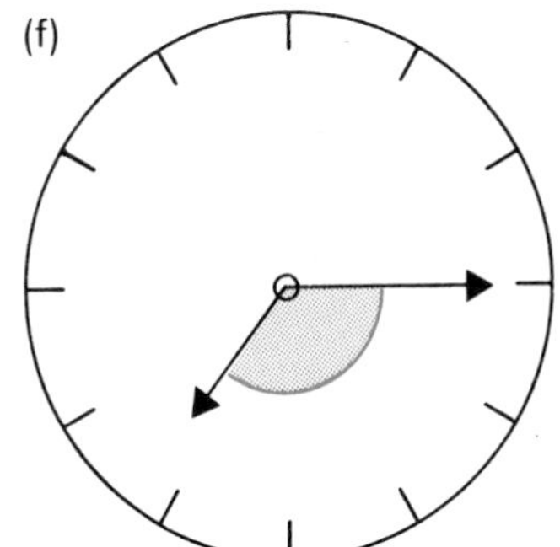

Fig. 27:15

7 Draw an interlacing polygon pattern like the one in Figure 27:16. We have used pentagons, but any regular polygon may be used.

Draw the outer circle first, then the two larger polygons. Draw the inside circle to just touch the sides of the larger polygons and draw the smaller polygons inside it.

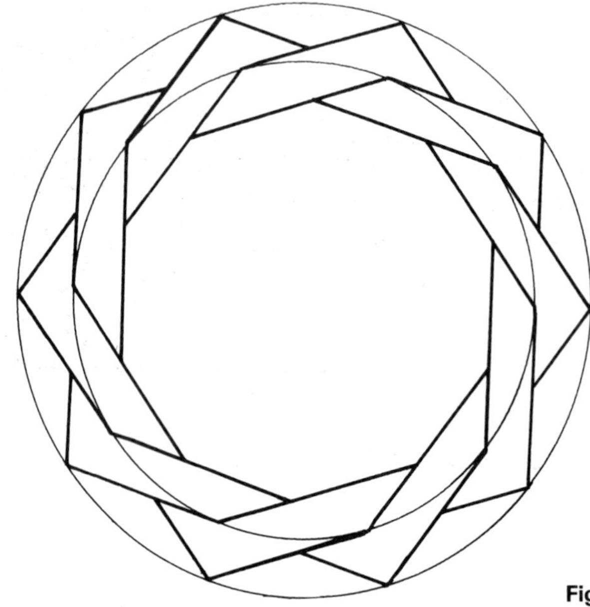

Fig. 27:16

28 Averages

A The mean

To remind you . . .

- **Calculating the mean**
  To find the average height of the pupils in your class you would probably add all the heights, then divide by the number of pupils. Mathematicians call this kind of average the arithmetic mean, or just the mean.

Points to discuss . . .

1 Which organisations or people might find the averages given in Figure 28:1 useful?

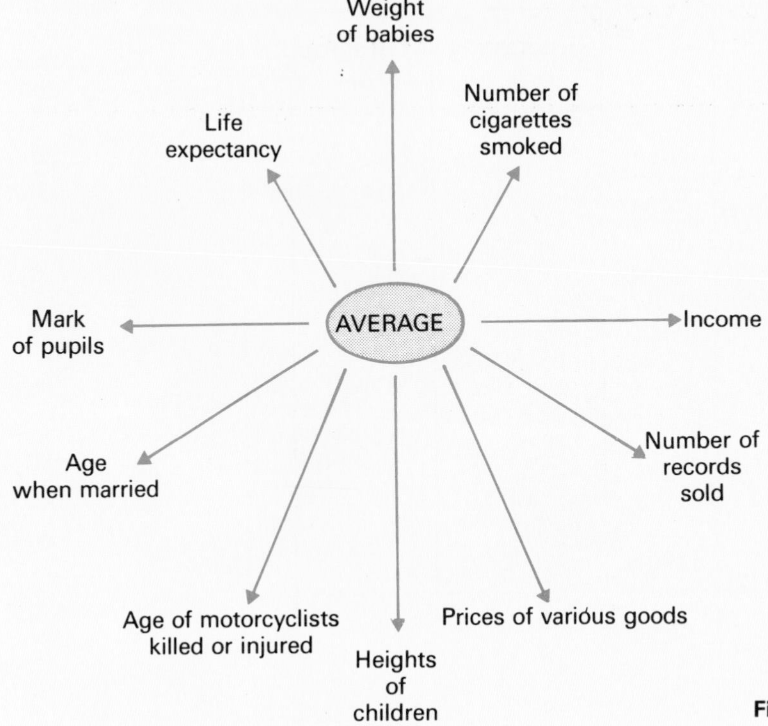

Fig. 28:1

2 **Frequency tables**

When finding the mean for a large amount of data (information) it is helpful to use a frequency table. A frequency table shows how many times things happen.

Example 100 pupils scored the following marks out of 10.

6	1	5	3	8	4	6	5	5	7
9	5	5	8	4	5	2	2	3	6
4	5	6	9	2	4	4	5	3	6
5	7	7	8	3	3	5	4	6	4
4	7	8	8	6	9	9	10	7	5
5	6	10	8	2	10	5	7	8	3
4	10	9	9	8	5	5	6	4	7
5	6	6	7	4	4	5	8	9	3
4	7	8	9	0	3	4	5	2	5
5	5	7	4	2	5	7	7	8	8

Copy and complete the frequency table. We have tallied the first 20 marks.

Mark m	Tally	Frequency f	Total marks $m \times f$
0			
1	/	1	$1 \times 1 = 1$
2	//		
3	//		
4	//		
5	~~////~~ /		
6	///		
7	/		
8	//		
9	/		
10			
	Totals	100	

$$\text{Mean} = \frac{\text{Total marks}}{\text{Total pupils}} = \qquad = $$

1 Link up each part with the correct letter from Figure 28:2.

(a) The average we are studying is called the . . .

(b) Basic information is called the . . .

(c) The number of times something happens is called the . . .

(d) In a frequency table, the tally marks are grouped in . . .

(e) The mean height of pupils in a class can be found by . . .

A	frequency
B	mean
C	$\dfrac{\text{sum of heights}}{\text{number of pupils}}$
D	raw data
E	fives

Fig. 28:2

2 What numbers are shown by the following tallies?

(a) ||| (b) 𝍸 (c) 𝍸 𝍸 𝍸

(d) 𝍸 |||| (e) || (f) 𝍸 𝍸 |

3 Write in tally form:

(a) 5 (b) 8 (c) 12 (d) 23 (e) 34

4 Work out the mean of each of these:

(a) 50 cm, 70 cm and 90 cm

(b) 1 m, $\frac{1}{2}$ m and $\frac{3}{4}$ m

(c) The first three even numbers

(d) The first three prime numbers

(e) The first three square numbers

(f) The first three triangular numbers

5 At a school fete, 1B ran a stall to guess the number of peas in a jar. The five teachers in the Mathematics Department all had a go. Here are their results:

Mr Newton 180 Mrs Hardy 150
Miss Euler 170 Ms Pascal 170
Signora Fibonacci 230

(a) Calculate the mean guess for the teachers.

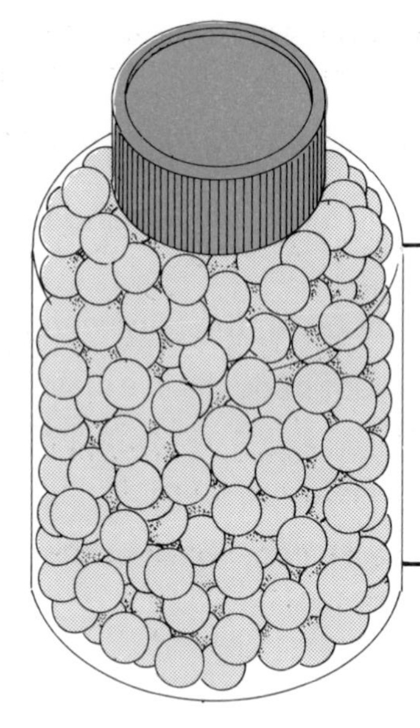

Fig. 28:3

Some of the children had a go. Here are their results:

100	100	110	110	110	110	120	180	200	130
150	140	130	130	170	150	130	170	150	140
160	140	140	170	140	160	130	160	130	200

(b) How many children had a go?

(c) Copy and complete this frequency table.

Guess	Tally	Total	Guess	Tally	Total
100	//	2	160		
110	////	4	170		
120	/	1	180		
130			190		
140			200		
150			210		

(d) Copy and complete the bar-chart in Figure 28:4, to show the information in the frequency table.

(e) Write down the most common guess made by the pupils.

(f) How many pupils thought there were more than 170 peas in the jar?

The jar had 169 peas in it. The mean guess for the children was 142.

(g) State, with a reason, whether the children under-estimated or over-estimated.

(h) State, with a reason, whether the teachers or the pupils were the better guessers. (SEG)

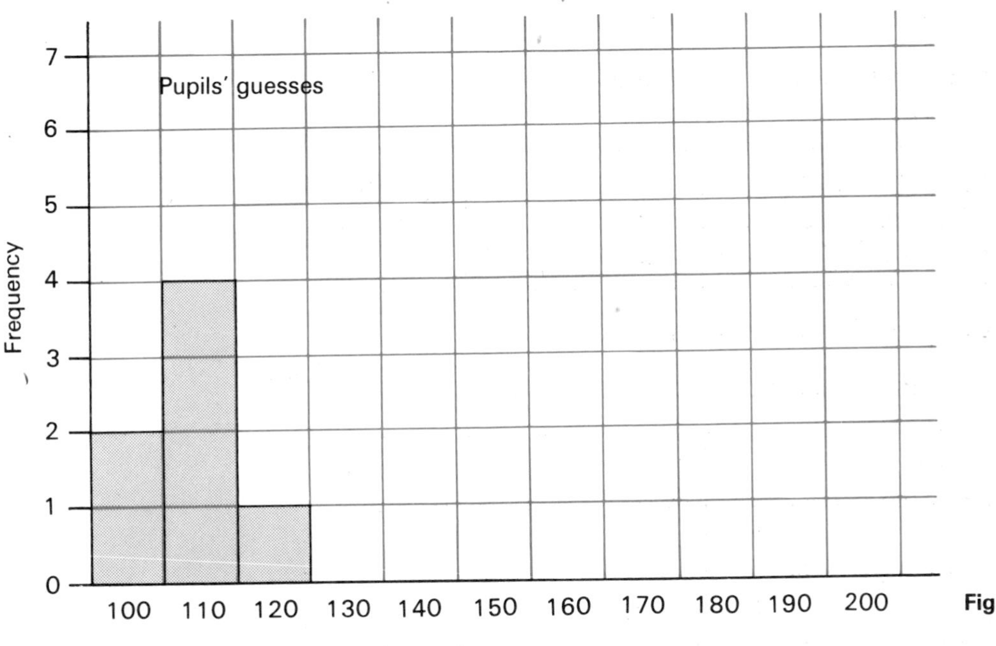

Fig. 28:4

6 The mean (average) height of seven young children is 103 cm.

(a) Calculate the total of the heights of the seven children.

(b) The mean height of three of these children is 107 cm.
 (i) Calculate the total of the heights of the other four children.
 (ii) Calculate the mean height of the other four children.
(WJEC)

7 Graph A in Figure 28:5 shows that a distance of 60 metres was covered in 5 seconds. This is a mean speed of

$\frac{60\text{ m}}{5\text{ s}} = 12\text{ m/s}$ (12 metres per second).

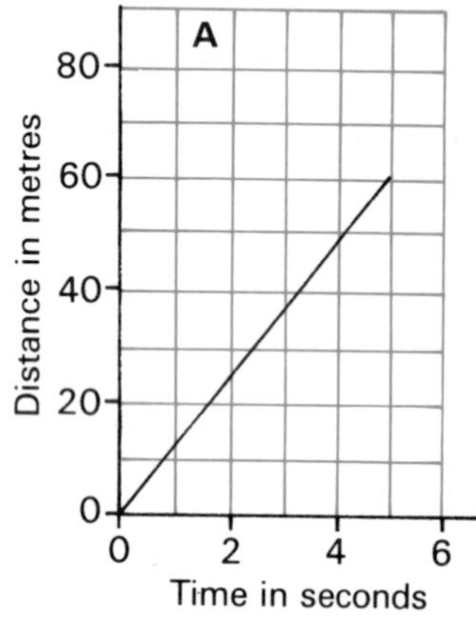

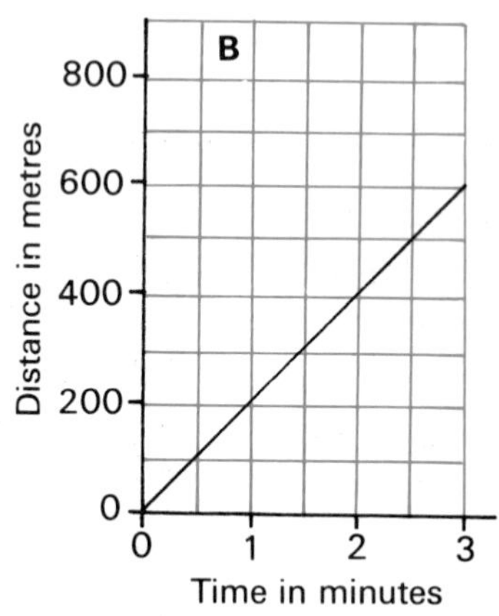

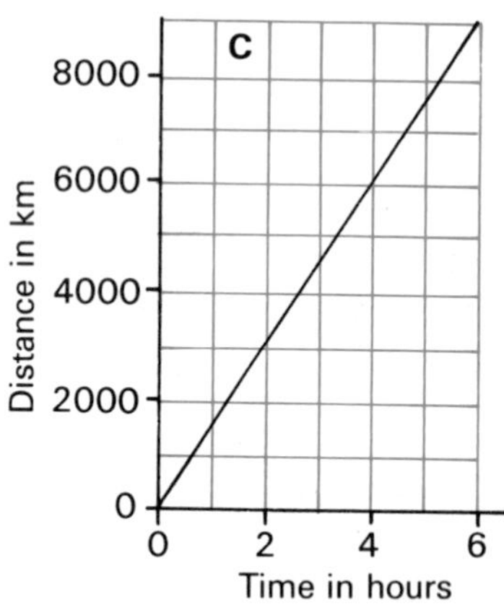

Fig. 28:5

(a) What mean speeds do graphs B and C show?

(b) If something travels at a constant speed of 12 m/s, how many metres would it cover in one minute?

(c) Graph C shows a speed in kilometres per hour. What is the speed in kilometres per **minute**?

8 Solve these clues to the word puzzle in Figure 28:6 and write down the answers.

(a) Groups of five.

(b) $4\overline{)24}$ is a form of this.

(c) Word for average.

(d) 1, 4, 9, 16, 25 are . . . numbers.

(e) Order of operation.

(f) Positive and negative whole numbers.

(g) Number of times something happens.

Fig. 28:6

(a)					A	L				S	
(b)					V						
(c)					E						
(d)		Q			R						
(e)	B		D		A						
(f)	I				G						
(g)					E	Q					

9 a, b, c, d and e represent five numbers. The mean of b and c is 12. The mean of d and e is 10. The sum of all five numbers is 70. Find the value of a.

10 The chart in Figure 28:7 shows the number of goals scored in league hockey matches on a certain Saturday.

(a) Write down the number of matches in which two goals were scored.

(b) Calculate the number of matches played.

(c) Calculate the number of goals scored altogether.

(d) Calculate the mean number of goals scored per match. (WJEC)

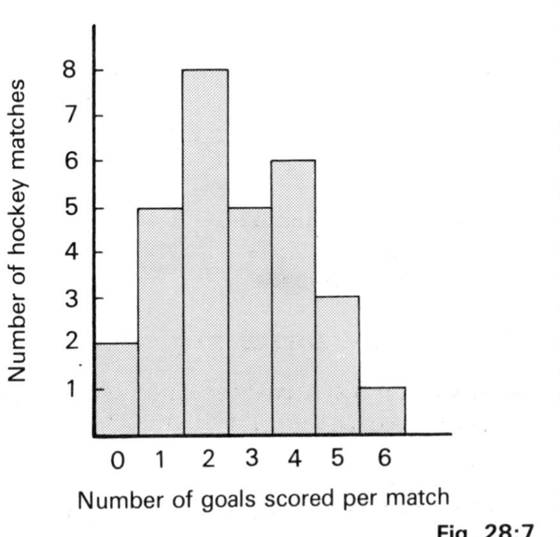

Fig. 28:7

B The mode and the median

● To remind you . . .

- **The median**
  The median is the midpoint of the values when they are arranged from smallest to biggest.
- **The mode**
  The mode is the value that occurs most often.

▶ Points to discuss . . .

1 The absences through sickness of nine girls in form 4T for one term were 1, 5, 51, 6, 7, 1, 4, 7 and 8 days. The school secretary worked out the mean absence in days as:

$$\frac{1 + 5 + 51 + 6 + 7 + 1 + 4 + 7 + 8 \text{ days}}{9}$$

$$= \frac{90 \text{ days}}{9} = \mathbf{10} \text{ days.}$$

The secretary then listed the absences in order:
1, 1, 4, 5, (6), 7, 7, 8, 51 days.
The middle value of 6 days is the median.

(a) Which is the better average, the mean or the median? Why?

(b) What would the median be if ten girls were involved, the tenth girl being absent for 7 days?

2 In one day a shop sold ladies' shoes in the following sizes: 3, 7, 5, 4, 5, 4, 8, 5, 5, 6, 5.

Why would the shop manager be interested in the **modal** average of size 5?

3 What is the modal shoe colour for the pupils in your class today? Could you find the mean or the median shoe colour?

1 Copy and complete the following, using the words listed on the right.

To find the median, list the values in order from . . . to . . . and then find the . . . value. If there is an even number of values, there are . . . middle values. The median is the . . . of these two middle values.

The . . . is the value that occurs most often.

2 (a) What do you think is the modal age in years of the pupils in your class?

(b) What is the modal hair colour of your class?

3 Find the mode of:

(a) 4, 3, 2, 4, 5, 4, 7, 4

(b) 2, 1·5, 3, $1\frac{1}{2}$, 6, 3, 1·5, 4

4 Rewrite in order, then find the median of:

(a) 3, 4, 1, 5, 2 (b) 1, 2, 3, 4, 5, 16

5 Find the median of:

(a) 3, 2, 5, 4, 1, 4, 3, 4, 1 (b) 7, 8, 7, 3, 4, 7

(c) 9, 5, 12, 3, 8, 4 (d) 6, 8, 0, 3, 5, 7, 3, 0

6 (a) Find the modes for parts (a), (b) and (d) in question 5.

(b) Why were you not asked for the mode of 5(c)?

7 Nine people received wages of £150, £160, £160, £160, £170, £170, £172, £175 and £420.

Find the median wage, the modal wage and the mean wage.

Which average gives a misleading picture of the wages? Why does this happen?

8 A shoe shop sold 35 pairs of ladies' shoes in one day. Here is a list of the sizes.

4, 3, 3, 3, 4, 3, 4, 4, 4, 4, 5, 4, 4, 4, 5, 4, 4, 7, 6, 5, 5, 6, 6, 6, 5, 5, 7, 5, 6, 6, 8, 7, 5, 5, 5

(a) Copy and complete this frequency table.

Shoe size	Tally	Frequency	Frequencies added
3	////	4	4
4	~~////~~ ~~////~~ /	11	(4 + 11) → 15
5	//		
6			
7			
8			

Total: Total:

(b) What is the modal size of shoe sold?

(c) Draw a bar-chart to illustrate the data in the frequency table.

(d) Thirty-five pairs of shoes were sold. The median value is the 18th pair of shoes when they are listed in order of size. Use the 'Frequencies added' column to find the median shoe size.

9 Find the mean, median and, where possible, the mode of each of these sets of data.

(a) 50 cm, 1 m, 0·5 m, 25 cm, $\frac{1}{2}$ m

(b) 1·8, 2·1, 3·4, 4·5, 1·8, 1·8, 0·9, 1·3

(c) $2\frac{1}{2}$, $1\frac{3}{4}$, $3\frac{1}{4}$, $2\frac{1}{3}$, $4\frac{2}{3}$, $\frac{1}{2}$

10 Jasmin and Angelo have an average age of 13 y 8 mth.

(a) How old is Jasmin if Angelo is 12 y 7 mth?

(b) Nishi is 13 y 2 mth. What is the average age of Jasmin, Angelo and Nishi?

(c) Jasmin, Angelo, Nishi and Janice have an average age of 14 y 11 mth. How old is Janice?

11 Alan has to travel 120 miles in 3 hours. He covers the first 95 miles in 2 hours, then is held up for 30 minutes. What speed in m.p.h. must he now average if he is not to be late?

12 Figure 28:8 shows the midday temperature at Northgate-on-Sea from the 11th to the 20th of June.

(a) Calculate the mean temperature to the nearest whole number.

(b) What would be the median temperature?

(c) Could you state the modal temperature? Give reasons for your answer.

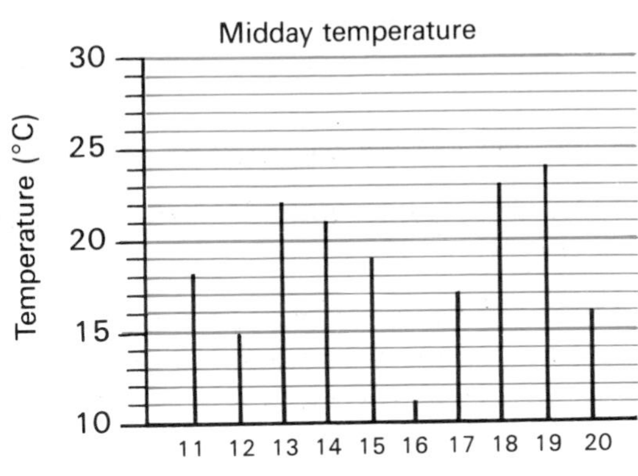

Fig. 28:8

Assignment 3

To remind you . . .

- Understand the problem.
- Plan your approach.
- Carry out the task.
- Communicate the results.

Two-way tables

Making a two-way table can be a useful way of showing a lot of information in a small space.

1 Figure A3:1 shows a Chinese menu.

The two-way table on page 183 allows the owner of The Dragon to total the bill for each customer and to find out which dishes are most popular.

Fig. A3:1

THE DRAGON

FU YUNG DISHES (CHINESE OMELETTE)

72	CHICKEN FU YUNG	£1·70
73	MUSHROOM FU YUNG	£1·60
74	SHRIMP FU YUNG	£2·00
75	KING PRAWN FU YUNG	£2·30

ENGLISH DISHES

76	ROAST CHICKEN WITH CHIPS	£1·80
77	SIRLOIN STEAK WITH CHIPS, ONION, MUSHROOM AND TOMATO	£3·50
78	SHRIMP OMELETTE AND CHIPS	£2·00
79	CHICKEN OMELETTE AND CHIPS	£1·80
80	MUSHROOM OMELETTE & CHIPS	£1·70
81	PLAIN OMELETTE AND CHIPS	£1·60
82	PLAICE AND CHIPS	£1·50

Order	Dish number											Total value of order
	72	73	74	75	76	77	78	79	80	81	82	
A	1		1			2						£10·70
B								2				
C	1			2	1						2	
D		2				1	1			1		
E			1			2			1	1	1	
Total number of dishes	2											

(a) Copy the table and complete the column for the total value of the orders and the row for the total number of dishes.

(b) Which dish was the most popular?

2 Six third-year pupils scored the following marks in an examination.

George	30 (M);	40 (Sc);	53 (Fr);	55 (H);	63 (E)
Elspeth	56 (M);	60 (Sc);	72 (Fr);	71 (H);	84 (E)
Hilary	72 (M);	78 (Sc);	37 (Fr);	56 (H);	55 (E)
Keith	67 (M);	90 (Sc);	67 (Fr);	84 (H);	52 (E)
Sapeena	66 (M);	72 (Sc);	70 (Fr);	51 (H);	80 (E)
Nadim	75 (M);	59 (Sc);	68 (Fr);	63 (H);	66 (E)

Abbreviations	
(M)	Mathematics
(Sc)	Science
(Fr)	French
(H)	History
(E)	English

(a) Make a two-way table to include all the information about the pupils and their marks.

(b) Use your table to total each pupil's marks and to find the mean (average) mark for each subject.

3 Make your own two-way table.

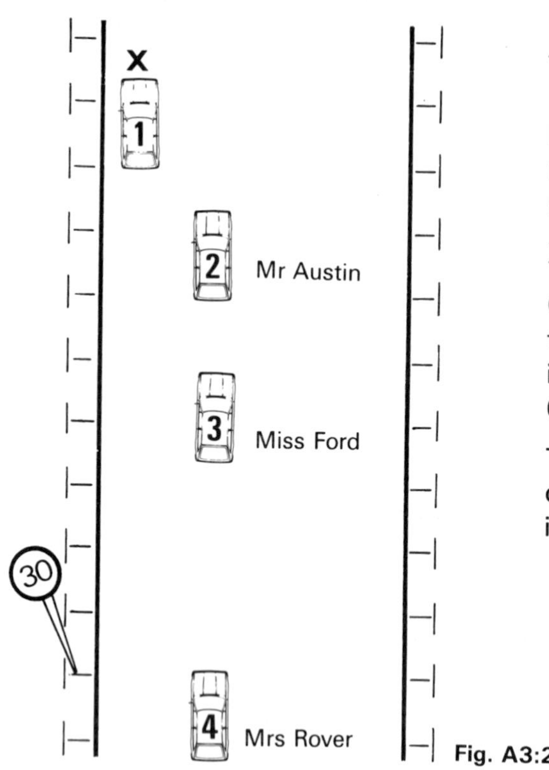

Fig. A3:2

What happened?

Figure A3:2 shows the scene just before a road accident. The road was wet, but it was not raining.

X represents an eight-year-old boy.

Car 1 is parked. Cars 2, 3 and 4 are all travelling at approximately 40 m.p.h. Car 3 is about 20 feet behind car 2. Car 4 is about 60 feet behind car 3.

The driver of car 4, Mrs Rover, is thinking deeply about a parent/teacher meeting she is going to attend that evening.

Figure A3:3 shows the scene just after the accident. The three drivers and the boy were all at fault.

1 Describe how you think the accident happened.

2 Describe the various faults involved.

3 The stopping distances are different for vehicles on dry or wet roads.

(a) How would you find out about such differences? (Chapter 10?)

(b) Describe two ways in which you could show the stopping distances.

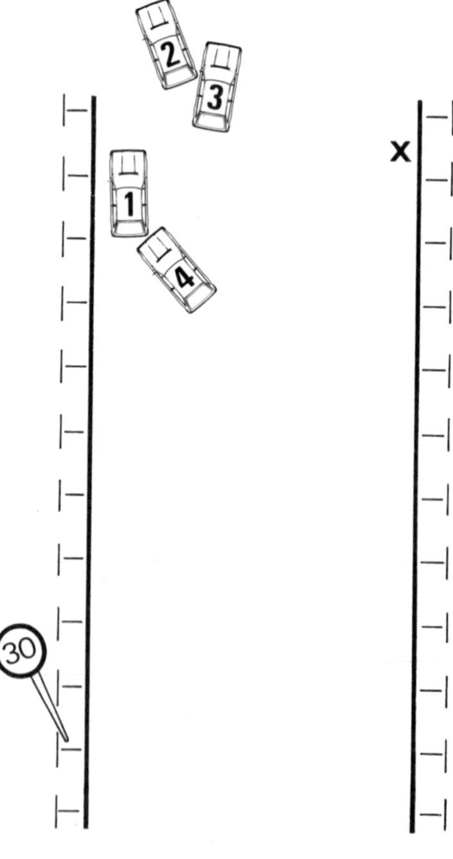

Fig. A3:3

29 Squares and square roots

▶ Points to discuss . . .

1 5^2 is read as 'five squared' and is short for 5×5. The small raised 2 is called the power or the index.

2 Your calculator may have a $\boxed{x^2}$ key. If it has, display 5, then press $\boxed{x^2}$. What does the $\boxed{x^2}$ key do?

3 How can you work out 5^2 if you do not have a $\boxed{x^2}$ key?

4 You now need a calculator with a key marked $\boxed{\sqrt{}}$ or $\boxed{\sqrt{x}}$. On some calculators you need to press the second function or inverse key before the $\boxed{\sqrt{}}$ key.

5 Display 25 on your calculator, then press $\boxed{\sqrt{}}$. What does the $\boxed{\sqrt{}}$ key do?

6 We write $\sqrt{25} = 5$, which is read as 'the square root of twenty-five is five'.

Check that:

(a) $6^2 = 36$ (b) $11^2 = 121$ (c) $1{\cdot}5^2 = 2{\cdot}25$

(d) $\sqrt{144} = 12$ (e) $\sqrt{400} = 20$ (f) $\sqrt{6{\cdot}25} = 2{\cdot}5$

7 The square root of one number is the same as the number. What is the number?

Look at Figure 29:1. Is $\sqrt{0{\cdot}25}$ greater or smaller than $0{\cdot}25$?

$\frac{1}{2}$ of $\frac{1}{2} = \frac{1}{2} \times \frac{1}{2} = \frac{1}{4}$

Fig. 29:1

29

1 Write in words:

(a) $2^2 = 4$ (b) $\sqrt{9} = 3$

2 Link up each part with the correct letter from Figure 29:2.

A 2 and 3	B greater	C 12 and 15
D 1, 4, 9, 16, 25, 36	E 30	F 40
G $21 \times 21 = 441$	H ends in 25	I 400

Fig. 29:2

(a) The first six square numbers are . . .

(b) $5^2 = 25$, $15^2 = 125$, $25^2 = 625$. The square of any whole number ending in 5 . . .

(c) An approximation for $(20{\cdot}9)^2$ is . . .

(d) $\sqrt{400} = 20$, so we know that $20^2 = \ldots$

(e) $\sqrt{9} = 3$, so $\sqrt{900} = \ldots$

(f) $\sqrt{16} = 4$, so $\sqrt{1600} = \ldots$

(g) $\sqrt{144} = 12$ and $\sqrt{225} = 15$, so $\sqrt{196}$ must lie between . . .

(h) $\sqrt{9} = 3$ and $\sqrt{4} = 2$, so $\sqrt{6{\cdot}25}$ must lie between . . .

(i) $\sqrt{0{\cdot}49}$ is . . . than 0·49.

3 Find:

(a) 21^2 (b) 32^2 (c) 35^2 (d) 50^2 (e) $12{\cdot}5^2$

(f) $\sqrt{2500}$ (g) $\sqrt{3600}$ (h) $\sqrt{4900}$ (i) $\sqrt{12{\cdot}25}$

(j) $\sqrt{20{\cdot}25}$

4 **Examples** An approximation for 32^2 is $30 \times 30 = 900$.
An approximation for $(5{\cdot}8)^2$ is $6 \times 6 = 36$.

Give an approximation for:

(a) 42^2 (b) 19^2 (c) 58^2 (d) $(8{\cdot}9)^2$

(e) $(12{\cdot}2)^2$

5 Copy the following, filling in the gaps with words and symbols from the list on the right.

5^2 is a . . . way of writing . . . .
The small raised . . . is called the . . . or the . . .

The . . . . on a . . . is pressed to find the . . . of a number.

The symbol . . . stands for the words . . . .

the square root of
short
x^2 key
square
$\sqrt{\ }$
calculator
power
five times five
2
index

6 A square has an area of 2500 square centimetres. Find the length of one side.

7 **Examples** 9·534 to the nearest whole number is **10**.
9·345 to the nearest whole number is **9**.

Approximate to the nearest whole number:

(a) 8·43 (b) 9·62 (c) 12·53 (d) 23·48

(e) $\sqrt{90}$ (f) $\sqrt{120}$ (g) $\sqrt{200}$ (h) $\sqrt{310}$

8 The area of a square is 80 square centimetres to the nearest whole number. Between which two consecutive whole numbers is the length in cm of one side of the square?

9 Without using your calculator evaluate the following:

(a) $\sqrt{36} + \sqrt{81}$ (b) $\sqrt{144} \times \sqrt{49}$ (c) $\sqrt{1} \times \sqrt{9}$

(d) $\sqrt{900} \times \sqrt{16}$ (e) $\sqrt{2500} \times \sqrt{121}$

(f) $\sqrt{6400} - \sqrt{225}$

Using your calculator

Insects

Insects can be helpful to us, like the bee fertilising fruits, or harmful, like the locust devastating crops. One thing is certain – there are billions of them!

An acre of normal pastureland will contain about 360 million (360 000 000) insects.

An acre is 4840 square yards, so to find the approximate number of insects in one square yard of pastureland we divide 360 000 000 by 4840.

Unfortunately, 360 000 000 has nine digits and most calculators will only show eight digits. To overcome this we can first divide both numbers by 10, giving
36 000 000 ÷ 484.

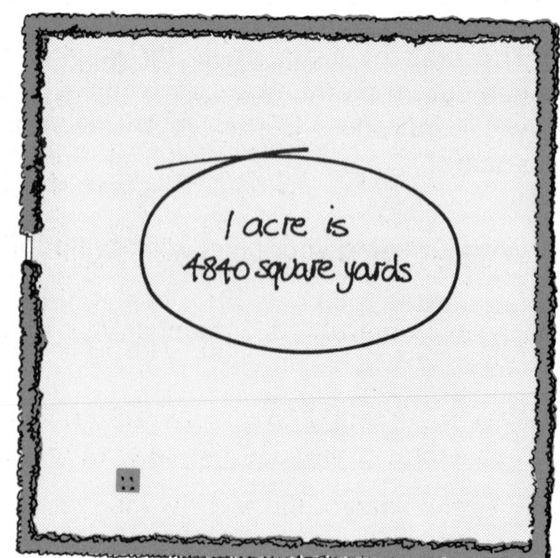

Fig. C2:1

1 Find, to the nearest whole number, the approximate number of insects in one square yard of pastureland.

2 You go for a picnic on a farm. On the grass you spread a tablecloth that is 3 yards square (meaning each side is 3 yards long).

(a) How many square yards does the tablecloth cover?

(b) Approximately how many insects will the cloth cover?

Use your answer to question 1 in questions 2 and 3.

3 You lay a one foot square handkerchief on the ground.

(a) How many square feet are there in one square yard?

(b) Approximately how many insects will the handkerchief cover?

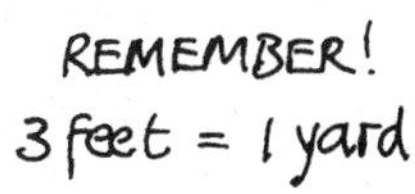

4 The acre in Figure C2:1 is shown as a square. What is the length of one side of the square, to the nearest yard?

5 A swarm of locusts can cover an area in the shape of a rectangle about 30 miles long and 5 miles wide. The swarm may contain an estimated 500 000 million insects and weigh about 80 000 tonnes.

(a) Approximately how many square miles does the swarm cover?

(b) Approximately how many million insects might there be to each square mile? Answer to the nearest million.

(c) To the nearest tonne, how many tonnes of locusts might there be in each square mile?

(d) One mile = 1760 yards. How many square yards are there in one square mile?

(e) Approximately how many locusts might there be in one square yard? Give your answer to the nearest 100.

30 Symmetry

A Line; rotational; point

What kind of symmetry has this butterfly?

Line symmetry

A plane (flat) shape has line symmetry when, after folding, the two halves fit exactly over each other. The fold line is called the line of symmetry, or the mirror line.

The shapes in Figure 30:1 have line symmetry.

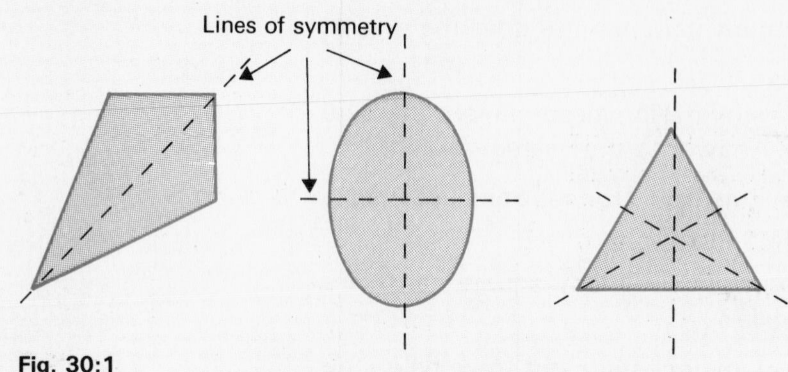

Fig. 30:1

These snowflakes have line and rotational symmetry.

Rotational symmetry

If a shape can be rotated and appear to be unchanged and in the same position, it is said to have rotational symmetry. The number of times it 'fits into itself' in a complete turn of 360° is called its order of rotational symmetry.

Figure 30:2 has rotational symmetry of order 3.

Fig. 30:2

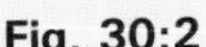

Point symmetry

A shape that can be rotated 180° and appear not to have moved is said to have point symmetry. This means that it will look the same when turned upside down.

Figure 30:3 has point symmetry.

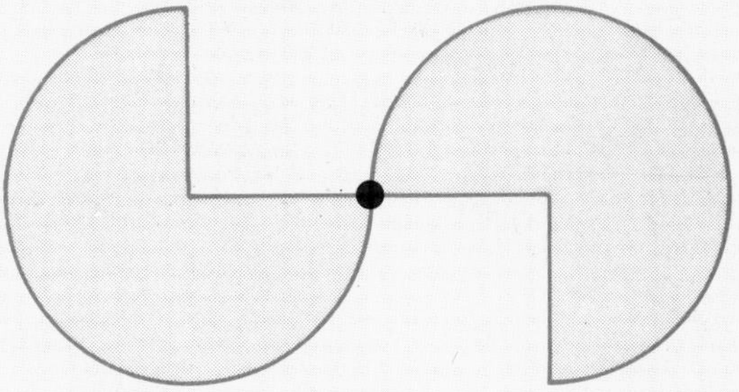

Fig. 30:3

Example Describe the symmetry of each shape in Figure 30:4.

(a)
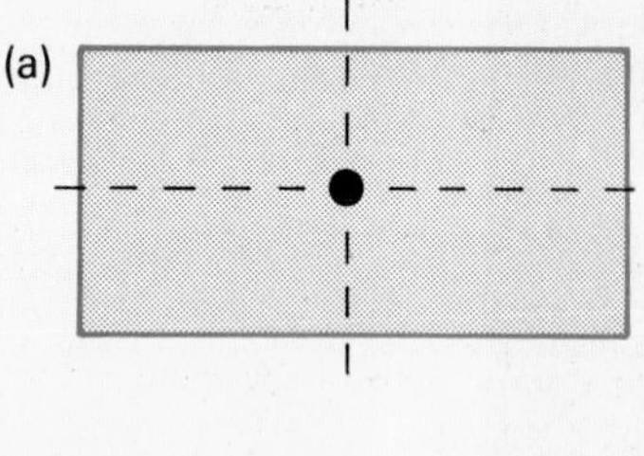
(b)
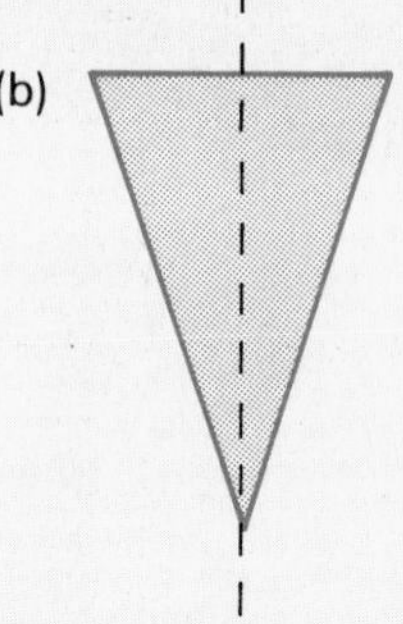
(c)
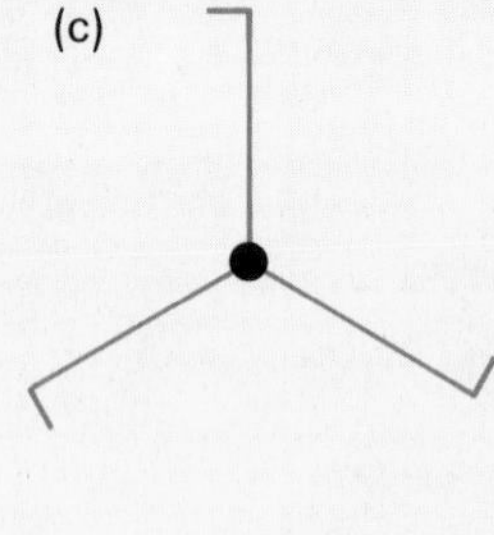

Fig. 30:4

(a) has 2 lines of symmetry
rotational symmetry of order 2
point symmetry

(b) has 1 line of symmetry
no rotational symmetry
no point symmetry

(c) has 3 lines of symmetry
rotational symmetry of order 3
no point symmetry

1 Which dashed lines in Figure 30:5 are lines of symmetry?

(a)
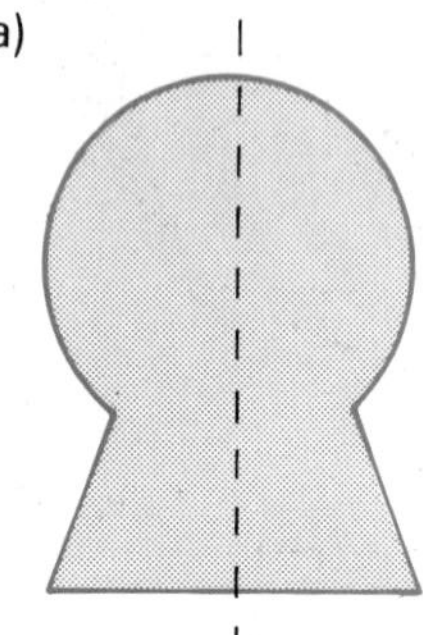
(b)
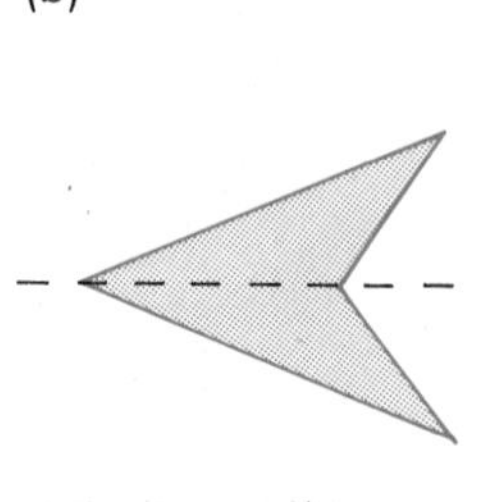
(c)
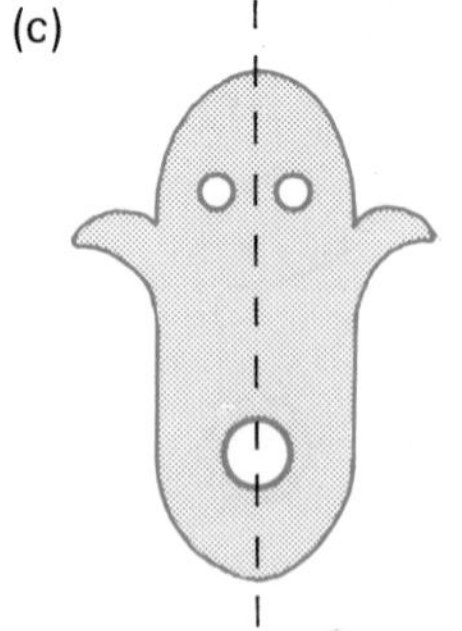
(d)
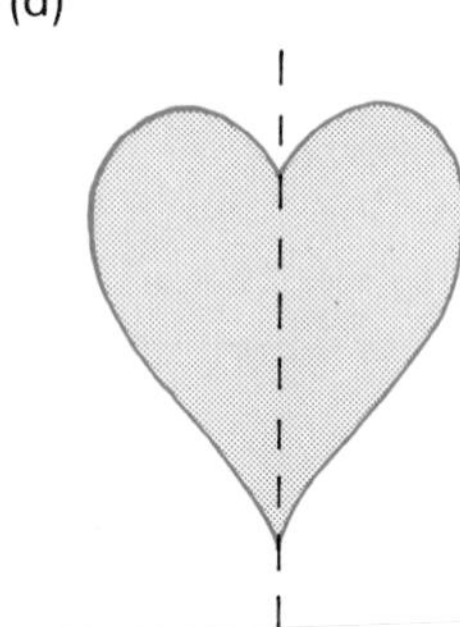
(e)
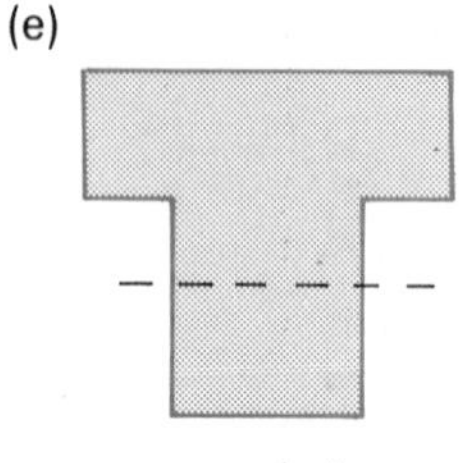
(f)
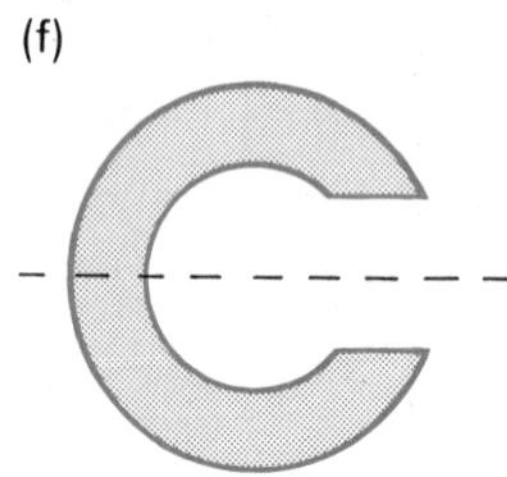
(g)
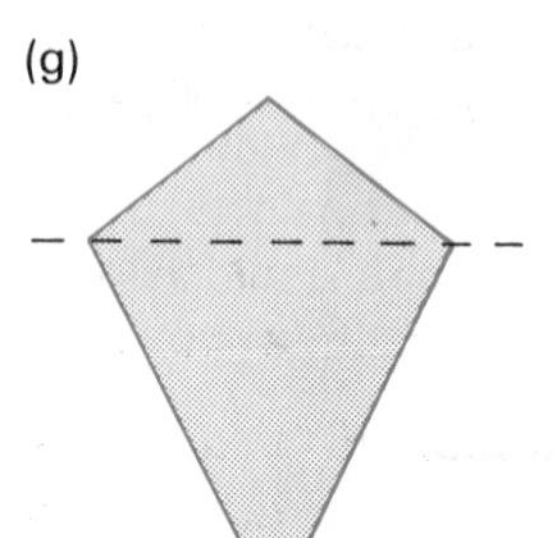
(h)
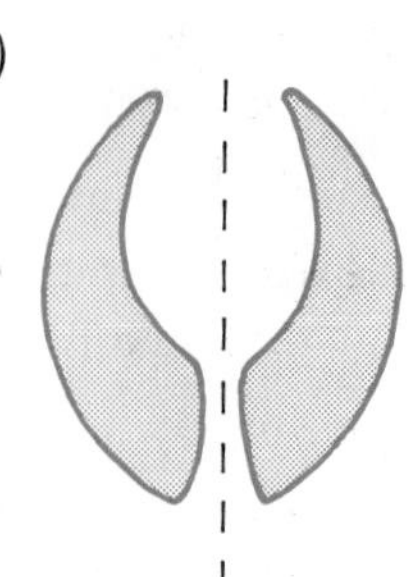

Fig. 30:5

2 Copy the drawings in Figure 30:6 onto squared paper. Complete each drawing so that each dashed line is a line of symmetry.

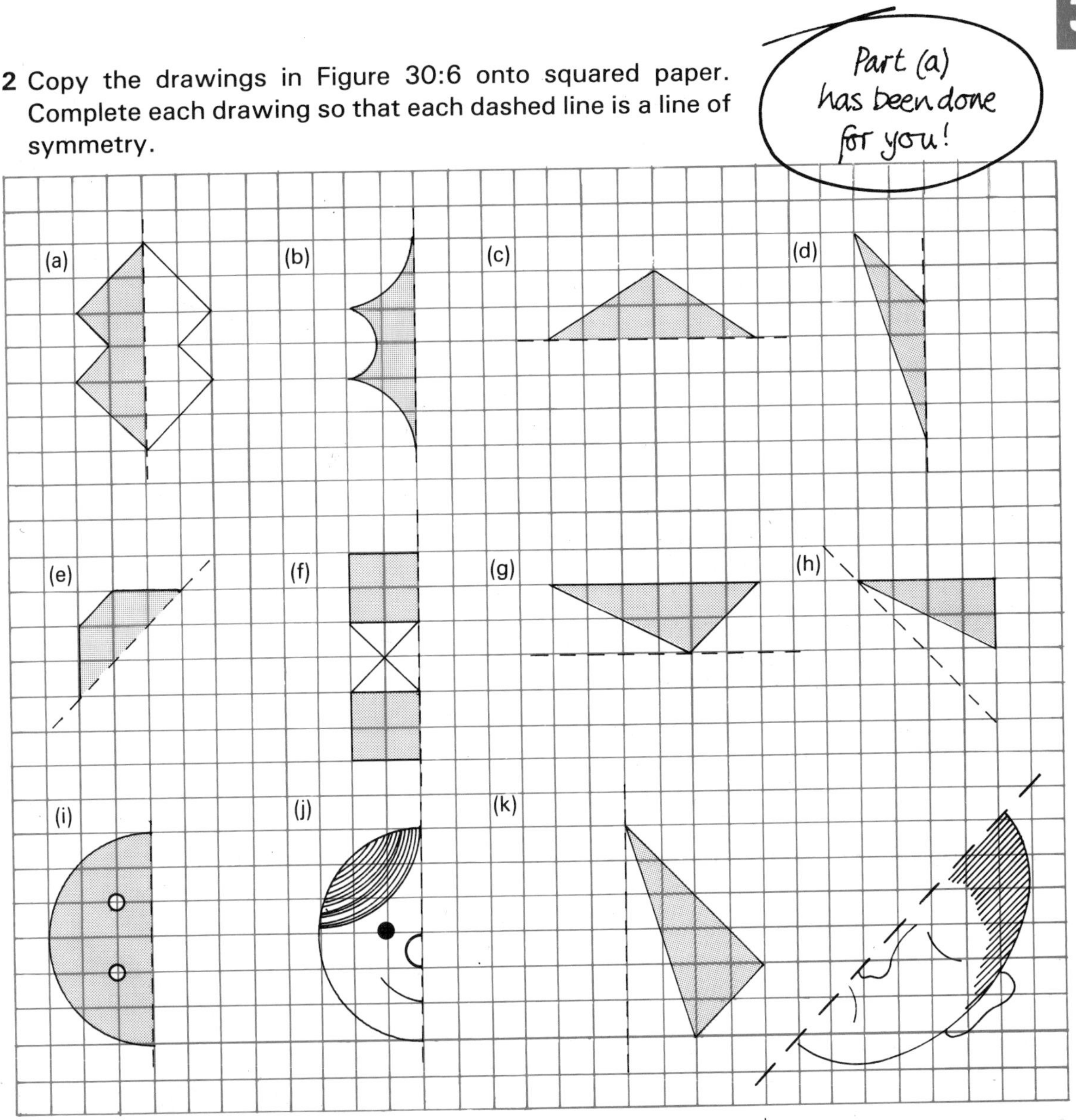

Part (a) has been done for you!

(a) (b) (c) (d)

(e) (f) (g) (h)

(i) (j) (k)

Fig. 30:6

3 Figure 30:7 shows a square bathroom tile with a vertical and a horizontal line of symmetry.

(a) Copy the tile and complete the shading to show the full pattern.

(b) When fully shaded, the tile has another symmetry. Describe this other symmetry. (SEG)

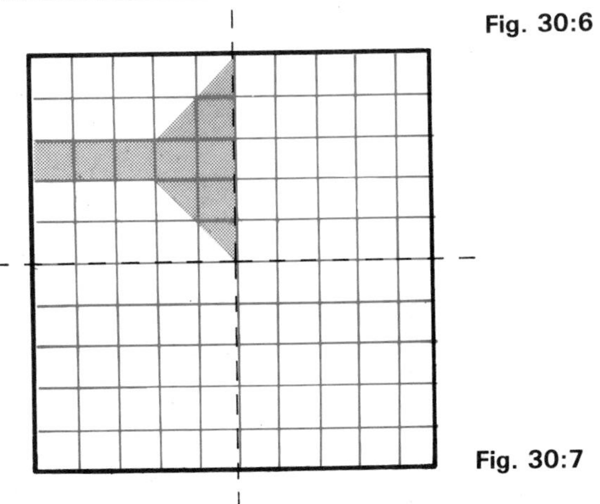

Fig. 30:7

4 Solve these clues to the word puzzle in Figure 30:8 and write down the answers.

(a) What this chapter is about.

(b) Reflected, as in a . . .

(c) 90°, a . . . angle.

(d) Perpendicular to horizontal.

(e) A quadrilateral with one line of symmetry.

(f) One kind of symmetry.

(g) Seen in a mirror.

(h) Triangle with no equal sides.

(i) One kind of symmetry.

(j) Triangle with two equal sides.

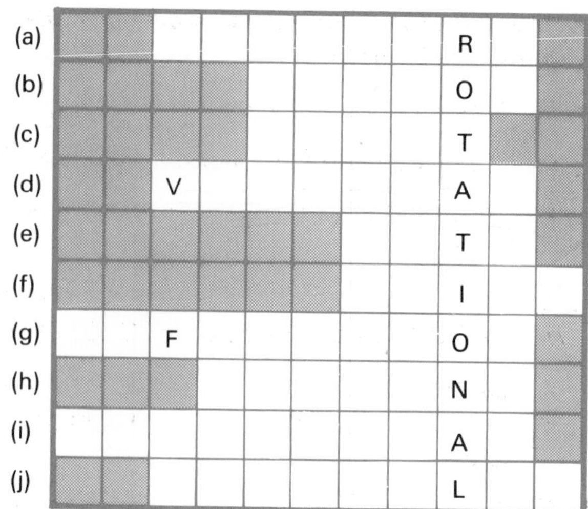

Fig. 30:8

5 Which of the letters in Figure 30:9 have:

(a) line symmetry

(b) point symmetry

(c) rotational symmetry?

Fig. 30:9

6 Pete the pirate thought, 'What a mess!' as he looked at himself in the mirror. Figure 30:10 shows what Pete saw in the mirror. Draw what Pete really looked like to Peg-leg, his captain.

Fig. 30:10

7 The circumference of a circle is made up of an infinite number of points.

(a) Does a circle have point symmetry?

(b) How many lines of symmetry has a circle?

(c) What is the order of rotational symmetry for a circle?

Infinite means 'more than can be counted'.

8 List the letters of the phrases describing each shape in Figure 30:11. For example, (a) C, G, M, O.

A square
B rectangle
C scalene triangle
D isosceles triangle
E equilateral triangle
F circle

G no line symmetry
H 1 line of symmetry
I 2 lines of symmetry
J 3 lines of symmetry
K 4 lines of symmetry
L infinite number of lines of symmetry

M no point symmetry
N point symmetry

O no rotational symmetry
P rotational symmetry of order 2
Q rotational symmetry of order 3
R rotational symmetry of order 4
S rotational symmetry of infinite order

(a)

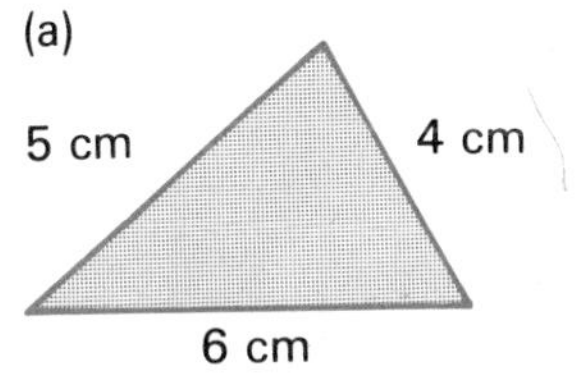

(b)

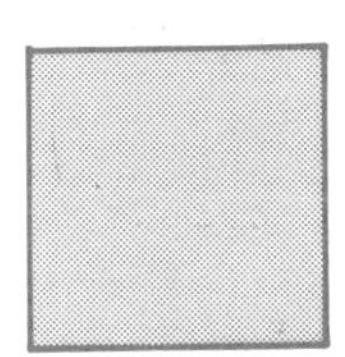

(c)

(d)

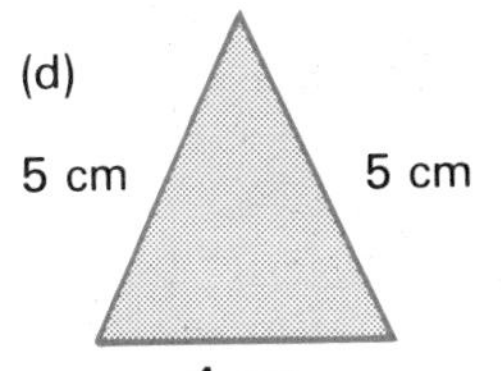

(e)

(f)

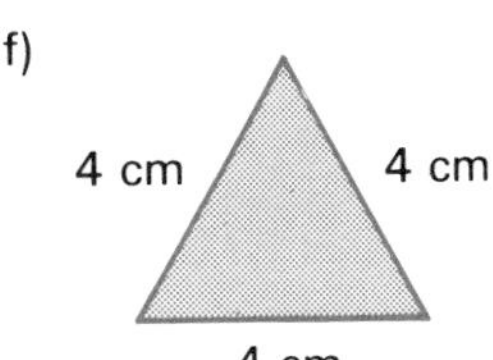

Fig. 30:11

9 Figure 30:12 shows a bathroom tile with part of the pattern shaded.

(a) Copy and complete the figure so that it is symmetrical about AB and CD, shading where appropriate.

(b) What fraction of the tile is shaded?

(WJEC)

Fig. 30:12

Worksheet 30A may be used here.

10 In Figure 30:13, triangle ABC is reflected in the mirror line WX to give the image $A_1B_1C_1$. Similarly, triangle $A_1B_1C_1$ is reflected in the mirror line YZ to give the image $A_2B_2C_2$.

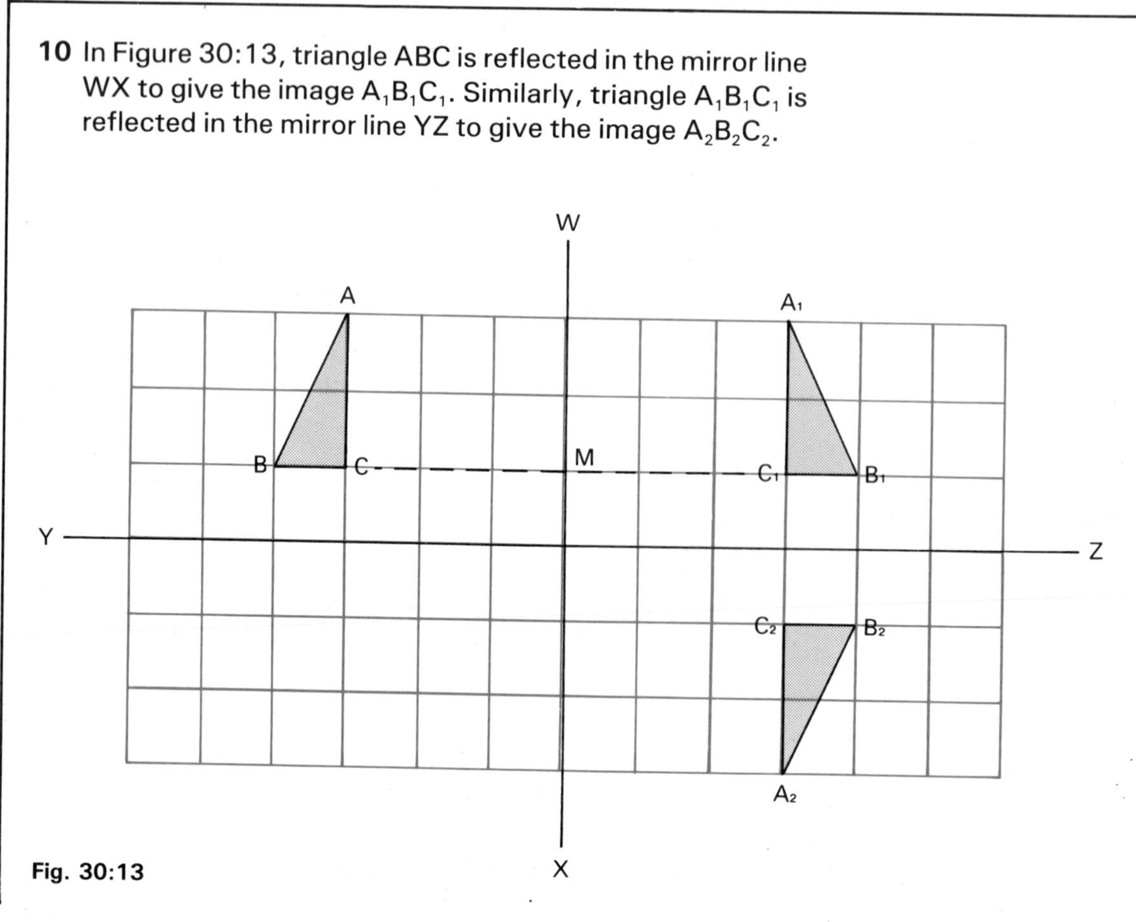

Fig. 30:13

Note Points with the same letter must be the same distance from the mirror line. For example, $BM = B_1M$.

Note The line joining points with the same letter must cross the mirror line at right angles. For example, $\angle WMC = \angle WMC_1 = 90°$.

(a) Copy Figure 30:13.

(b) Reflect $A_2B_2C_2$ through the mirror line WX and draw the image $A_3B_3C_3$.

(c) Is $A_3B_3C_3$ an image of ABC? If so, what is the mirror line?

11 (a) Copy Figure 30:14. Write the coordinates of points A, B, C and D.

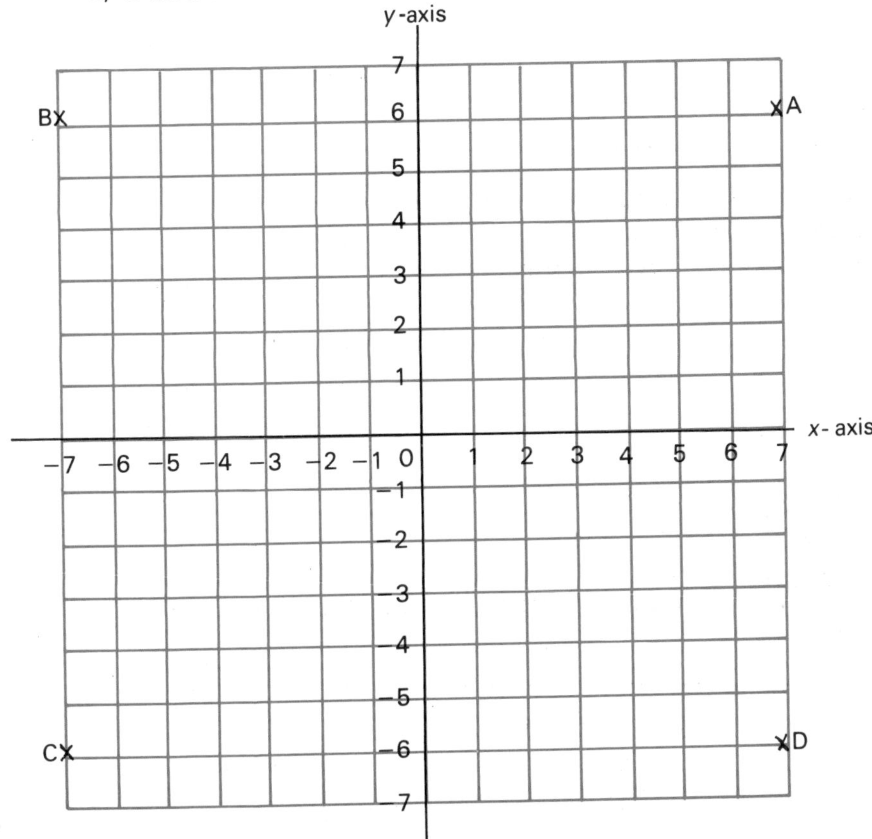

Fig. 30:14

(b) Mark and label the points:
E (3, 0) F (4, 2) G (6, 3) H (4, 4)
I (3, 6) J (2, 4) K (0, 3) L (2, 2)
Join the points with straight lines, E to F to G etc., and back to E.

(c) (i) How many lines of symmetry has the shape you have drawn?

(ii) Mark in the point of symmetry and give its coordinates.

(iii) Give the rotational order of symmetry.

(d) Find the area of the shape in square units.

(e) Reflect the shape through the x-axis and give the new coordinates, for example K_1 (0, −3) and so on.

B Symmetry of polygons

● To remind you . . .

- A polygon is a plane (flat) shape with three or more straight sides.

- Figure 30:15 shows a **regular** pentagon (all its sides and angles are **equal**) and an **irregular** pentagon.

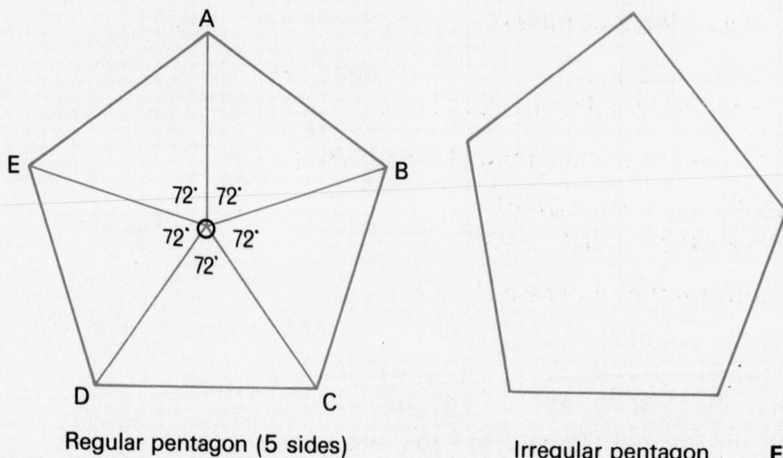

Regular pentagon (5 sides)   Irregular pentagon   **Fig. 30:15**

1 (a) Draw a regular hexagon (see Figure 30:16).

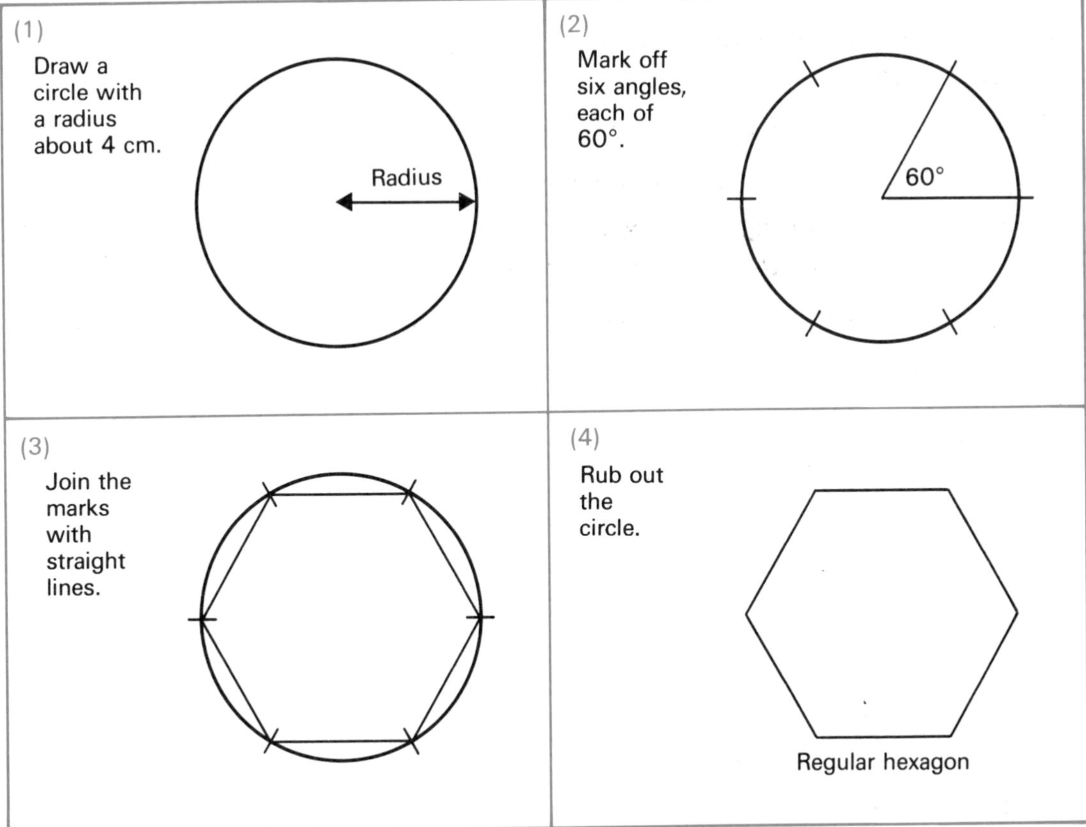

Fig. 30:16

(b) How many lines of symmetry has a regular hexagon?

(c) Three of the lines of symmetry each join two corners. The angles at those corners are **bisected** by the lines of symmetry. What does bisected mean?

2 (a) Draw a regular pentagon (see Figure 30:15).

(b) How many lines of symmetry has a regular pentagon?

(c) Look at Figure 30:15. Give the size of
(i) ∠AOB (ii) ∠ABO (iii) ∠BAO

(d) Is triangle ABO equilateral or isosceles?

3 Copy and complete the table.

Name	Sketch	Sides	Size of angles	Lines of symmetry
(a) Equilateral triangle		3	$\frac{180°}{3} = 60°$ at corners	
(b) Square			at corners	4
(c) Regular pentagon			$\frac{360°}{5} = 72°$ at centre	
(d) Regular hexagon			at centre	
(e) Regular octagon		8	at centre	
(f) Regular decagon		10	at centre	

4 Figure 30:17 shows two different tiles, A and B. Tile A is a regular five-sided polygon. Tile B is a regular six-sided polygon.

(a) Calculate the sizes of the angles marked x and y.

(b) Explain why tiles in the shape of a regular six-sided polygon will fit together on a floor without any gaps between them, whereas tiles in the shape of a five-sided regular polygon will not. (WJEC)

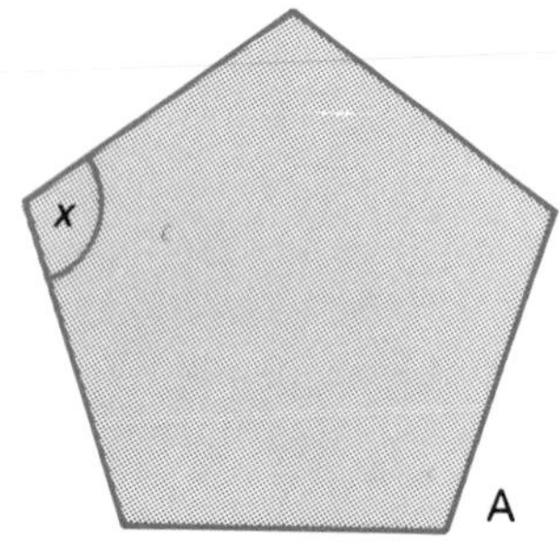

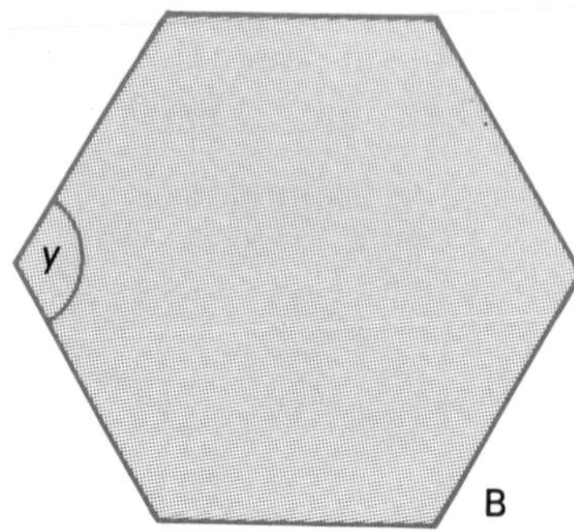

Fig. 30:17

5 Figure 30:18 shows a cube with a horizontal plane of symmetry marked ABCD. ABCD cuts the cube into two identical, symmetrical halves.

Draw the cube five times and sketch a different plane of symmetry in each cube. Do not include the example in Figure 30:18.

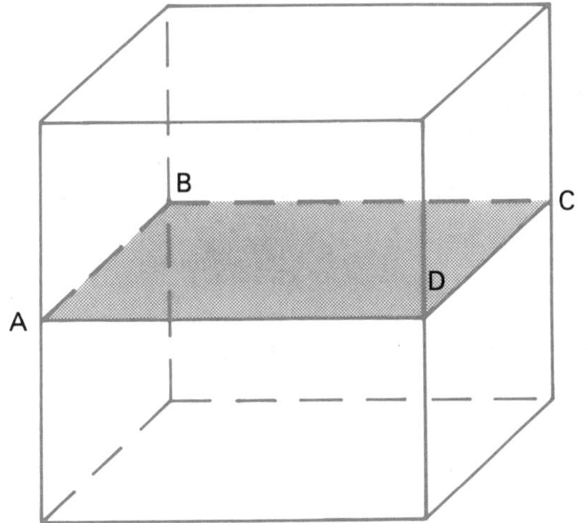

Fig. 30:18

A Hopscotch

Ali has invented a new game of hopscotch! He decides to find out how many ways he can get to each circle.

The number of ways has been completed for the first few circles in Figure B5:1. Copy the diagram and fill in the number of ways that each circle can be visited.

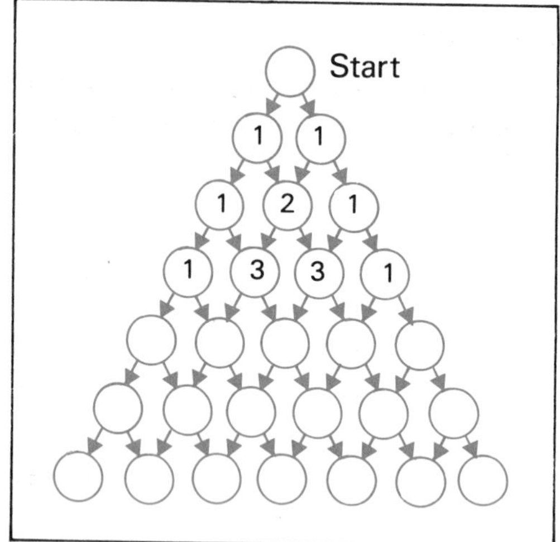

Fig. B5:1

B Half-full

A cylindrical glass is shown in Figure B5:2. How could you pour water from a tap into the glass to make the glass half-full?

There are no measuring marks on the glass and you must not use any aid.

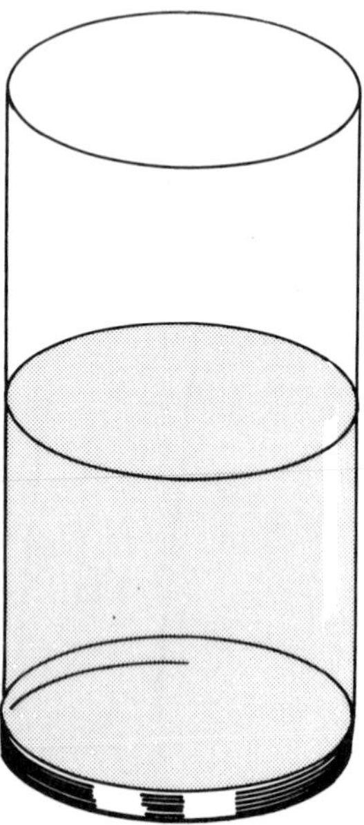

Fig. B5:2

C Rooms

Figure B5:3 shows twenty people arranged in eight rooms, with six people in each row of three rooms.

Re-arrange the people so that there are seven people in each row of three rooms.

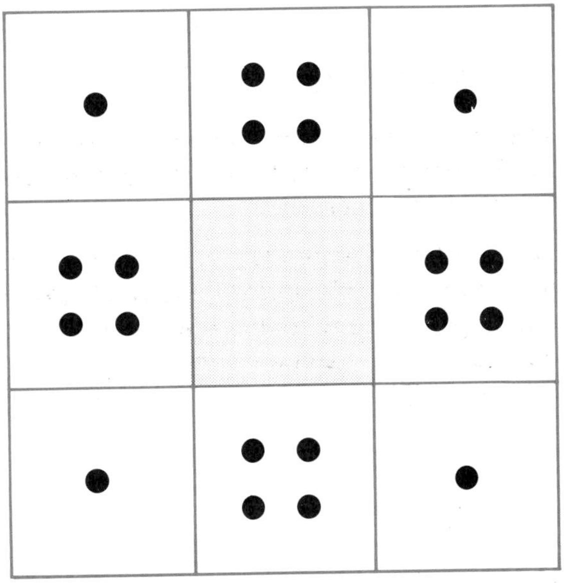

Fig. B5:3

D Sharing

Two mothers and two daughters shared £300 between them. Each of them received exactly £100. How was this possible?

31 The metric system

A Length

The British imperial system measures with units such as inches, pounds, and pints. Arithmetic is difficult in this system because the connections between units vary. For example, 16 ounces make 1 pound weight, 12 inches make 1 foot, 8 pints make 1 gallon.

Britain has now largely changed to the metric system which has an easy-to-use base of ten.

The metric system has base units which are increased and decreased in tens.
The base unit for length is the metre.

The base unit for mass (weight) is the kilogram.
The base unit for capacity (liquid volume) is the litre.

Prefixes for the base units include:

micro – a millionth
milli – a thousandth (as in millimetre)
centi – a hundredth
deci – a tenth
deca – ten
hecta – a hundred
kilo – a thousand (as in kilogram)
mega – a million

1 State whether you would use kilometres, metres, centimetres or millimetres to measure (a) to (l) in Figure 31:1.

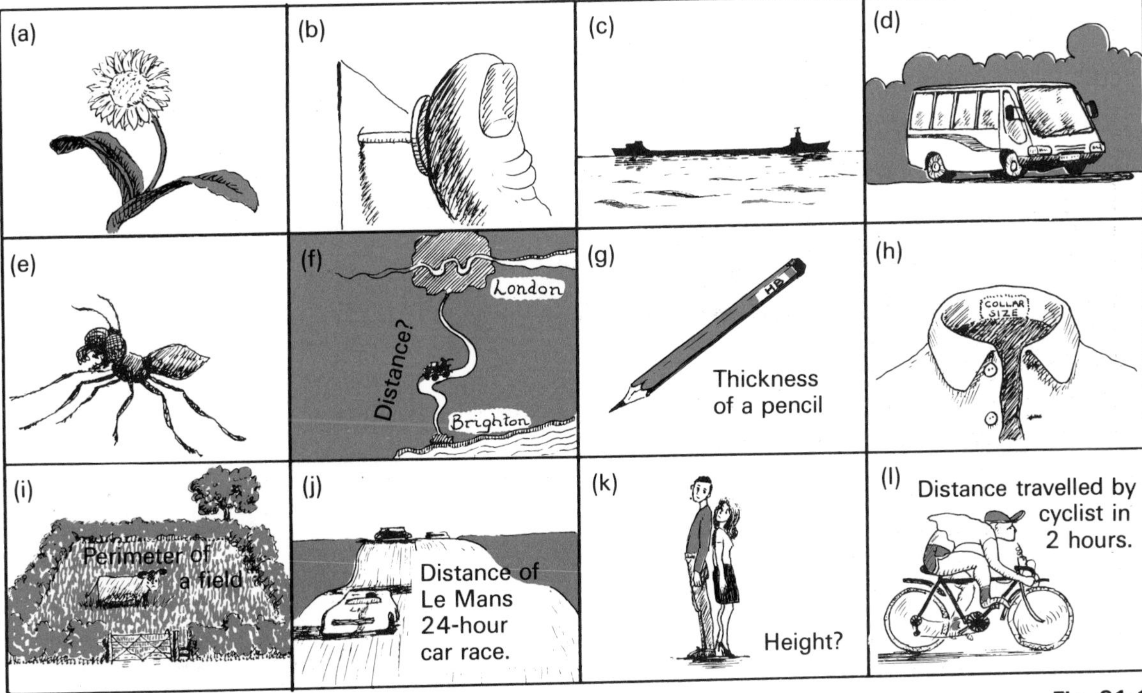

Fig. 31:1

2 Examples $5 < 8$ is read as '5 is less than 8'.
$8 > 5$ is read as '8 is greater than 5'.

Copy the following, inserting the correct symbol, $<$ or $>$.

(a) 75 cm 0·5 m (b) 25 mm 2 cm

(c) 2500 m 3 km (d) 30 mm 4 cm

(e) 3·3 km 3150 m (f) 9·3 cm 100 mm

3 Copy and complete:

(a) 100 cm = . . . m (b) . . . mm = 1·5 cm

(c) 400 cm = . . . m (d) . . . m = 1·5 km

(e) 8·3 m = . . . cm (f) 1·5 m = . . . mm

4 Put a decimal point (and zeroes if needed) in the statements below so that they make sense. Part (a) has been done for you.

(a) The beetle was 25 cm (2·5 cm) long.

(b) The boy was 175 m tall.

(c) The English Channel between Dover and Calais is about 330 km wide.

(d) The window glass was 553 mm thick.

(e) The cat was 65 m long.

(f) The garden pond is 153 m deep.

(g) The ant was 53 m long.

(h) The pencil was 185 cm long.

5 Figure 31:2 is not the correct size. Use a ruler and protractor to draw it the correct size. Measure the length of BC.

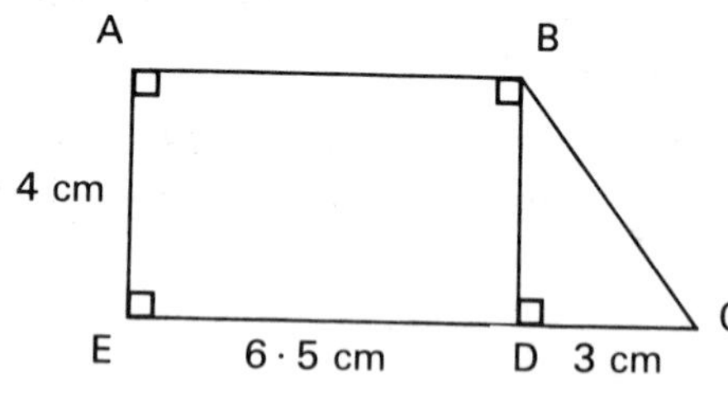

Fig. 31:2

6 A car is travelling at 22·5 m per second.

(a) How long will it take to travel 4·5 km?

(b) How many minutes will it take to travel 270 km?

7 The scale of a map is 1 to 10 000. What distance, in metres, is represented by a line on the map of length:

(a) 1 cm (b) 2·5 cm (c) 4·7 cm?

8 Example To enter 6 cm 9 mm on a calculator we need to change it to 6·9 cm.
To enter 3 m 8 cm we change it to 3·08 m.

With or without a calculator evaluate:

(a) 16 cm 9 mm × 28 (b) 17 cm 6 mm × 263

(c) 5 m 18 cm × 37 (d) 9 m 4 cm × 105

Worksheet 31A may be used here.

9 Make a chart showing ten objects you would measure in metres, or centimetres, or millimetres.
Write a size for each object. Do not repeat any of the objects mentioned so far.

B Weight and capacity

The base units for mass (weight) and capacity are connected to the metre.

1000 cubic centimetres (cm^3) of water has a mass of 1 kilogram and a capacity of 1 litre.

▶ Points to discuss . . .

1 When **gravity** acts on the mass of an object, then the object has **weight**. On Earth, objects with the same mass have the same weight.

2 What do we mean by, 'The aeroplane's test pilot experienced **7G**'?

3> If you landed on the Moon you would weigh about one-sixth of your Earth weight. What differences might this make to the way you live?

1 Some measurements are given below. Which measurement belongs to each part of Figure 31:3?

1 cubic metre (1 m^3)   20 litres   200 ml

1500 g   5 ml   1500 kg

Fig. 31:3

2 Copy and complete the table.

g	1000	2000		4500	3700	5300		12 900		800
kg	1		2·5		3·7		9·1		10	

3 Copy and complete the table.

litres	1		4·5		6·3			7·25		8·37
millilitres (ml)	1000	3000				7700		7250		
cubic centimetres (cm³)	1000			5000			12 500	7250	6250	

4 Solve these clues to the word puzzle in Figure 31:4 and write down the answers.

(a) 1000 metres make this.

(b) Just under two pints.

(c) A medicine spoon is 5 of these.

(d) 1000 . . . = 1 cubic metre.

(e) About the length of a drawing pin.

(f) Scientists sometimes use this instead of weight.

(g) 1000 millimetres.

(h) About the mass of a car.

(i) A thousandth of a kilogram.

(j) Gravity acting on an object gives it this.

Fig. 31:4

5 A garden pond holds 4500 litres of water. The pond is to be emptied for cleaning using a bucket which holds 20 litres.

(a) How many buckets of water will be needed to empty the pond?

(b) Express the capacity of the pond in cubic metres.

(c) If it takes, on average, 40 seconds to empty one bucket of water, how many (i) minutes and (ii) hours and minutes will it take to empty the pond?

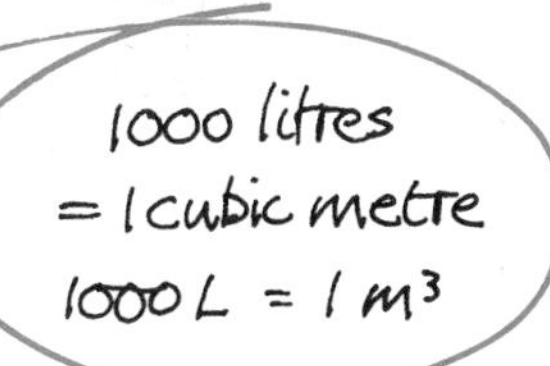

6 Jean has to take two 5 ml spoons of medicine three times a day. How many days will a 0·45 litre bottle of medicine last?

7 For the articles shown in Figure 31:5 find the total weight **in kilograms** of:

(a) 3 packets of flour

(b) 3 packets of flour and 1 jar of savoury

(c) 2 jars of jam and 2 jars of coffee

(d) 1 packet of detergent, 2 jars of savoury, 3 jars of jam and one jar of coffee

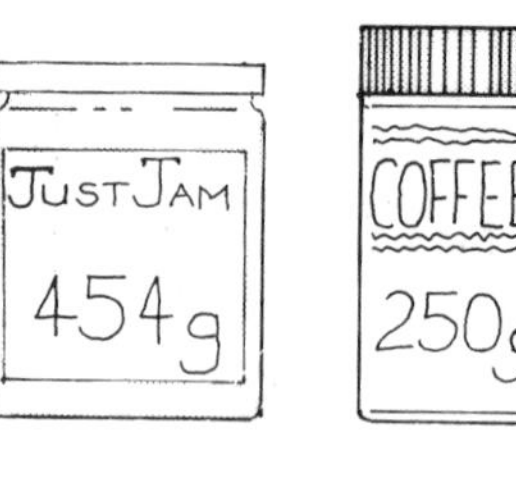

Fig. 31:5

8 How many tubs, B, can be filled from the packet of salt, A, in Figure 31:6? (SEG)

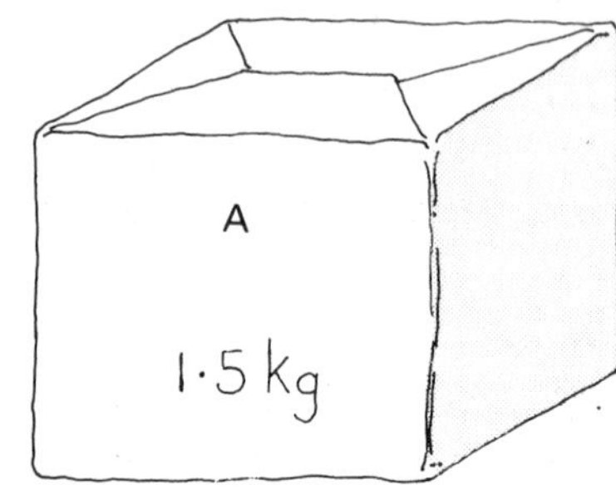

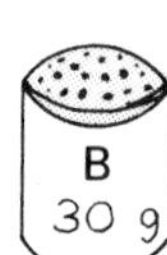

Fig. 31:6

9 Copy and complete the following sentences with a weight chosen from:

7 g   250 g   1 kg   2·5 tonne
45 kg   0·80 tonne

(a) Bert's car weighs . . .

(b) A 2p coin weighs . . .

(c) A packet of butter weighs . . .

(d) Esmerelda is 12 years old and weighs . . .

(e) Eddy the elephant weighs . . .

(f) A bag of sugar weighs . . .

10 Study Figure 31:7.

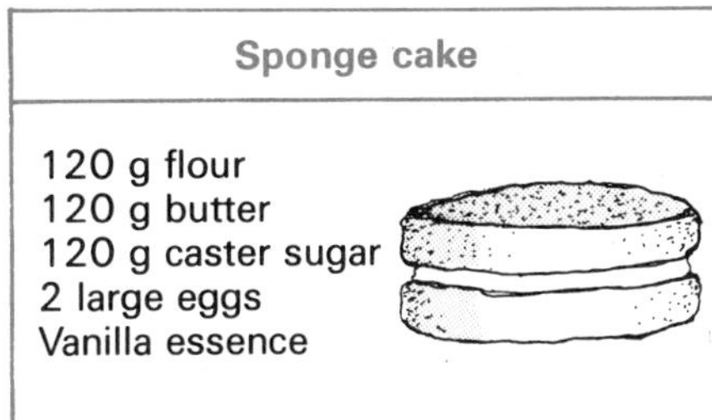

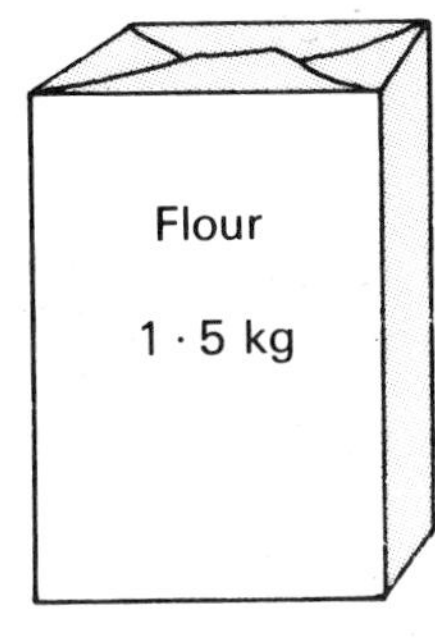

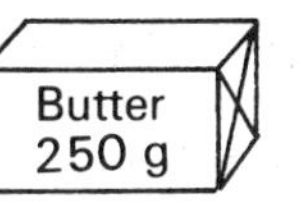

Fig. 31:7

(a) How many whole sponge cakes could you bake using one bag of flour?

(b) How many packets of butter would you need to buy to bake this number of cakes? (SEG)

11 The lava from a volcanic eruption is flowing down a mountain at the rate of 2·35 m per second.

(a) How far will the lava flow in 2·4 minutes?

(b) A house is directly in the path of the lava, 3·76 km from the start of the flow. How long will the lava take to reach the house? Give your answer in (i) seconds, (ii) minutes.

12 Mr Sells uses 7200 litres of petrol a year at £0·43 a litre. The quantity of engine oil he uses is in the ratio of 1 : 120 compared to the quantity of petrol. The oil costs £0·92 a litre.

Find the cost of:

(a) the petrol (b) the oil

(c) If the cost of both petrol and oil rises by 5%, what will be the new total cost of the same quantities of petrol and oil?

13 An elephant weighs 4·57 tonnes.

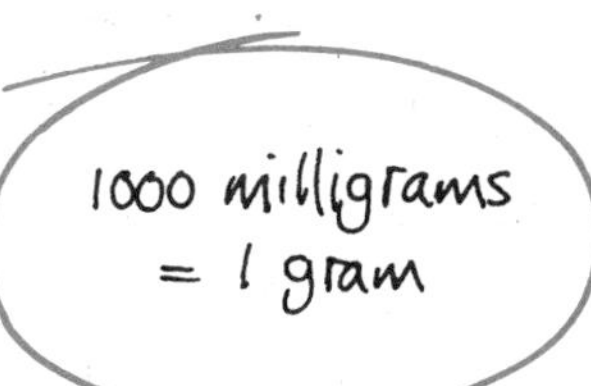

(a) How much is its weight in
(i) kilograms (ii) milligrams?

(b) On average, the elephant eats 65 kg of food per day. What total weight of food, in tonnes, will it eat in June, July and August?

(c) If its food costs 31p per kg, what would be the cost of the food over eight weeks?

14 Some metric/imperial approximate conversions are given below.

2 inches ≈ 5 cm 2 kg ≈ $4\frac{1}{2}$ pounds
1 mile ≈ $1\frac{3}{5}$ km 1 litre ≈ $1\frac{3}{4}$ pints

Rewrite the following, converting metric to imperial and vice versa.

Frank Muscles, believed (by Frank's mum) to be the world's strongest man, is 2 m 2·5 cm tall, has a chest measurement of 57·5 inches and weighs 243 pounds.

His daily training includes running 8 kilometres and lifting 100 kg weights.

He eats approximately $2\frac{1}{2}$ kg of steak a day and drinks 7 pints of milk.

Frank recently saved a young child's life by lifting one end of a 1·1 tonne car.

Worksheet 31B may be used here.

32 Probability

A Taking a chance

We all try to improve the probability of good, rather than bad, things happening to us.

▶ Points to discuss . . .

1 How could you make it more probable that:

(a) you stay healthy

(b) you improve your test results?

2 What examples of probability and chance in everyday life can you think of?

3

Studies well	Lazy
Untidy	Hard working
Weak at maths	Strong legs
Self conscious	Nervous
Frowns a lot	Hates losing
Friendly	Good at maths
Practical	Complains a lot
Healthy parents	Likes to run
Good with machines	Smart appearance
Impatient	Self reliant
Stamina	Determined
Likes people	Good organiser

Choose five items from the above list that could make it more probable that:

(a) Hassan can become an engineer

(b) Susan can become a hotel receptionist

(c) a horse can win a race

You may use the same item more than once.

4 When a heatwave in Britain has lasted for four months, is rain more probable than usual over the next six months?

What are your reasons for giving the answer you do?

32

1 Many people like to gamble, despite the fact that most of them lose money.

Figure 32:1 shows the names of six horses running in the 3:30 p.m. race at Mid-River and the 'odds' given for each horse. Odds of 5–1 (five-to-one) means that, if the horse wins, a £1 bet would win £5. The original £1 would also be returned.

Fig. 32:1

(a) Which horse is the favourite to win?

(b) Is there a high or a low probability of Green Flash winning? Give reasons for your answer.

(c) If you placed a £1 bet on each horse, what is the maximum amount you could receive for each bet, including the return of the £1?

2 A football pools coupon is filled in with

1	for a home win,
2	for an away win,
X	for a draw.

Home	Away	No.	4 DRAWS MARK X	10 HOMES MARK 1	5 AWAYS MARK 2
	Chelsea	1			
Barnsley	Wimbledon	2			
Birmingham	Bourn'm'th	3			
Blackpool	Tottenham	4			
Bradford C	Leeds	5			
Brighton	Hull	6			
Cardiff	Liverpool	7			
Carlisle	Oldham	8			
Charlton	Aston Villa	9			
Crewe	South'pton	10			
Derby	Sheff Utd	11			
Hudd'field	Halifax	12			
Kettering	Grimsby	13			
Middlesbro	Luton	14			
Millwall	Watford	15			
Newcastle	Ipswich	16			
Nott'm F	Camb'ge U	17			
Plymouth	Swindon	18			
Portsmouth	Norwich	19			
Port Vale	Crystal P	20			
Stoke	Oxford Utd	21			
Sunderland	Coventry	22			
Sutton Utd	Everton	23			
West Brom	Chester	24			
Fulham	Bury	25			
North'pton	Chest'field	26			
Wigan A	Lincoln	27			
Rochdale	Scunthorpe	28			
Stockport	Northwich	29			
		30			
		31			

(a) Copy and complete the table of all possible results for three matches.

Match 1	1	1	1	1	1	1	1	1	1	2	2	2	2	2	2	2	2	2	X	X	X	X	X	X	X	X	X
Match 2	1	1	1	2	2	2																					
Match 3	1	2	X	1	2	X																					

(b) Copy and complete this table.

Number of matches	Possible number of results	Probability of choosing correct result with one entry
1	3	1 chance in 3, or $\frac{1}{3}$
2	9	1 chance in 9, or $\frac{1}{9}$
3		1 chance in 27, or $\frac{1}{27}$
4	81	
5		
6		
7		
8		
9		
10		

3 A football pool offers a 'Lucky 10' entry in which the client has to forecast the results of ten matches.

(a) What is the least number of lines the client will have to enter to make sure of getting an all-correct forecast?

(b) If each entry line costs 3p, how much will the client have to spend to be certain of making an all-correct forecast?

B The probability line

All probabilities can be shown on a scale between 0 and 1.

Examples Next year will be 1980. Probability 0
You can read. Probability 1

Some other probabilities are shown in Figure 32:2.

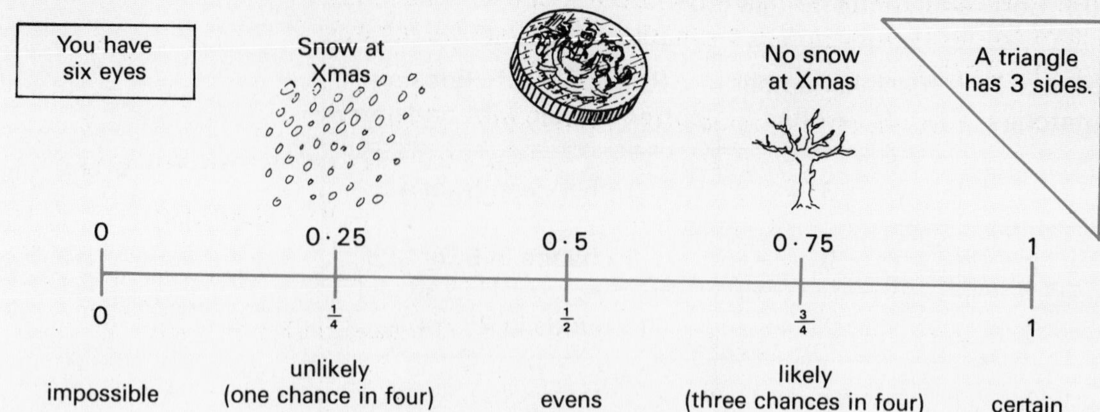

Fig. 32:2

The probability of something happening added to the probability of it not happening totals 1.

Example An unbiased coin is just as likely to come down heads as tails.

A biased (or loaded) coin would usually land the same way up.

The probability of an unbiased coin coming down heads is one chance in two, or $\frac{1}{2}$.

The probability of throwing a tail is also $\frac{1}{2}$.

So the probability of throwing a head added to the probability of not throwing a head is $\frac{1}{2} + \frac{1}{2} = 1$.

Example The probability of throwing a three with an unbiased die is one chance in six, or $\frac{1}{6}$.

The probability not throwing a three with the same die is five chances in six, or $\frac{5}{6}$.

$\frac{1}{6} + \frac{5}{6} = 1$.

Example The probability of drawing a heart from a well-shuffled pack of cards is thirteen chances in fifty-two, or $\frac{13}{52} = \frac{1}{4}$.

The probability of not drawing a heart is (52 – 13) chances in fifty-two, or $\frac{39}{52} = \frac{3}{4}$.

$\frac{1}{4} + \frac{3}{4} = 1$.

In this exercise a die (plural 'dice') is a cube marked 1 to 6, and a pack of cards has four suits (hearts, diamonds, spades, clubs), each of 13 cards.

1 Link each part with the correct letter from Figure 28:3.

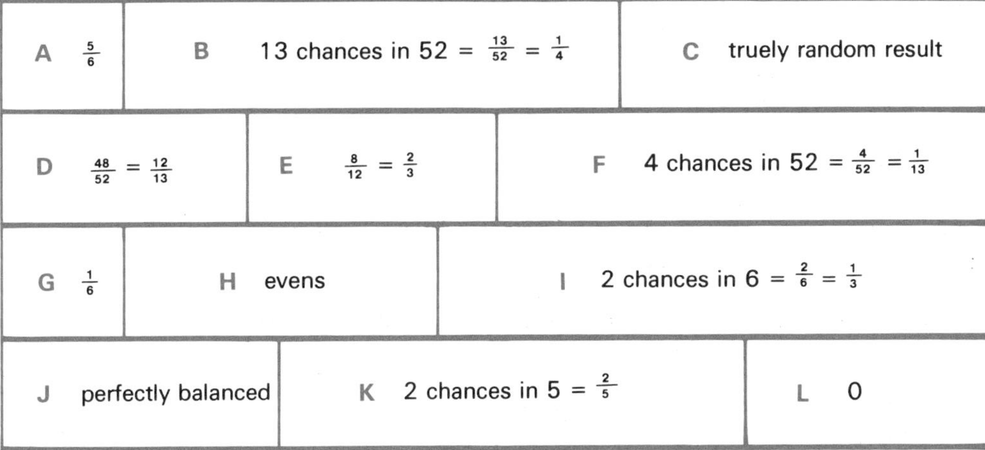

A $\frac{5}{6}$	B 13 chances in 52 = $\frac{13}{52} = \frac{1}{4}$	C truely random result
D $\frac{48}{52} = \frac{12}{13}$	E $\frac{8}{12} = \frac{2}{3}$	F 4 chances in 52 = $\frac{4}{52} = \frac{1}{13}$
G $\frac{1}{6}$	H evens	I 2 chances in 6 = $\frac{2}{6} = \frac{1}{3}$
J perfectly balanced	K 2 chances in 5 = $\frac{2}{5}$	L 0

Fig. 32:3

(a) A die should be 'unbiased'. This means it should be . . .

(b) The chance of throwing a six with a die is . . .

(c) The chance of not throwing a six with a die is . . .

(d) The chance of throwing a two or a three with a die is . . .

(e) The chance of drawing a diamond from a well-shuffled pack of cards is . . .

(f) The pack should be well shuffled in order to obtain a . . .

(g) The chance of drawing an ace from a pack of cards is . . .

(h) The probability of not drawing an ace from a pack of cards is . . .

(i) The probability that the next stranger you meet was born in a month with an 'r' in it is . . .

(j) The probability that the stranger was born on the 31st April 1951 is . . .

(k) The probability of a number, picked at random from 2, 3, 4, 6, 8, being a prime number is . . .

(l) The probability of there being an even number of seeds in a packet is . . .

2 State the chance of the following.

(a) Picking a diamond from a pack of cards.

(b) Picking a queen from a pack of cards.

(c) Picking the six of hearts from a pack of cards.

(d) Scoring 7 with a throw of a die.

(e) An unborn baby being a girl.

(f) Scoring an odd number with one throw of a die.

(g) Picking a red ball from a bag holding one red and nine green balls.

(h) Picking a ball that is not red from the bag in (g).

(i) Picking a soft-centre chocolate from a box containing eight soft-centres and twelve hard-centres.

(j) Picking a chocolate that is not soft-centred from (i).

3 A bag contains thirty marbles of the same size. Fifteen are red, ten are black and five are white. Giving your answers as fractional probabilities where possible, what is the probability of choosing at random:

(a) a red marble (b) a black marble

(c) a white marble (d) a black or a white marble

(e) a red, black or white marble (f) a green marble?

4 Two unbiased dice are thrown. Their scores are added to make a total between 2 and 12.

There are 36 possible totals with only one chance of 12. So the probability of a total of 12 is one chance in thirty-six, or $\frac{1}{36}$.

(a) Copy and complete the table.

(b) Write down the probability of throwing a total of:

(i) 2 (ii) 3 (iii) 4 (iv) 5
(v) 6 (vi) 7 (vii) 11

+	1	2	3	4	5	6
1	2	3	4			
2		4				
3			6			
4						
5						
6						12

5 The probability of not winning a raffle is 0·92. What is the probability of winning it?

6 The numbers from 1 to 30 inclusive are written on equal sized pieces of cards. The cards are well shuffled before each random choice.

(a) What is meant by 'from 1 to 30 inclusive'?

(b) Giving each answer, where appropriate, as a probability fraction state the probability of choosing:

(i) an even number (ii) an odd number

(iii) a square number (iv) a prime number

(v) an odd or an even number

(vi) a square or a prime number

7 One letter is chosen at random from the word PROBABILITY. What is the probability that it is:

(a) the letter R (b) the letter P (c) the letter Y

(d) the letter B (e) the letter I?

8 What is the probability that one of the angles of a right-angled triangle is 90°?

9 Figure 32:4 shows a game at a fete. A player spins the pointer and wins whatever sum of money the pointer indicates when it comes to rest. What is the probability of:

(a) winning 7p (b) winning nothing

(c) winning 5p or less

(d) winning 10p?

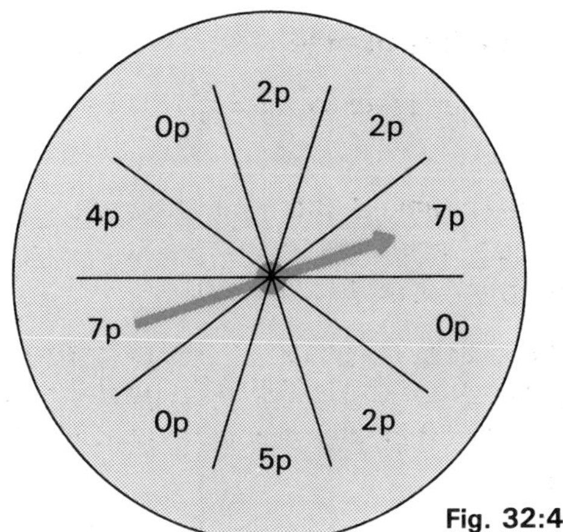

Fig. 32:4

10 Jane won a £50 prize in the Premium Bond draw in January, then £100 in March. She decided that this was all the luck she could expect as she knew lots of people who had never won anything, so she cashed in her bonds and bought some new dresses.

Was Jane's reasoning correct or incorrect? Write down why you think this.

11 Comment on the following statements:

(a) The probability of a rainy day in December is 0·6, so the probability of three rainy December days in a row is 1·8.

(b) Jim and Sasha have a family of three boys, and now Sasha is pregnant again. She thinks she is almost certain to have a girl this time, as she does not know anyone who has a family of four boys.

12 During a 30-day period a fire brigade had to attend fires as shown in the table:

Number of fires in one day	0	1	2	3	4	5	6
Frequency	3	?	6	4	2	2	1

Work out the missing frequency, then find the probability that on any day taken at random from the sample shown above the fire brigade attended:

(a) no fires (b) fewer than 3 fires (SEG part)

13 Last year a particular school entered 240 candidates for a mathematics examination. The number of candidates awarded grades A and B are shown in Figure 32:5.

Fig. 32:5

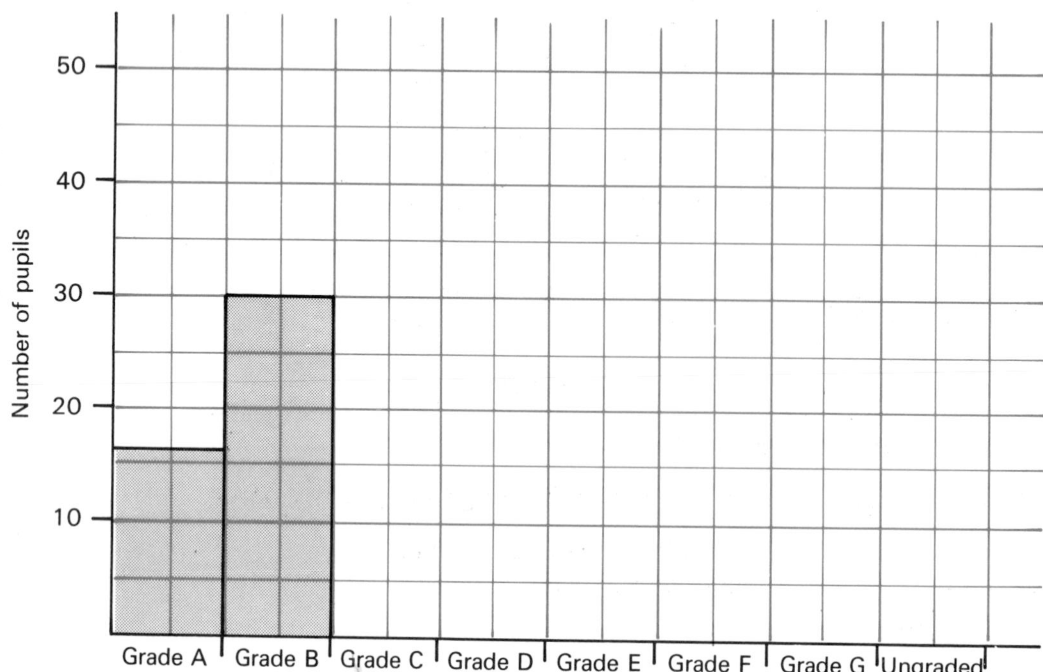

The remainder were awarded grades as follows:

Grade C	38	Grade F	32
Grade D	36	Grade G	26
Grade E	42	Ungraded	20

(a) Using this information, copy and complete the bar-chart.

(b) Write down the number of candidates who were awarded (i) grade A (ii) grade B.

(d) Write down the probability that a pupil chosen at random from the 240 candidates was awarded a grade D.

(LEAG)

14 A coin is tossed four times. The 'tree diagram' in Figure 32:6 shows all the possible results and the probability of each result.

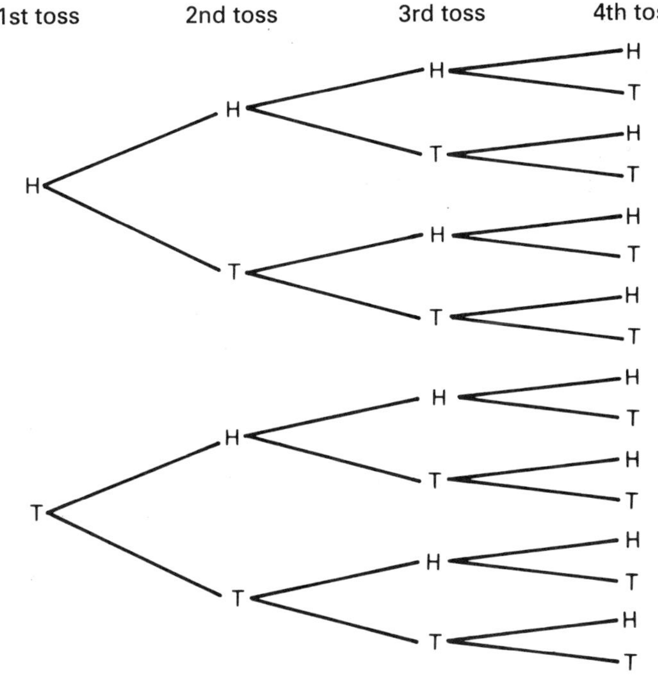

Fig. 32:6

(a) Copy and complete Figure 32:6.

(b) Use the tree diagram to find the probability of getting, *in any order*:

(i) 2 heads and 2 tails (ii) 3 heads and 1 tail
(iii) 4 heads (iv) 1 head and 3 tails
(v) no heads

33 Directed numbers

● To remind you . . .

- The Celsius thermometer in Figure 33:1 uses directed numbers.
  The two directions are above zero, shown with a plus sign (positive numbers), and below zero, shown with a minus sign (negative numbers).

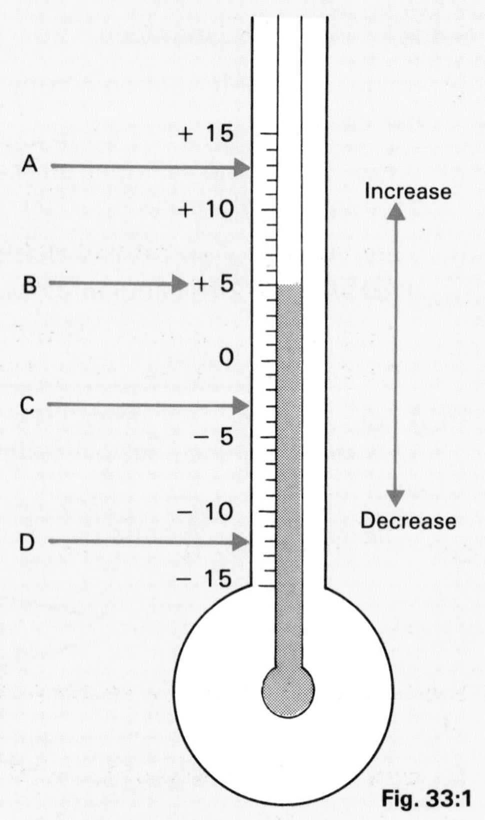

Fig. 33:1

▶ Points to discuss . . .

1. The mercury in the thermometer shows a temperature of 5 °C. What is 5 °C in words?

2. What are the temperatures at A, B, C and D?

3. A to B shows a temperature decrease of 8 degrees. Give the temperature change from A to C, B to D, D to C, C to B, and D to A.

4. How can you work out the final temperature when the mercury level starts at 0 °C, moves through an increase of 5 degrees, then a decrease of 9 degrees, followed by an increase of 6 degrees.

5 Figure 33:2 shows addition as a move to the right and subtraction as a move to the left.

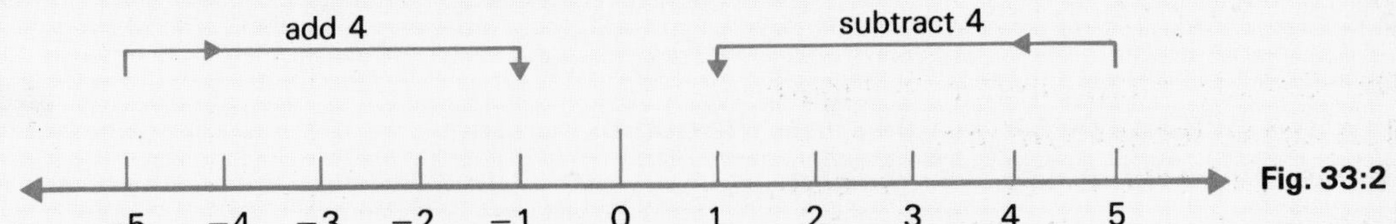

Fig. 33:2

Starting at −5 a move of add 4 brings us to −1.
We can write this as −5 + 4 = −1.

Starting at +5 a move of subtract 4 brings us to +1.
We can write this as +5 − 4 = +1.

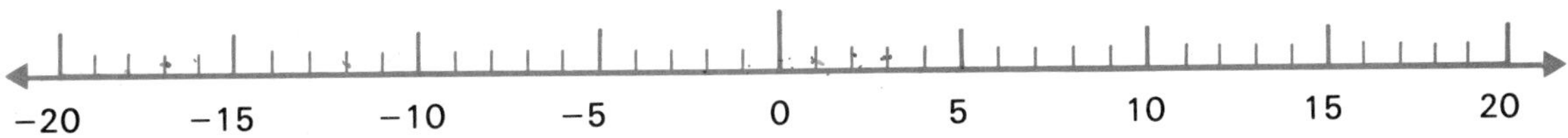

Fig. 33:3

Copy the number line in Figure 33:3 for questions 1 to 6.

1 Starting each time at +5, where would you be after a move of:

(a) add 4 (b) subtract 5 (c) add 10

(d) subtract 10?

2 Starting each time at −5, where would you be after a move of:

(a) subtract 5 (b) add 5 (c) add 10

(d) subtract 7?

3 Starting each time at +5, where would you be after moves of:

(a) add 5 then add 2

(b) subtract 5 then add 3

(c) subtract 7 then subtract 2

(d) subtract 3 then subtract 4 then add 5?

4 Repeat question 3 with a starting point of −8.

5 Question 1(a) can be written +5 + 4 = +9.
Question 2(a) can be written as −5 − 5 = −10.

Write similar number statements for the rest of questions 1 and 2.

6 For any two numbers on the number line, the number on the left is less than the number on the right.

Check on Figure 33:3 that:
2 < 5 (2 is less than 5).
5 > 2 (5 is more than 2).
3 > −2 (3 is more than −2).
−9 < −6 (−9 is less than −6).

Copy the following numbers, and write < or > between them to make a true statement.

(a) 6 4 (b) 3 7 (c) 1 0 (d) 0 2

(e) −3 0 (f) 2 −1 (g) −4 6

(h) −5 −8 (i) −9 −1 (j) −6 −4

7 Mr Potter noticed that the reading on the thermometer one midday was 4 °C. The following morning the temperature was −3 °C. By how many degrees had the temperature fallen? (WJEC)

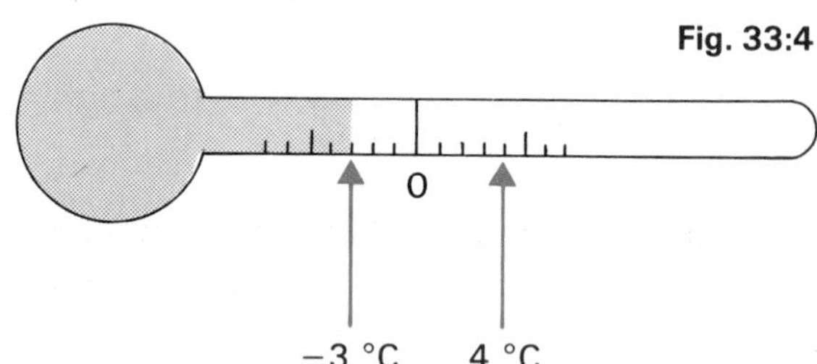

Fig. 33:4

8 In Moscow the temperature during the day was 6 °C. By midnight it had dropped 9 degrees. What was the temperature at midnight?

9 A pot plant will die if the temperature falls below −3 °C. Which of these temperatures mean death for the plant?

2 °C −5 °C −0·4 °C

−2·7 °C −3·9 °C (SEG)

10 Seven people each take 2 chocolates from a box. Altogether 14 chocolates have been subtracted from the box.
This story shows that 7 × −2 = −14.

Write a story to show that 6 × −4 = −24.

11 Pair the opposites from the list below. For example, *Add* pairs with *Subtract*.

Credit	Over	Height	Add	Descend
Subtract	Profit	Debit	Forwards	Under
Depth	Ascend	Above	Plus	Loss
Backwards	Positive	Minus	Below	Negative

12 Figure 33:5 shows a simplified bank statement.

MISS MOSS 15 HIGH STREET			Dogger Bank Low Tide Branch	
Date	Details	Debit	Credit	Balance
1 Oct	Balance brought forward			00.00
3 Oct	Salary cheque		363.50	363.50 C
4 Oct	Owens Garage	63.70		299.80 C
10 Oct	Cash	100.00		199.80 C
11 Oct	Gas	77.29		122.51 C

Fig. 33:5

The debit column shows amounts paid out, or subtracted, from the account. The credit column shows amounts paid in, or added, to the account. The balance column shows the differences between the debit and credit columns.

(a) Write the headings for a simplified bank statement, using your name.

(b) Enter the following items in the correct debit or credit column:

Salary cheque for £483·60
Cheque for £79·50 to pay the gas bill
Cheque for £46·73 to pay the telephone bill
Cash withdrawal of £120
£25 cheque from an aunt for your birthday

(c) Complete the balance column.

Inequalities on a number line

$a \geqslant -4$ means that a is equal to or greater than -4, or a is not less than -4.

Example List the values of a where $-4 \leqslant a < 3$.

$-4 \leqslant a < 3$ means that a is at least -4 but is less than 3. Note that $a = 3$ is not allowed. Always read the letter first, then look left and look right.

All the possible values for $-4 \leqslant a < 3$ are shown by the heavy line in Figure 33:6.

Fig. 33:6

You can see from Figure 33:6 that the set of integer values for a is $\{-4, -3, -2, -1, 0, 1, 2\}$.

13 (a) Describe in words:
(i) $0 \leqslant a \leqslant 6$ (ii) $-5 \leqslant x < 4$ (iii) $-4 < a \leqslant 5$

(b) Show parts (i), (ii) and (iii) of section (a) on separate number lines. Remember to include the solid and empty circles.

(c) Write the set of integer values represented on each number line.

14 Look at Figure 33:7.

(a) Write down the six temperatures shown on the chart.

(b) What was the likely temperature at
(i) 2230 (ii) 0030?

(c) Copy Figure 33:7 and shade in the region
2 °C $\geqslant$ temperature $\geqslant$ -2 °C.

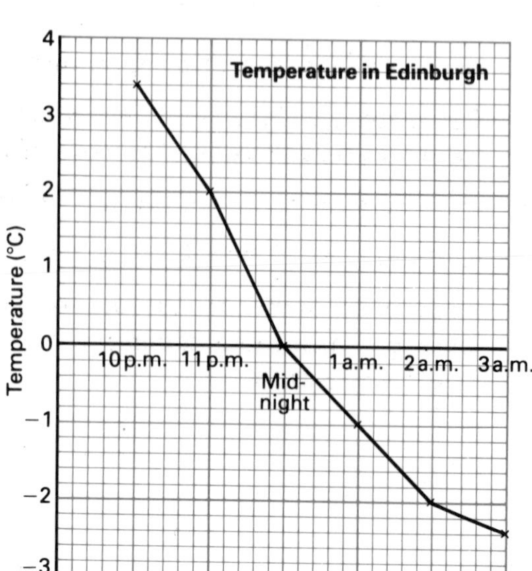

Fig. 33:7

15 **Example** Evaluate 5 − 3 − 7 − 2 + 6.

Instead of using a number line to work out +5 then −3 then −7 then −2 then +6, we can find the sum of the positive numbers and then the sum of the negative numbers, as follows:
+5 and +6 = +11.
−3 and −7 and −2 = −12.
We can now write the original problem as
5 − 3 − 7 − 2 + 6 = + 11 − 12 = − 1

Check this on a number line, if you like.

When using a calculator we simply press the keys
5 ⊟ 3 ⊟ 7 ⊟ 2 ⊞ 6 ⊜

Evaluate:

(a) 2 − 3 + 4 − 1 (b) 29 − 40 + 12

(c) 18 − 2 − 10 (d) 1 − 2 − 4 + 6 − 9 + 10

(e) $\frac{1}{2} + 3\frac{1}{2} - 3\frac{1}{4} + \frac{3}{4}$ (f) 0·5 + 1·3 − 2·4 + 0·2

16

	Maximum temp. °C	Minimum temp. °C
Bayford	8	−4
Lakestone	13·5	−3
Northfield	9	−8
Eastonham	10	−9
Rivermouth	12	−5·5

(a) What was the lowest temperature recorded?

(b) Calculate the differences between the maximum and minimum temperatures for each of the five places.

(c) Find the sum of the maximum temperatures.

(d) Find the sum of the minimum temperatures.

(e) Using your answers to (c) and (d), find the mean (average) maximum temperature and the mean minimum temperature.

17 Figure 33:8 shows a Celsius/Fahrenheit thermometer with some equivalent temperatures marked.

(a) Draw a Celsius ↔ Fahrenheit conversion graph using scales of:
Horizontal: 2 cm to each 10 °C, from −10 to +30
Vertical: 1 cm to each 10 °F, from +0 to +90
The graph has been started in Figure 33:9.

(b) Mark on your graph the locations of the five equivalent pairs of temperatures.

(c) Draw a straight line through the five points. Give your graph a suitable title.

(d) Using your graph state as accurately as you can the Celsius equivalent temperatures for:
(i) 5 °F (ii) 15 °F (iii) 25 °F
(iv) 28 °F (v) 18 °F

(e) One of the following formulae provides a good approximation for the conversion of everyday Celsius temperatures (C) to Fahrenheit temperatures (F).

(i) $F \approx (3 \times C) + 30$ (ii) $F \approx (2 \times C) - 30$
(iii) $F \approx (2 \times C) + 30$

Which is the correct formula? Give your reasons.

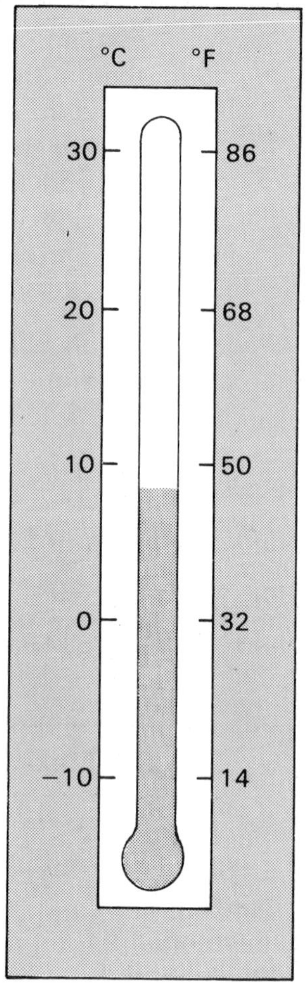

Fig. 33:8

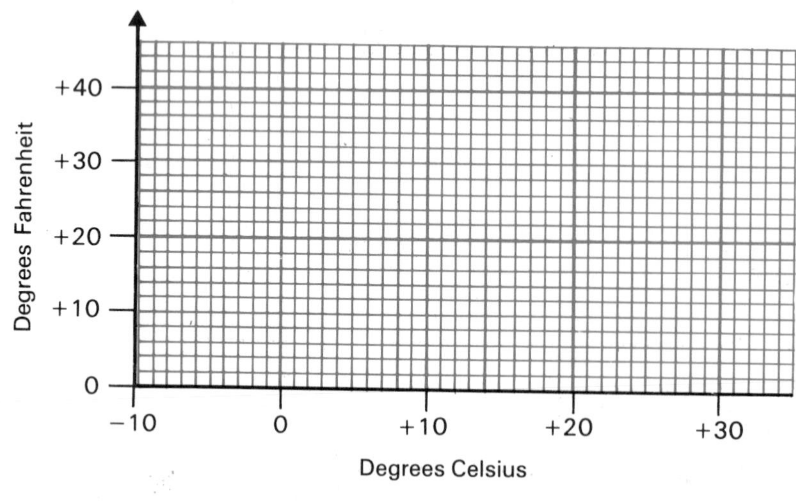

Fig. 33:9

18 The positions of nine different things, marked A to I, are shown in Figure 33:10. The positions are shown in metres above and below sea level. Sea level is marked as 0 m (zero metres).

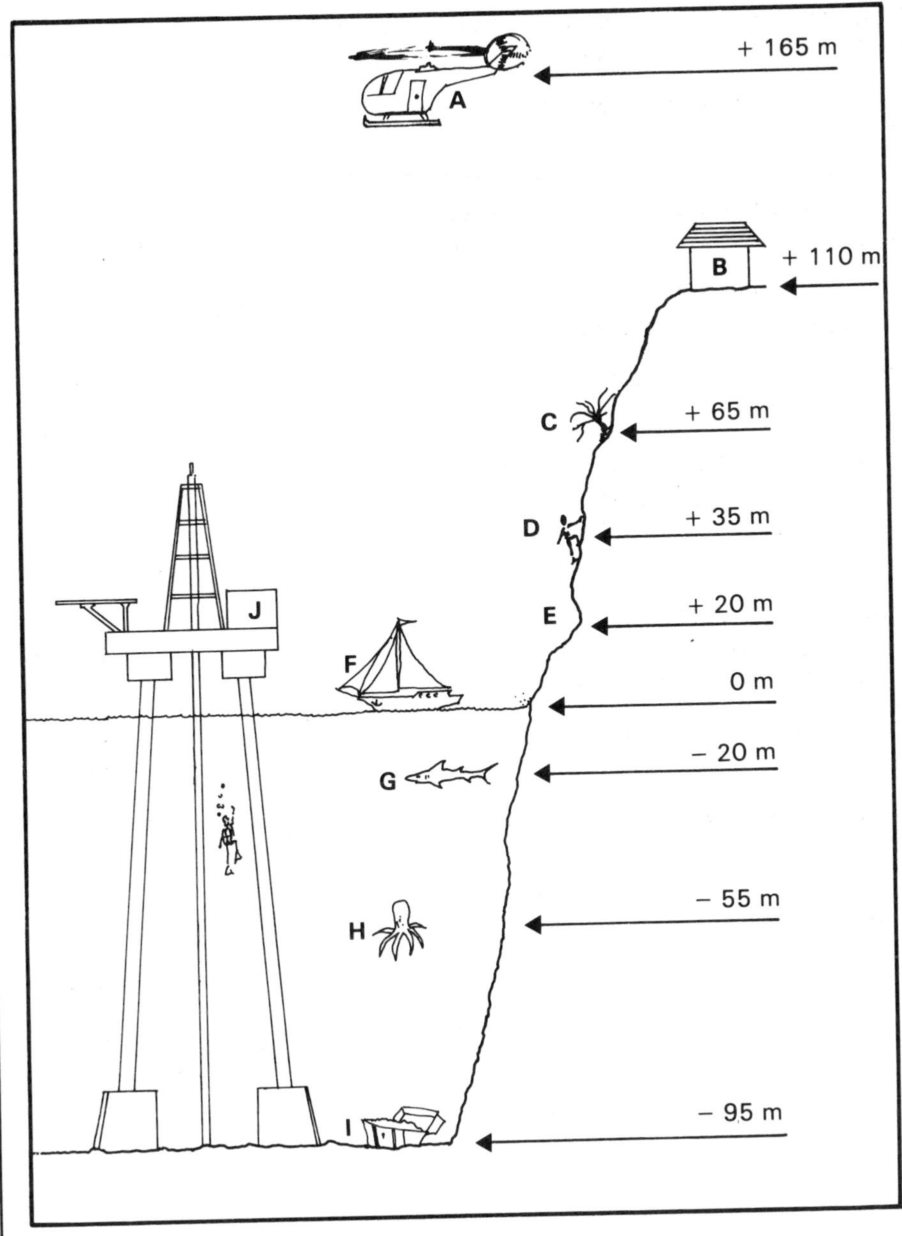

Fig. 33:10

The position of the climber at D is +35 m.
The position of the octopus at H is −55 m.
The difference in vertical height between D and H is 90 m.

What is the difference in vertical height between:

(a) D and E (b) D and G (c) I and G

(d) A and B (e) A and I?

(f) The climber falls (ouch!) to the cave at E, from where he climbs to the hut at B (relief!). How much further is his ascent compared to his descent?

A diver is checking the legs of the oil-rig (J) at intervals of 5 metres.
At the sixth check the diver's position will be at
−5 m × 6 = −30 m.

(g) Work out:

(i) 7×-5 m (ii) $-6 \times 4\frac{1}{2}$

(iii) 6×-9 °C (iv) $5\frac{1}{4} \times -12$ m

(v) $6{\cdot}75 \times -10$ °C (vi) $8 \times -12{\cdot}5$

(vii) $-4\frac{1}{3} \times 15$ (viii) $16 \times -1{\cdot}25$

(ix) $100 \times -0{\cdot}1$

Worksheet 33 may be used here.

34 Using letters

A Letters for numbers

Let the length of a side of this square be s.

The perimeter of the square is
$s + s + s + s \rightarrow 4 \times s \rightarrow 4s$.

The area of the square is
$s \times s \rightarrow s^2$ (read as 's squared').

1 (a) For this square s is 2 cm. Why?

(b) The perimeter of a square of side s is $4s$, which is short for $4 \times s$. This square has $s = 2$ cm so its perimeter is 4×2 cm $= 8$ cm.
What is the perimeter of a square with $s = 3$ cm?

(c) The area of a square of side s is s^2, which is short for $s \times s$. This square has $s = 2$ cm so its area is 2 cm $\times$ 2 cm $= 4\text{ cm}^2$.
What would be the area of a square with $s = 3$ cm?

2 (a) e is 3. What number is e^2?

(b) f is 5. What number is f^2?

(c) g^2 is 16. What number is g?

(d) m^2 is 100. What number is m?

3 Emperor Chung punishes his slaves in an odd way.
The first one to annoy him is forgiven.
The second one to annoy him has 3 hairs pulled out.
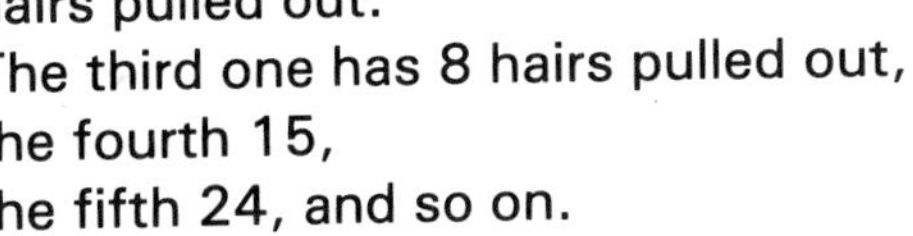
The third one has 8 hairs pulled out, the fourth 15, the fifth 24, and so on.

We can write this as:

Slave number	1	2	3	4	5
Hairs lost	0	3	8	15	24

(a) Copy the table, then write the columns for slaves 6 and 7.

(b) Explain how you worked out the hair losses for slaves 6 and 7.

(c) A mathematical slave works out that slave number n loses $n^2 - 1$ hairs.
For instance, slave number 3 loses 8 hairs. n is 3, so n^2 is 9, and $n^2 - 1$ is 8.
Check the rule for slaves number 1, 2, 4, 5, 6 and 7.

(d) Emperor Chung has 100 slaves. How many hairs would be pulled out of the 100th slave who annoyed him?

4 (a) John has £5. He needs £8. How much more must he earn?

(b) We can write the problem in part (a) as:
'Find x if $5 + x = 8$.'
What would x be if $4 + x = 9$?

(c) What would e be if $4 + e = 9$?

5 Find the number for each letter:

(a) $2 + a = 6$ (b) $3 + b = 12$ (c) $4 + c = 5$

(d) $8 + d = 8$ (e) $e + 7 = 9$ (f) $3 + f = 13$

6 $2n$ is a short way to write $2 \times n$ (2 times n).
When n is 3 then $2n$ is $2 \times 3 = 6$.

Find:

(a) $2n$ when n is 5 (b) $2n$ when n is 10

(c) $3n$ when n is 4 (d) $10n$ when n is 10

7 If k is 7 then $2k$ is 14 and $2k + 1$ is 15.
$2k + 1 = 15$ is true when $k = 7$.
Can you find another number for k so that $2k + 1 = 15$ is true?

8 If $2a + 1 = 13$ then $2a$ must be 12.
(Why? Because $12 + 1 = 13$.)

If $2a = 12$ then a must be 6.
(Why? Because $2a$ means 2 times a and $2 \times 6 = 12$.)

So $2a + 1 = 13$ when $a = 6$.

(a) What is g when $2g + 1 = 15$?

(b) What is m when $2m + 2 = 8$?

(c) What is v when $2v + 5 = 7$?

(d) What is w when $2w + 3 = 12$?

9 Can you work out what each letter is?

(a) $2a + 7 = 11$ (b) $3b = 6$

(c) $3c + 2 = 14$ (d) $3d = 12$

(e) $3e + 10 = 19$ (f) $2f - 1 = 7$

(g) $2g - 1 = 9$ (h) $3h - 7 = 14$

10 $3x + y = 20$

This is true when x is 4 and y is 8, because $3x$ would be 12, and $12 + 8 = 20$.

Can you find any other numbers for x and y? Who in your class can find the most?

B Flow diagrams

Example $6 \xrightarrow{\times 2} 12 \xrightarrow{+3} 15$

If we read the arrow as 'becomes', then we can read this flow diagram as '6 times 2 becomes 12 then 12 plus 3 becomes 15'.

34

1 Copy these flow diagrams and fill in the gaps.

(a) $4 \xrightarrow{\times 2} \ldots \xrightarrow{+3} \ldots$

(b) $5 \xrightarrow{\times 2} \ldots \xrightarrow{+3} \ldots$

(c) $3 \xrightarrow{\times 3} \ldots \xrightarrow{+1} \ldots$

(d) $8 \xrightarrow{\times 10} \ldots \xrightarrow{+2} \ldots$

(e) $2 \xrightarrow{\ldots} 6 \xrightarrow{\ldots} 10$

(f) $6 \xrightarrow{\ldots} 18 \xrightarrow{\ldots} 19$

2 **Example** $n \xrightarrow{\times 2} 2n \xrightarrow{+3} 2n + 3$

Copy and complete:

(a) $a \xrightarrow{\times 3} 3a \xrightarrow{+2} \ldots$

(b) $b \xrightarrow{\times 2} \ldots \xrightarrow{+5} \ldots$

(c) $c \xrightarrow{\times 2} \ldots \xrightarrow{+4} \ldots$

(d) $d \xrightarrow{\times 5} \ldots \xrightarrow{-1} \ldots$

3 We can use flow diagrams to 'change the subject' of an equation. Your teacher will explain this to you.

Example If $e = n + 6$ we say that e is the subject. We can change the subject to n like this:

$$\begin{array}{ccc} n & \xrightarrow{+6} & n + 6 \\ & & \downarrow \\ e - 6 & \xleftarrow{-6} & e \end{array}$$

So $n = e - 6$.

Note how $\xrightarrow{+6}$ changes to $\xleftarrow{-6}$.

Example $f = 2a + 7$

$$\begin{array}{ccccc} a & \xrightarrow{\times 2} & 2a & \xrightarrow{+7} & 2a + 7 \\ & & & & \downarrow \\ \dfrac{f-7}{2} & \xleftarrow{\div 2} & f-7 & \xleftarrow{-7} & f \end{array}$$

Note (i) how the $\xrightarrow{\times 2}$ changes to $\xleftarrow{\div 2}$.

(ii) that the $\div 2$ becomes 'over 2' in $\dfrac{f-7}{2}$.

Copy and complete:

(a) $c = h + 5$

$$h \xrightarrow{+5} \ldots$$
$$\downarrow$$
$$\ldots \xleftarrow{-5} c$$

$h = c - 5$

(b) $d = k - 3$

$$k \xrightarrow{-3} \ldots$$
$$\downarrow$$
$$\ldots \xleftarrow{+3} d$$

$k = d + 3$

(c) $e = m + 1$

$$m \xrightarrow{\ldots} \ldots$$
$$\downarrow$$
$$\ldots \xleftarrow{\ldots} \ldots$$

$m = \ldots\ldots$

(d) $a = 2n + 3$

$$n \xrightarrow{\times 2} 2n \xrightarrow{+3} 2n + 3$$
$$\downarrow$$
$$\ldots \xleftarrow{\div 2} \ldots \xleftarrow{-3} a$$

$$n = \frac{a - 3}{2}$$

(e) $p = 3q - 4$

$$q \xrightarrow{\times 3} \ldots \xrightarrow{-4} \ldots$$
$$\downarrow$$
$$\ldots \xleftarrow{\div 3} \ldots \xleftarrow{+4} p$$

$q = \ldots\ldots$

4 Change the subject:

(a) $a = b + 4$ (b) $c = f + 5$ (c) $d = g - 1$

(d) $e = 2m + 3$ (e) $f = 4n + 2$ (f) $g = 2h - 6$

35 Bar-charts

100 pupils were asked which sport they liked best. This frequency table shows the results.

Sport	Frequency
Football	30
Cricket	15
Netball	25
Hockey	20
Athletics	10
Total	100

The results are shown as a bar-chart in Figure 35:1 and as a proportionate bar-chart in Figure 35:2.

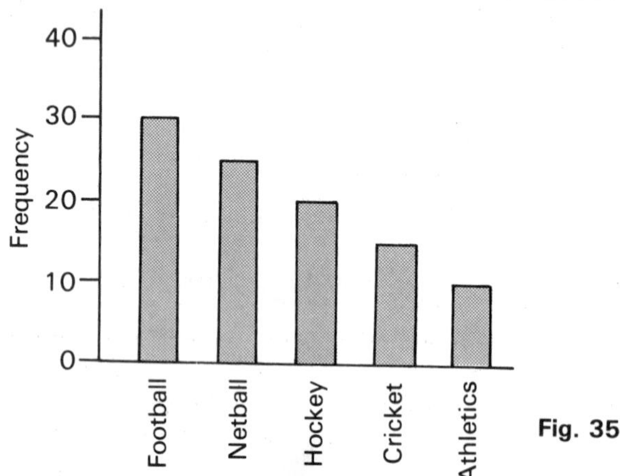

Fig. 35:1

Fig. 35:2

▶ Points to discuss . . .

1. Could the frequency table also be shown by a pictogram?

2. The bars in Figure 35:1 are in a different order from the frequency table. Why do you think the order was changed?

3. Why is Figure 35:2 called a **proportionate** bar-chart?

4 Figure 35:3 shows a bar-chart that compares some road casualties in 1971 with those in 1984. What is the scale on the horizontal axis?

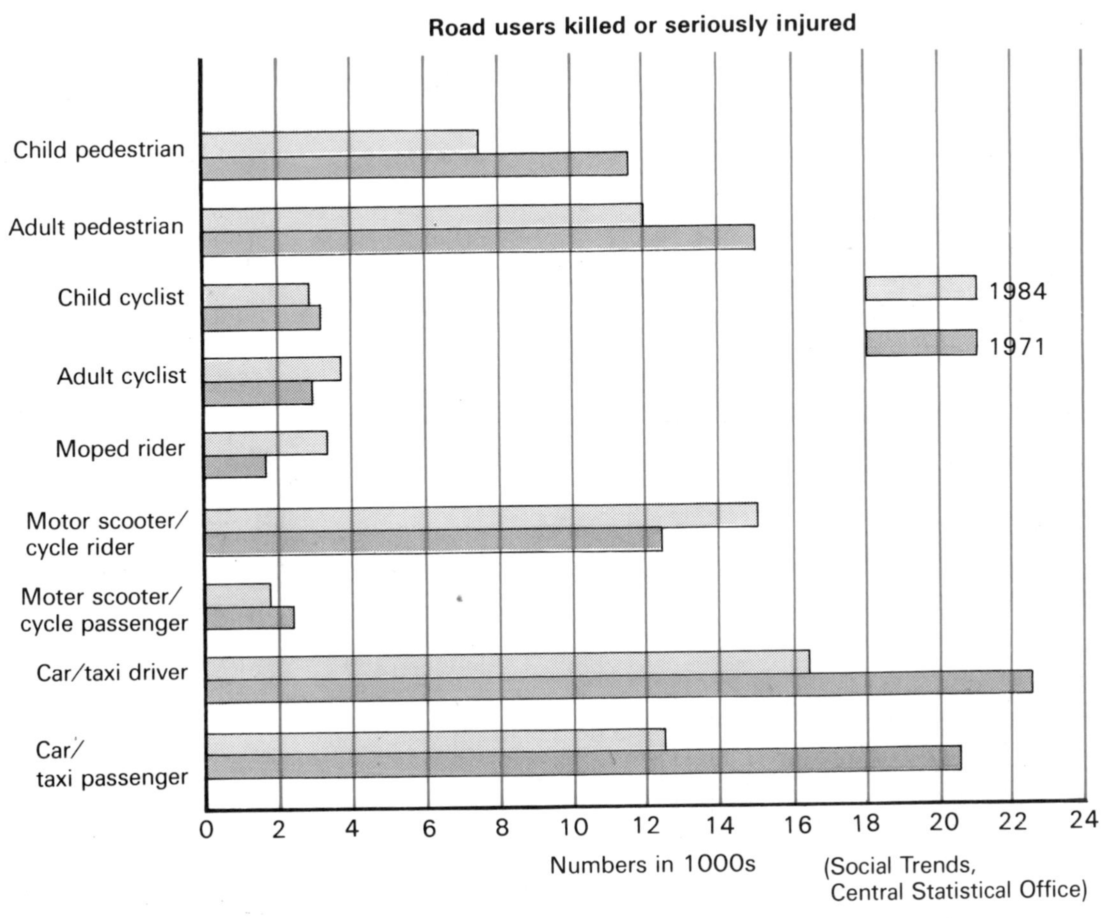

Fig. 35:3

5 Approximately how many of the casualties were:

(a) child pedestrians in 1971

(b) child pedestrians in 1984

(c) motor scooter/cycle riders in 1984?

6 (a) Which classes of road user suffered more casualties in 1984 than in 1971?

(b) Which classes suffered fewer casualties?

7 (a) Which class of road user showed the greatest increase in casualties between 1971 and 1984?

(b) Which class showed the greatest decrease?

8 Would you say that the overall differences between 1971 and 1984 are encouraging or discouraging? Why?

1 Figure 35:4 shows the total sales of petrol made by the Bamon Service Station during one week.

(a) What was the greatest amount of petrol sold in one day?

(b) What was the total amount of petrol sold that week?

(LEAG)

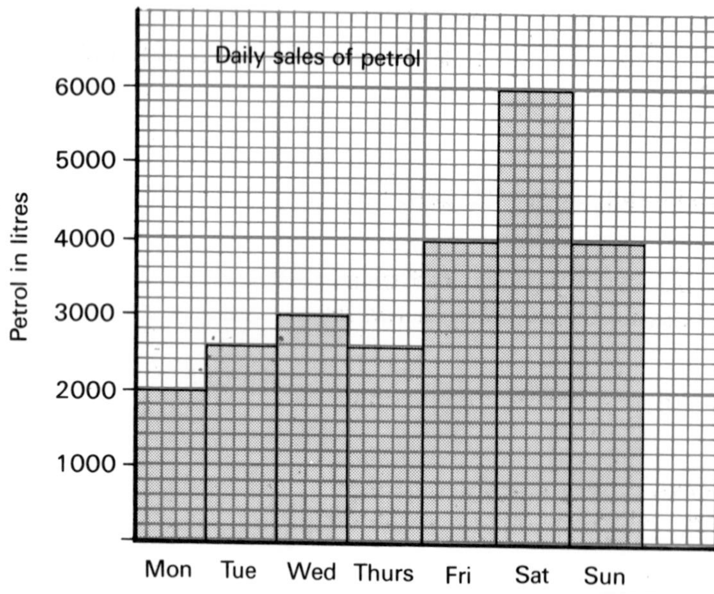

Fig. 35:4

2 Copy and complete the paragraph below, choosing the correct words from the list.

Bar-charts are a way of showing . . . The bars are shown vertically or . . . The information is sometimes shown in . . . bar, called a . . . bar-chart. A frequency table shows how many . . . various things happen.

times
one
horizontally
data
proportionate

3 Figure 35:5 shows the age of dwellings in Great Britain for three years.

(a) What type of bar-chart is used in Figure 35:5?

(b) What is meant by:
(i) pre 1891 (ii) post 1970?

(c) Write down the approximate percentages that represent the five age groups in 1984.

Fig. 35:5

(Social Trends, Central Statistical Office)

4 The air we breathe out is approximately 80% nitrogen, 15% oxygen and 5% carbon dioxide.

(a) How long would be each bar if we represented these percentages by three bars drawn to a scale of 1 cm to 10%?

(b) Show the percentages as simplified common fractions.

5 A student asked 30 people leaving a football ground how much they had paid to see the match. Their replies are listed below.

£5 £5 £4 £3 £4 £3 £5 £2 £2 £5
£3 £6 £6 £6 £2 £5 £2 £5 £5 £3
£3 £5 £3 £5 £5 £3 £4 £2 £2 £4

(a) Copy and complete this table.

Amount paid	£2	£3	£4	£5	£6
Number of people	6				

(b) Copy and complete Figure 35:6, showing the information in your table.

(c) Write down the mode of the amounts paid by the 30 people.

(MEG)

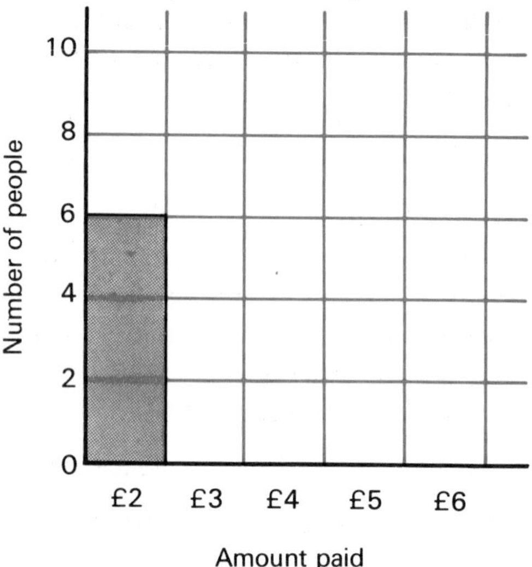

Fig. 35:6

6 (a) Copy the table on the right and complete the totals column.

(b) Draw a bar-chart, numbered from 0 to 10, to illustrate the table.

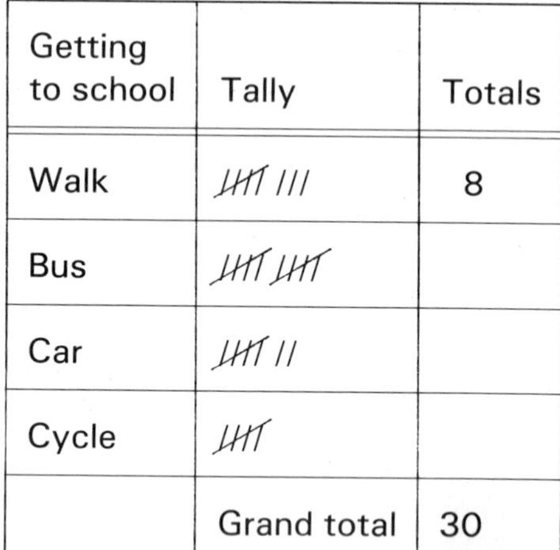

Getting to school	Tally	Totals
Walk	𝍸 ///	8
Bus	𝍸 𝍸	
Car	𝍸 //	
Cycle	𝍸	
	Grand total	30

7 Figure 35:7 shows the number of cars sold per day in one week by a large garage in Aberystwyth.

(a) How many cars were sold on Friday?

(b) On which day was the greatest number of cars sold?

(c) On which day was the least number of cars sold?

(d) How many cars were sold altogether during the week?

(e) What was the average number of cars sold per day?

(f) Mr Austin, the sales manager, would like to increase by 2 the average number of cars sold per day. How many cars would he have to sell in a working week to do this?

(WJEC)

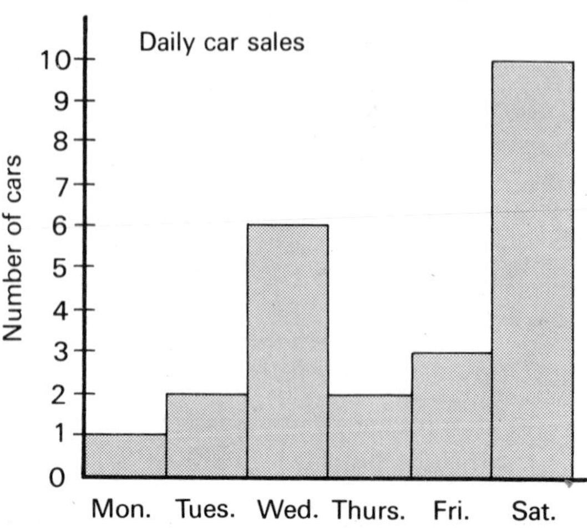

Fig. 35:7

8 The sales of a record in the Top Forty over five weeks are shown below. (The numbers are given to the nearest 10 000.)

Week	1	2	3	4	5
Sales in 1000s	250	320	440	470	410

(a) Show the sales in a bar-chart using scales of:
Horizontal: 1 cm to 1 week
Vertical: 2 cm to 100 000 records

(b) Find the mean (average) sales per week.

(c) Show the sales in a line graph.

9 Figure 35:8 shows the results of a random survey in Lutonbury into the ages of 30 people.

Fig. 35:8

(a) Copy and complete the table.

Age	Tally	Frequency
1–10		2
11–20		7
21–30		
31–40		
41–50		
51–60		
61–70		
71–80		
over 80		
	Total	30

(b) How many people were aged 51 to 60?

(c) Copy and complete the bar-chart in Figure 35:9.

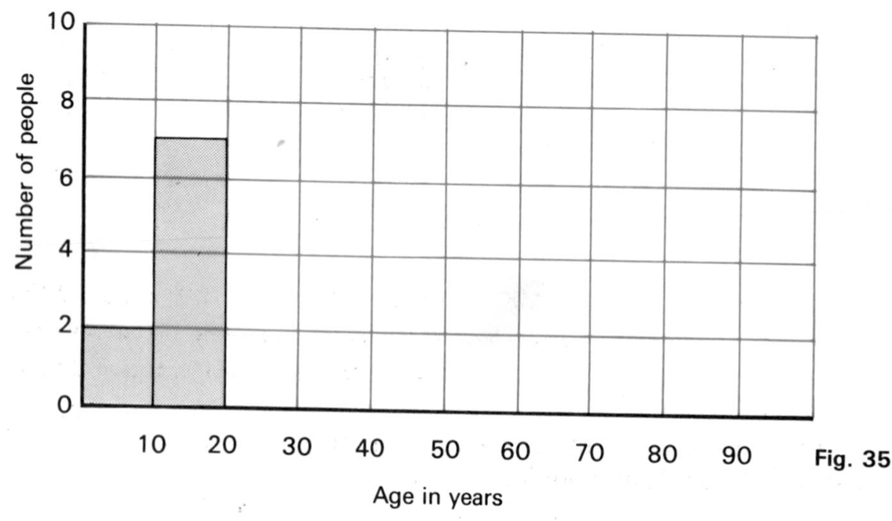

Fig. 35:9

(d) (i) What fraction of those surveyed are aged 51 to 60?

(ii) If the survey is typical of the 30 000 people in Lutonbury, how many of the population are aged 51 to 60?

(iii) What percentage of the population is aged 31 to 40? (LEAG)

Worksheet 35 may be used here.

10 Figure 35:10 shows world population growth since 1950 with projections up to 2025.

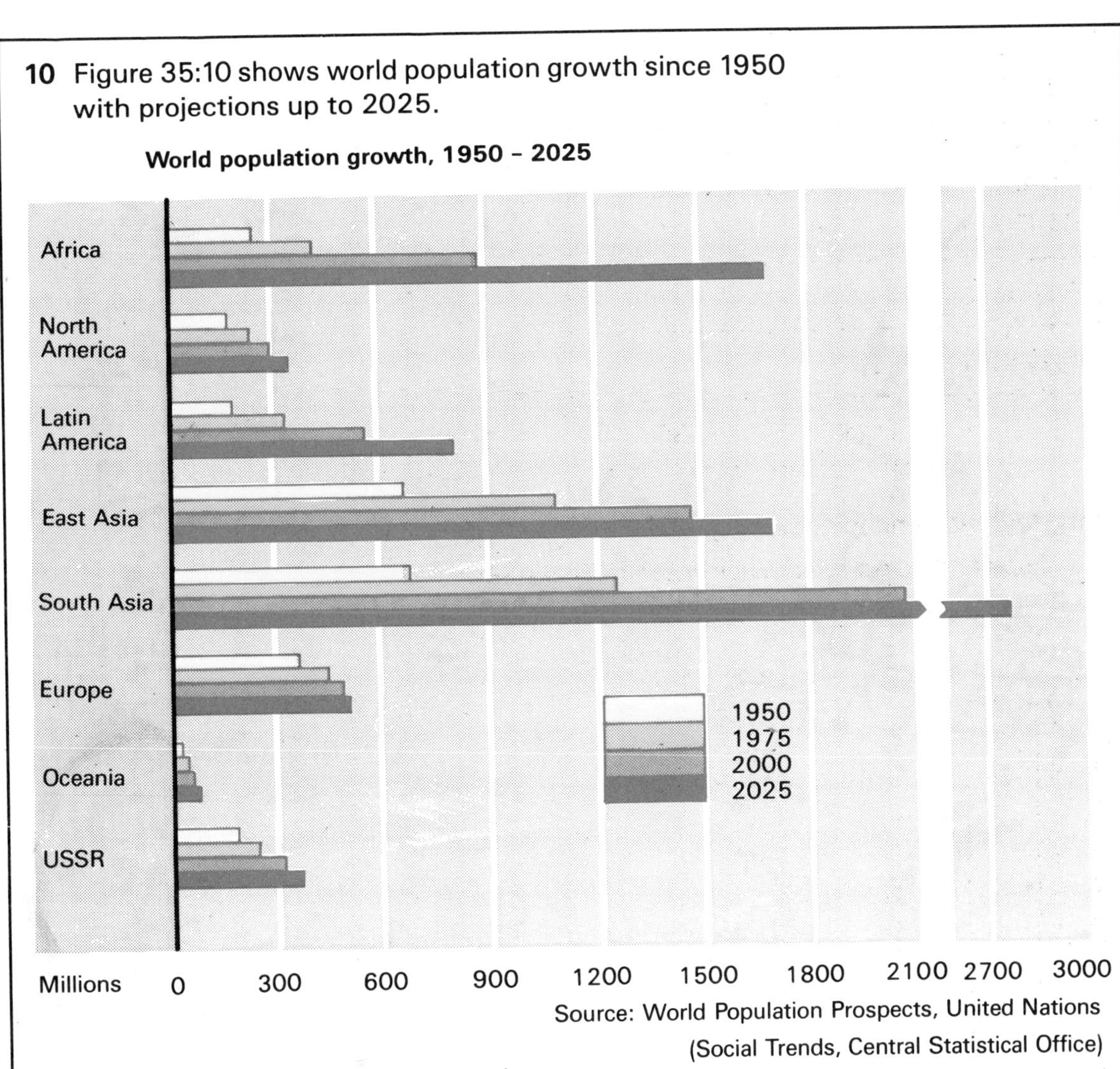

Source: World Population Prospects, United Nations (Social Trends, Central Statistical Office)

Fig. 35:10

(a) State as accurately as you can the scale used on the horizontal axis per 100 million people.

(b) What part of the world is named Oceania?

(c) Why is the 2025 projection for South Asia shown with a 'broken' bar?

(d) Approximately what is the total projected world population for AD 2000?

(e) State the approximate population for Africa in
(i) 1950 (ii) 2025

(f) Write a short report on how you would cope with some of the problems involved with the increase in world population.

Assignment 4

Exploring sequence

REMEMBER!

- Look for the pattern in the sequence.
- It often helps to look at the differences between consecutive terms.

A **sequence** is a set of numbers connected by a pattern or a rule.

The pattern in the sequence 1, 3, 5, 7, . . . is easy to see. Each term in the sequence is formed by adding 2 to the previous term.

We can find the 10th term in the sequence 1, 3, 5, 7, . . . by adding nine differences to the **first** term, like this:

10th term $= 1 + (2 \times 9) \rightarrow 19$

By using this formula we can find any term in the sequence 1, 3, 5, 7, . . .

We could say the nth term is $1 + 2(n - 1)$.

Testing the pattern

Claire investigated the number of regions created by drawing chords across a circle. She drew three circles, like this.

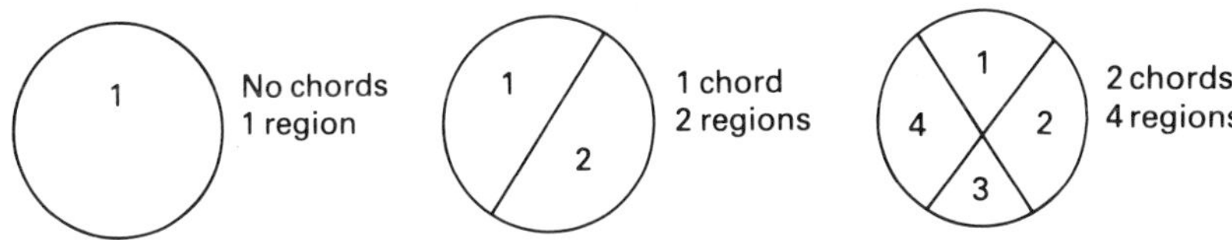

She concluded that the regions follow a doubling sequence of 1, 2, 4, . . .

Test the pattern by drawing another circle with three chords. Was Claire right?

Investigate the sequences detailed below. Write a clear report on what you find in each section. Include any tables, diagrams etc., that you think necessary.

1 Use a formula to find the 10th, 15th and 20th terms of the sequence:

(a) 2, 4, 6, 8, . . . (b) 1, 3, 5, 7, . . .

(c) 1, 4, 7, 10, . . .

2 If you drink, on average, 5 containers of liquid a day your liquid intake could be represented by the sequence 5, 10, 15, 20, . . .

(a) Write down patterns representing:
(i) heartbeats (ii) sleep
(iii) the renewal of the lining of your stomach

(b) Investigate bio-rhythms.

3 (a) Write down the first ten terms of the sequence which shows the numbers of your **direct** ancestors (parents, grandparents and so on). The first term is 2.

(b) (i) How many direct ancestors were there in the 20th generation of ancestors?
(ii) About how long ago did they live?

4 Figure A4:2 shows five table-tennis players and the ten ways they could be paired off in a tournament.

Fig. A4:2

(a) Make a table showing the number of possible pairs with 2, 3, 4, 6 and 7 players.

(b) Can you predict the number of possible pairs with
(i) 10 players (ii) 15 players?

5 An nth term is represented by $\frac{n(n+1)}{2}$.

(a) Find the kind of number represented by the formula $\frac{n(n+1)}{2}$.

(b) Find the 10th, 15th and 30th terms in the sequence.

Information for aural tests

1

The food and drink sold in 1985 by British Rail station catering division included:

Hot food dishes	368 368
Hot snacks	3 320 980
Pies	1 050 504
Pints of draught beer and lager	5 149 656
Sandwiches	6 963 216
Cups of tea	19 500 000
Cups of coffee	16 594 136
Casey Jones burgers	7 131 904

(British Rail)

2

(a)	1	2	5	6	9	10	11	12
(b)	13	14	15	16	18	20	21	24
(c)	25	27	28	29	30	31	32	33
(d)	35	36	37	40	41	42	43	44
(e)	49	50	51	53	55	59	60	61
(f)	63	64	65	67	68	72	73	75

3

Seventeen

These documentary films show how the lives of teenagers change and develop at the age of 17.
Teacher's notes*
Monday 1.33—1.58pm, 6 programmes from 27 April
Repeated Thursday 12.12—12.37pm from 30 April

Maths at Work

These documentary films show a range of mathematical techniques and concepts being applied by young people at work.
Teacher's notes*
Wednesday 11.40am—12 noon,
5 programmes from 4 March
Repeated Thursday 9.30—9.50am from 5 March

Job Bank

These programmes are about a wide range of jobs and occupations suitable for young people of mixed abilities leaving school or college.
Teacher's notes*
Monday 1.38—1.58pm,
15 programmes from 22 September
Repeated Wednesday 12.25—12.45pm
from 24 September

Daytime on Two (BBC Education)

4

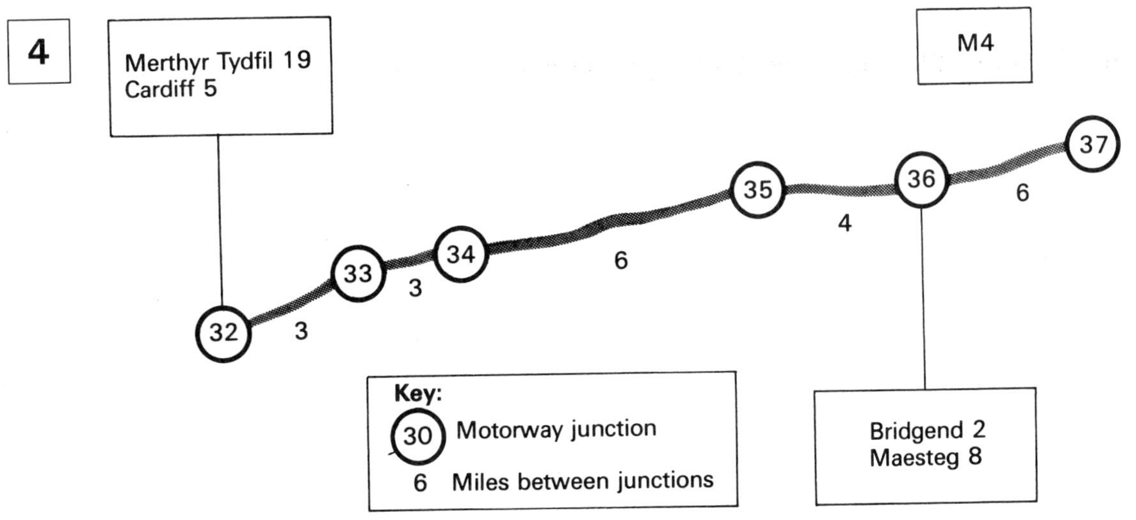

5

Liverpool—Chester—Crewe-London 6

Catering available for all or most of journey

⊘ Restaurant (Mondays to Fridays) serving meals
Ⓑ Buffet serving hot dishes, drinks and light refreshments
☕ Buffet serving drinks and light refreshments

Sundays from February 22	☕	☕	☕	☕	☕	☕	☕	☕	☕	☕
Liverpool Lime Street	—	—	0745	—	0955	—	—	1155	—	—
Runcorn	—	—	0804	—	1014	—	—	1214	—	—
Chester	—	—	—	—	1040	—	—	1157	—	—
Crewe	—	—	0908	—	1118	1145	—	1318	1338	—
Stafford	—	—	0932	1031	—	—	1226	—	—	1426
Tamworth	—	—	—	—	—	—	—	—	—	—
Nuneaton	—	—	0950g	—	—	1225g	—	—	—	—
Rugby	0926	1008	1043d	1137d	—	1313	—	—	1514	1531
Milton Keynes Central	0951	1032	1159	1259	—	1414	—	—	—	1620
Watford Jn (arrive)	1034	1112	1150	1250	1349	1500	—	1553	—	1657
Kensington Olympia	1121	1159	—	—	—	—	—	—	—	—
London Euston	—	—	1220	1318	1417	1440	1454	1615	1644	1658

Sundays all dates	☕	☕	☕	☕	C ☕	☕	☕	C ☕	☕	☕
Liverpool Lime Street	—	—	1442h	1600	—	—	—	—	—	1700
Runcorn	—	—	1502k	1617	—	—	—	—	—	1717
Chester	—	1441n	—	—	—	—	—	1626	1626	1712
Crewe	—	1559	1618	—	1645	—	1705	1713	1720	1743
Stafford	1602	1620	—	1657	—	1720	—	—	1743	1804
Tamworth	—	1639	—	—	—	—	—	—	—	—
Nuneaton	—	1651	—	—	—	—	1751	—	1810	1831
Rugby	—	—	—	—	—	—	—	—	1823	—
Milton Keynes Central	—	—	—	—	—	1820	—	—	1852	—
Watford Jn (arrive)	1732	—	—	1821	1826	1849	—	1859	1920	1933
Kensington Olympia	—	—	—	—	—	1922	—	—	—	—
London Euston	1755	1813	1818	1844	1849	—	1916	1923	1944	1956

Sundays all dates	☕	☕	☕	☕	☕	☕	☕	☕	2 🛏
Liverpool Lime Street	—	—	—	1800	—	1915	—	—	0015
Runcorn	—	—	—	1817	—	1932	—	—	—
Chester	—	—	—	—	1816	1925	—	—	—
Crewe	1807	1823	1837	—	1901	1958	2033	2040	0110
Stafford	—	—	—	—	1922	2019	—	—	0208
Tamworth	—	—	—	1922	—	—	—	—	—
Nuneaton	—	—	—	—	—	2046	—	2124	0241
Rugby	—	—	—	—	1959	—	—	2137	0258
Milton Keynes Central	1930	1945	—	—	2114	—	—	2309	0341
Watford Jn (arrive)	—	—	2013	2027	2048	2144	2208	2226	—
Kensington Olympia	—	—	—	—	—	—	—	—	—
London Euston	2014	2029	2037	2051	2112	2207	2231	2250	0442

A Mondays to Fridays.
B Saturdays only.
C Until October 26.
d Calls to set down only.
g Bus Nuneaton → Coventry
h 1456 until October 26, also from February 22.
k 1516 until October 26, also from February 22.
n 1512 until February 15.

Ⓟ InterCity **Pullman** (Mondays to Fridays) quality at-seat-meal-service to First Class ticket holders.
🛏 InterCity **Sleepers** 1st and 2nd Class (occupation and vacation of cabins, see page 95). Second Class seating only.

(InterCity timetable. British Rail)

7

PASSENGER SERVICES
(Channel Link)

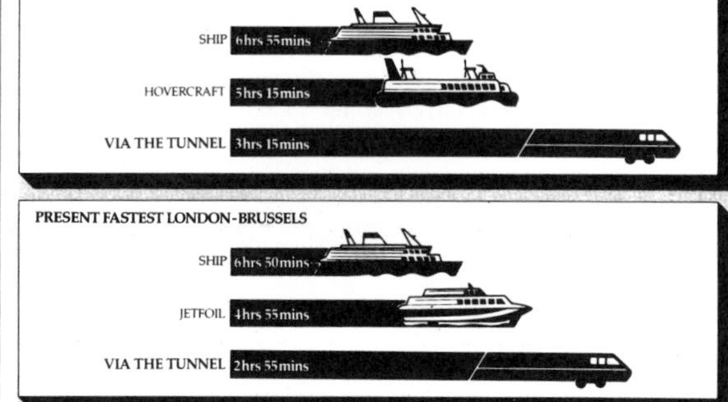

(British Rail)

8

Price of inland letter post

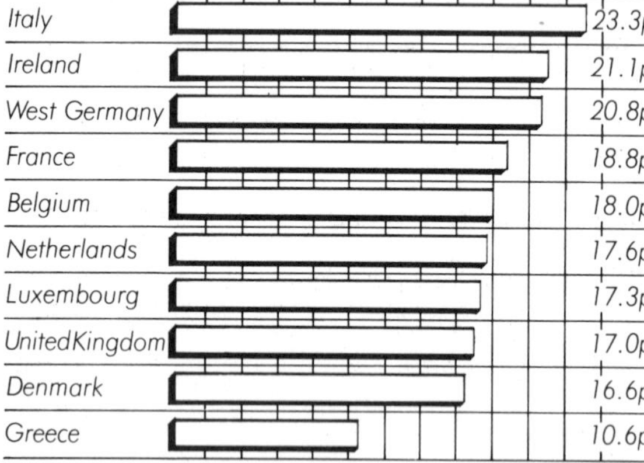

Tariffs adjusted to reflect purchasing power of currencies

(Royal Mail)

6

9

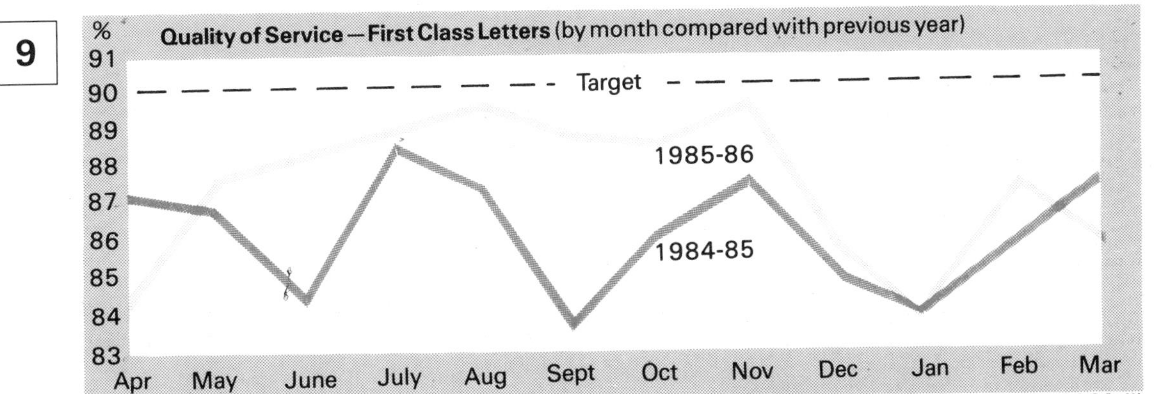

(Royal Mail)

10

Use this "Ready Reckoner"
to decide which life insurance plan is right for you

	PLAN A	PLAN B	PLAN C	PLAN D	PLAN E
Minimum Cover You Get	£10,000	£20,000	£35,000	£50,000	£65,000
Double Cover if Death Accidental	£20,000	£40,000	£70,000	£100,000	£130,000
Age (nearest)	Amount you pay monthly				
20-30	£5.00	£6.00	£7.35	£10.50	£13.65
31-35	£5.00	£6.20	£9.10	£13.00	£16.90
36-40	£5.40	£8.40	£12.95	£18.50	£24.05
41-45	£6.00	£12.00	£19.25	£27.50	—
46-50	£9.30	£18.60	£30.30	—	—
51-55	£14.70	£29.40	—	—	—

(Northern Ireland SEC)

11

1984/85*

PASSENGER

GOVERNMENT GRANT 1172

FREIGHT 408

PARCELS 149

OTHER 358

TOTAL INCOME £3594m

1985/86

PASSENGER

GOVERNMENT GRANT 896

FREIGHT 528

PARCELS 127

OTHER 292

TOTAL INCOME £3176m

(British Rail)

12

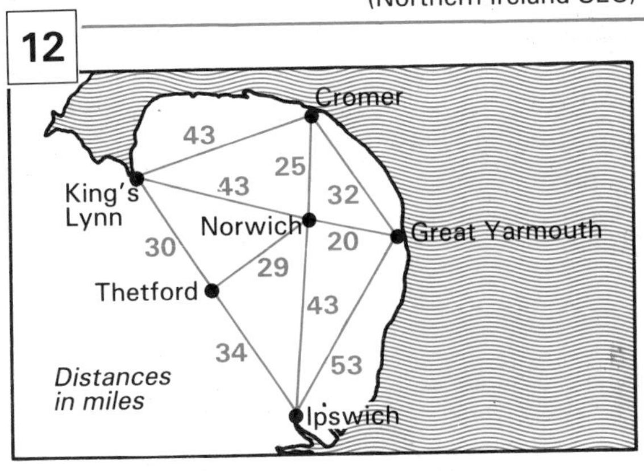

13

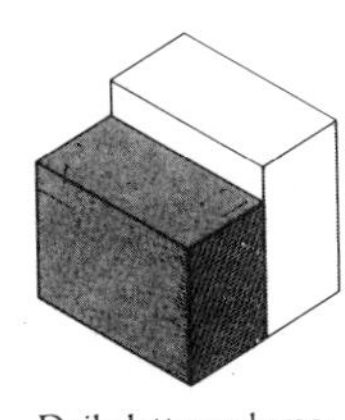

Daily letter volume: 42 million (average)

Mail collection points: 100,000

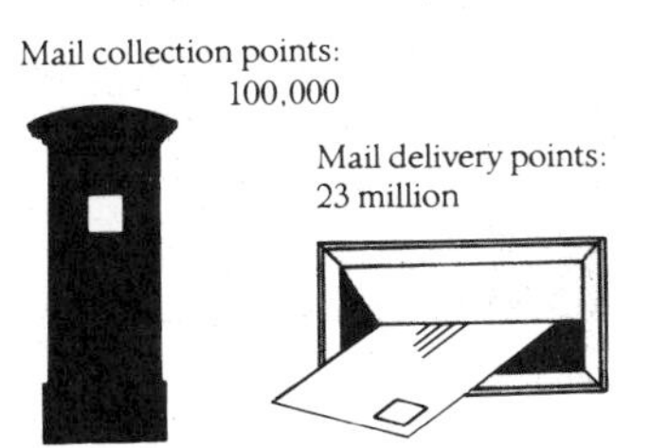

Mail delivery points: 23 million

Size of vehicle fleet: 28,000

(Royal Mail)

14

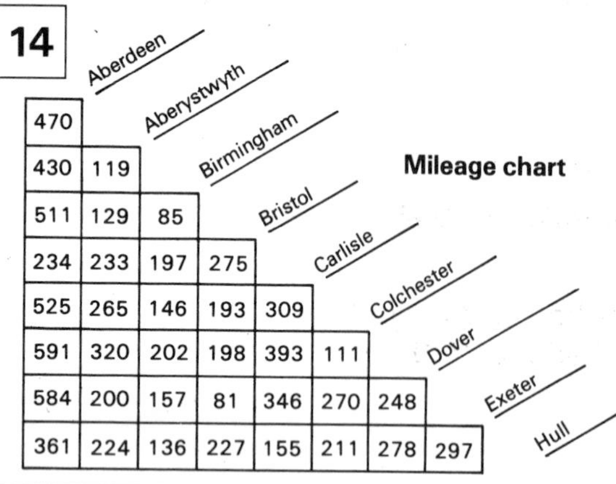

Mileage chart

	Aberdeen	Aberystwyth	Birmingham	Bristol	Carlisle	Colchester	Dover	Exeter
Aberystwyth	470							
Birmingham	430	119						
Bristol	511	129	85					
Carlisle	234	233	197	275				
Colchester	525	265	146	193	309			
Dover	591	320	202	198	393	111		
Exeter	584	200	157	81	346	270	248	
Hull	361	224	136	227	155	211	278	297

15

Rectangle drawn to scale

3 cm

16

Rates for letters

Weight not over	First class	Second class
60g	18p	13p
100g	26p	20p
150g	32p	24p
200g	40p	30p
250g	48p	37p
300g	56p	43p
350g	64p	49p
400g	72p	55p
450g	82p	62p

Weight not over	First class	Second class
500g	92p	70p
600g	£1.15	85p
700g	£1.35	£1.00
750g	£1.45	£1.05
800g	£1.55	Not admissible over 750g
900g	£1.70	
1000g	£1.85	
Each extra 250g or part thereof	45p	

The Post Office aims to deliver (Monday to Saturday) 90% of first class letters by the working day following the day of collection and 96% of second class letters by the third working day following the day of collection.

(Royal Mail)

17

FARES

Standard Single Fares

VEHICLES AND THEIR PASSENGERS	E TARIFF £	D TARIFF £	C TARIFF £	B TARIFF £
Cars, Minibuses and Campers				
Up to 4.00m (13′1″) in length/Motorcycle combination	20.00	30.00	39.50	48.00
Up to 4.50m (14′9″) in length	20.00	35.00	47.50	57.00
Up to 5.50m (18′) in length	20.00	40.00	56.50	67.00
Over 5.50m : per extra metre or part thereof	10.00	10.00	11.00	12.00
Caravans and Trailers				
Up to 4.00m (13′1″) in length	19.00	24.00	26.00	28.00
Up to 5.50m (18′) in length	19.00	36.00	38.00	40.00
Over 5.50m : per extra metre or part thereof	10.00	10.00	10.00	10.00
Motorcycle, Scooters and Mopeds	11.00	11.00	12.00	13.00
Each Adult	11.50	11.50	11.50	11.50
Each Child (4 but under 14 yrs)	6.00	6.00	6.00	6.00

(Southern EG)

18

Dry Cleaning

Two-piece (plain skirt)	£2·50
Two-piece (pleated skirt)	£3·20
Blouse	£0·60
Two-piece suit	£2·70
Jacket	£1·45
Trousers	£1·35

19

Admission Prices

Stalls £1.40
Back Circle £1.80
Front Circle £2.40
Children under 14 ... half price.

CLASSIC CINEMA
"SIX SHOOTER"

20

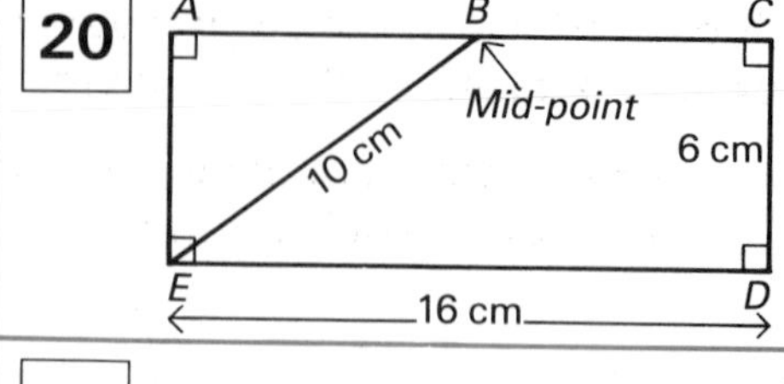

21

X
b
a
Y
120°
p
q

Summaries

1 Base ten: the denary system

Digits (the figures 0 to 9) change in value according to their place in a number.

Example In 65 903 the 6 stands for 6 ten-thousands, or 60 000; the 9 stands for only 9 hundreds, or 900.

2 Line graphs

Figures 2:1 and 2:2 (pages 5 and 6) are examples of line graphs.

In Figure 2:1 points between the crosses have a meaning. For example, at $3\frac{1}{2}$ years old the child was probably about 95 cm tall.

In Figure 2:2 points between the crosses have no meaning. For example, there was no football match on January 7th, so you cannot say how many people attended it!

3 Types of number

Make sure that you know the following. (They can be looked up in the glossary and in chapter 3.)

Even odd triangular number square number integer prime number infinity consecutive positive negative

4 Addition and subtraction: which operation?

You should be able to add and subtract without a calculator. Practise if you need to – make up your own questions, do them, then check your answers with a calculator.

Remember Always think about your answer before you leave it. Is it a sensible answer?

Take a break 1 (Networks)

A network is traversable when

(a) it has two odd nodes, or

(b) all its nodes are even.

5 Pictograms

Figure 5:1 (page 22) shows a pictogram. A symbol represents a number. Make sure you choose a sensible number; if you want to show 1000 cars it would be silly to draw one car to represent 10 cars. Why?

6 Multiplication and division: which operation?

You should be able to multiply two-digit numbers together (like 45×73), and divide by a single digit (like $351 \div 9$), without need for a calculator. Make sure that you know your tables too!

You need to know whether or not your calculator saves up $+$ and $-$ until after it has done any $\times$ or $\div$. Does it say that $7 + 3 \times 2$ is 20 or 13?

7 Time

You need to understand the 24-hour clock system (add 12 to p.m. times).

Remember that April, June, September and November have only 30 days, and that February has 28, with 29 in a leap year.

When doing arithmetic in time remember that there are 60 minutes in an hour, so a calculator is not much help. (3 hours 30 minutes is 3·5 hours not 3·3 hours, and 3 hours 40 minutes + 2 hours 50 minutes is 6 hours 30 minutes, not 5·90 hours.)

8 Calculators

Learn to use your own calculator, not a borrowed one. Always watch the display to see what is happening as you press the keys.

Make sensible estimates. For example, if $x^2 = 20$, then x must be between 4 and 5 because $4^2 = 16$ and $5^2 = 25$.

9 Decimal fractions

You should learn how to add, subtract, and multiply decimal fractions.

Adding and subtracting

As for whole numbers, but make sure you line up the units column figures.

Multiplying

Work the multiplication without any decimal points, then put the decimal point in the answer using the rule; 'Same number of figures to the right of the point in the answer as in the question'.

10 Conversion graphs

Figure 10:1 (page 51) shows a conversion graph. By going up to the conversion line from one axis, then going at right-angles to the other axis, you can convert from one unit to another. In Figure 10:1 you can convert between gallons and litres.

11 Common fractions: cancelling

$\frac{3}{4}$ → The whole one has been divided into 4 parts.

→ Three of these parts make up the fraction.

When possible cancel fractions to make them simpler.

$\frac{15}{35}$ divide both numbers by 5 → $\frac{3}{7}$

12 Flow-charts

Figure 12:2 (page 60) shows a flow-chart.

Note the different shape boxes used for start/stop, instructions and decisions.

Start/Stop

Instructions

Decisions

13 Ratio and enlargement

A ratio of boys to girls of 2 to 3, written 2 : 3, means that there are 2 boys to every 3 girls, perhaps 20 boys and 30 girls, or perhaps 10 boys and 15 girls.

Ratios can be cancelled like fractions.

Similar shapes are the same shape but not the same size.

An enlargement of, say, factor 3 can be made using the 'ray' method or by the 'squares' method (see page 68).

14 Common fractions: add; subtract; multiply

Check with your teacher whether you may use a calculator for common fraction arithmetic.

Adding and subtracting

Make them the same kind of fraction (same bottom number).

Multiplying
Convert mixed numbers to top-heavy fractions.
Multiply top numbers together and bottom numbers together.
Remember to cancel if you can.

15 Scales

Map scales
1 : 100 000 means 1 cm represents 100 000 cm, or 1 inch represents 100 000 inches, and so on.

100 000 cm = 1000 m = 1 km, so a scale of 1 : 100 000 is the same as 1 cm represents 1 km.

When written as $\frac{1}{100\,000}$ it is called the representative fraction.

If 1 cm represents 500 m, then 2·5 cm represents

2·5 × 500 m = 1250 m.

7000 m will be represented by

7000 ÷ 500 = 14 cm.

Model scales
These are like map scales, but usually are not such big reductions.

16 Proportional division

Add the parts; divide to find one part; multiply to give the answer.

Example Divide £169 in the ratio 4 : 9.

4 + 9 = 13, so £169 ÷ 13 gives £13 as 1 part.
4 × £13 = £52 and 9 × £13 = £117

17 Travel graphs

Travel graphs are sometimes called journey graphs or distance/time graphs.

Time is always on the horizontal (across) axis.

Label the distance axis to say where the distances are measured from, e.g. Distance from Dudley, in km.

The slope of the graph line represents speed, that is, distance over time.

18 Proportional changes; scatter graphs

Direct proportion

Halve the ingredients to make half as big a cake.
Double the petrol to go twice as far.

Indirect proportion

Double the speed to take half the time.

The unitary method

Find the amount for one part.

Example Reduce £120 in the ratio 3 : 4.

£120 is 4 parts.
So £30 is 1 part.
So 3 parts is £90.

Scatter graphs

These are drawn when there might be a link, or correlation, between two lots of information. A line of best fit through the plotted points illustrates the link.

19 Fraction conversions

Decimal to common

Write over 10, 100, 1000, etc. depending on the column of the last figure.

Example 0·072 is $\frac{72}{1000}$ as the 2 is in the thousandths column.

Cancelling makes the fraction simpler:

$$\frac{72}{1000} \xrightarrow{\text{divide both by 2}} \frac{36}{500} \xrightarrow{\text{divide both by 4}} \frac{9}{125}$$

Common to decimal

Divide the top number by the bottom.
$\frac{3}{8} \rightarrow 3 \div 8 \rightarrow 0{\cdot}375$

Decimal places

Long decimal numbers are best reduced to 2 or 3 decimal places.

Examples 1·0496 → 1·0 to 1 d.p.
1·0496 → 1·05 to 2 d.p.
1·0496 → 1·050 to 3 d.p.

Take a break 3 (Congruency)

Two shapes are congruent if they are identical, regardless of their position.

S

20 Money

A calculator omits the final zero in decimal amounts, so £4·60 is shown as 4·6.

When adding or subtracting, make sure the amounts are in the same units, e.g. all pounds or all pennies.

Example £16 + 25p is not 16 + 25, but either £16 + £0·25 or 1600p + 25p

21 Fraction division

Decimals

Divide by powers of 10 by moving the figures to the right.

Examples 18·2 ÷ 10
move 1 place → 1·82

18·2 ÷ 1000
move 3 places → 0·0182

Divide by decimals by changing the question to dividing by a whole number.

Example 48·603 ÷ 0·03
multiply both by 100
→ 4860·3 ÷ 3 → 1620·1

Common fractions

Multiply by the inverse.

Example $3\frac{1}{2} \div 5$

$$\frac{7}{2} \div \frac{5}{1} \rightarrow \frac{7}{2} \times \frac{1}{5} \rightarrow \frac{7}{10}$$

$$\frac{2}{7} \div \frac{3}{4} \rightarrow \frac{2}{7} \times \frac{4}{3} \rightarrow \frac{8}{21}$$

If using a calculator, put brackets round the fractions.

Example for the last example above:
[(] 2 [÷] 7 [)] [÷] [(] 3 [÷] 4 [)] [=]

Assignment 2 (Nets)

Remember how to use compasses to draw a right-angle, a triangle and a regular hexagon (Figure A2:2, page 126).

Figure A2:4 (page 127) shows one net for a cube.

22 Percentages

% means out of 100.

1% of £1 is 1p.
23% of £500 is 23p × 500 = £115·00.

Learn to use the % key on your calculator.

One number as a percentage of another

Example £4 as a percentage of £16 is

$$\frac{4}{16} \times \frac{100\%}{1} = 25\%$$

23 Approximating

Make sure your answer *is* approximately the same.

Be especially careful to put in zeros.

Example 9936·4 to the nearest thousand is 10 000.

24 Foreign currency

When converting make sure you choose correctly whether to multiply or divide. An easy check is whether £1 is more, or less, than one unit of the foreign currency.

Example If £1 = 8 francs, then £2 **cannot** be 8 ÷ 2 = 4 francs.

25 Perimeters; areas; volumes

The area of a triangle is half of the length of the base line multiplied by the length of the altitude to that line. We usually remember this as 'Half the base times the height'! See Figure S25:1.

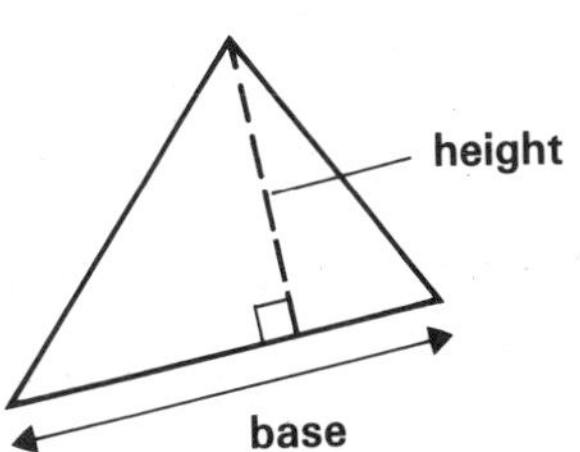

Fig. S25:1

The area of a parallelogram and a rectangle is the length of one side multiplied by the shortest distance from that side to the parallel one. We usually remember this as 'base times height'! See Figure S25:2.

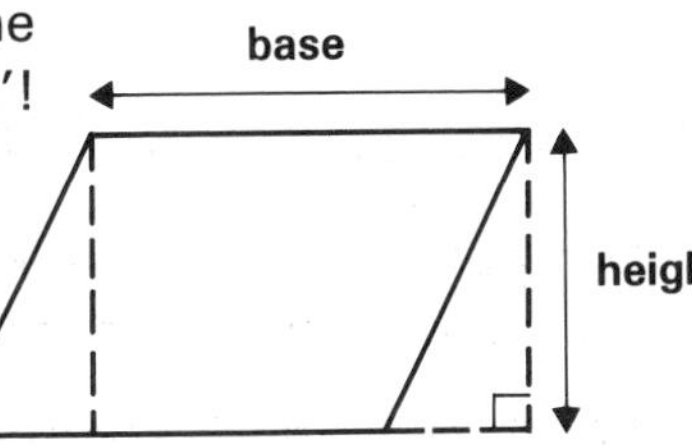

Fig. S25:2

A prism is same shape all the way through. The volume of a prism is the area of its cross-section multiplied by its length.

Circle
The circumference of a circle is $\pi \times d$ (use 3·14 or 3 for π; d means diameter).

The area of a circle is $\pi \times r \times r = \pi r^2$ (r is the radius).

The volume of a cylinder is $\pi r^2 \times h$ (height).

26 Best buys

To find the best buy compare the prices for the same amount. This can be 1 unit, or an easy multiple, like 50 g or 1 kg.

27 Angles

When using a protractor always decide first whether the angle is more or less than a right-angle, so that you read the correct number.

28 Averages

There are three types of average: **mean, mode** and **median.**

For the values 2, 2, 3, 5, 8,

the mean is $\frac{2 + 2 + 3 + 5 + 8}{5} = \mathbf{4}$,

the median (middle value) is **3**,
the mode (most frequent value) is **2**.

Two-way tables
These are useful for showing a lot of information in a table.

29 Squares and square roots

Use the ☑ key on your calculator.

Many numbers do not have an exact square root. They are irrational numbers.

30 Symmetry

Lines of symmetry
These are the fold (or mirror) lines when a figure is folded in half so that one half lies exactly on the other.

Rotational symmetry

The order of rotational symmetry is the number of times a figure fits into itself in one complete turn.

Point symmetry

A figure has point symmetry if it looks identical when turned upside down.

31 The metric system

You probably know most common units. Do you know that:

1000 kg = 1 tonne (about the weight of a family car)

1000 cubic centimetres = 1 litre (just under 2 pints)

10 000 square metres = 1 hectare

1 000 000 tonnes = 1 megatonne

1 000 000 micrometres = 1 metre

32 Probability

Probabilities are given as a fraction between 0 (impossible) and 1 (certain).

The probability of an event happening if all outcomes are equally likely is

$$\frac{\text{the number of successful outcomes possible}}{\text{the total number of different possible outcomes}}$$

Example The probability of throwing a one with a balanced die is $\frac{1}{6}$.

The probability of an event happening + the probability of the same event not happening = 1.

33 Directed numbers

-8 (negative, or minus, eight) is 8 units below zero,
-5 is 5 units below zero,
so $-8 < -5$ (we say '-8 is less than -5').

Adding is moving up the number line (or to the right).
Subtracting is moving down the number line (or to the left).

Examples $-4 + 2 = -2$
$-4 - 2 = -6$ See Figure S33:1.

$-4 \leq a < 3$ means a is not less than -4, and less than 3.

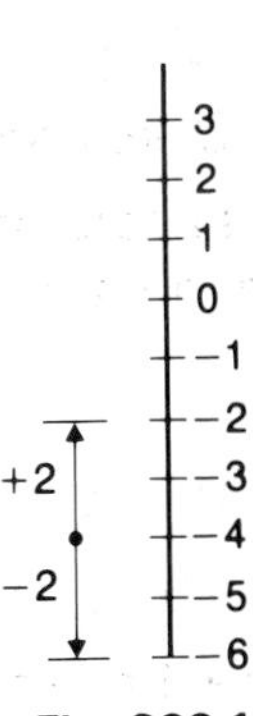

Fig. S33:1

34 Using letters

The perimeter p of this square is $4s$ (short for $4 \times s$).

If $s = 2$ cm, then $p = 4 \times 2$ cm $= 8$ cm.
The area is $s^2 = 2$ cm $\times$ 2 cm $= 4$ cm^2.

s

If $2a + 7 = 11$, then $2a = 4$, so $a = 2$.

35 Bar-charts

The proportionate bar-chart is made by joining all the bars of an ordinary bar-chart end to end. Figures S35:1 and S35:2 show the same information in a normal bar-chart and in a proportionate bar-chart.

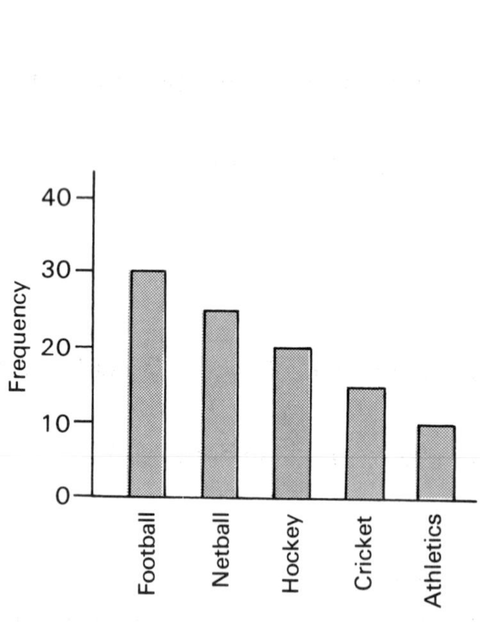

Fig. S35:1

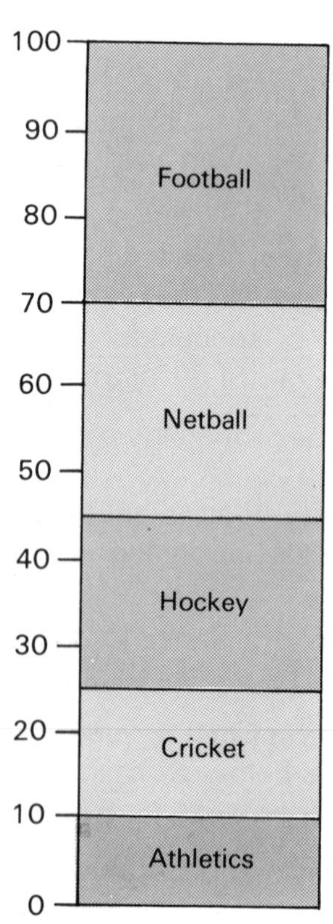

Fig. S35:2

Glossary

If you cannot remember what a word or a phrase means, this glossary should help you.

Numbers in brackets refer to the chapter and summary where that topic is taught. Words in *italic* can be looked up in this glossary.

A

Acute An angle between 0° and 90°.

Acre An *area* of 4840 *square yards*.

AD Anno Domini ('In the year of our Lord').

Annually Yearly.

Approximately equal to About the same: usually shown by $\approx$ or $\doteq$.

Arc Part of the *circumference* of a circle.

Area (25) The space covered by a flat shape.

Ascending order of magnitude Putting values in order, from the smallest to the largest.

Average (28) See *mean*, *mode* and *median*.

Axis (Axes) The *horizontal* (x) and *vertical* (y) lines on a graph. The distances of a point from these lines give the *coordinates* of the point.

B

Bank statement A communication from a bank showing the state of your account.

Bar-chart (28, 35) A way of showing information (data) in bars.

Base unit *Metre* – *Kilogram* – *Litre*.

BC Before Christ.

Bisected Divided into two equal parts.

BODMAS (6) Order of operations: **B**rackets – **O**f – **D**ivide – **M**ultiply – **A**dd – **S**ubtract.

British Summer Time An hour in advance of Greenwich Mean Time (GMT).

C

Calendar month January, February, March, etc.

Cancelling Simplifying *fractions* by dividing the top and bottom numbers, e.g.

$$\frac{\cancel{12}^{1}}{\cancel{36}_{3}} = \frac{1}{3}.$$

Capacity The measurement of liquid volume, e.g. in litres.

Celsius A temperature scale where 0 °C marks the freezing point and 100 °C marks the boiling point of water.

Centimetre *Metric* measurement of length; 100 cm = 1 m.

Centimetre square A *square* with each side 1 cm.

Century 100 years. The 20th century is from 1901 to 2000.

Chain *Imperial* measurement of 22 *yards*.

Chord A straight line joining two points on the *circumference* of a circle.

Circle Circumference = $\pi \times$ diameter.
Area = $\pi \times r \times r = \pi r^2$ (r is the radius).

Compasses (pair of) Used for drawing circles and arcs.

Consecutive Following on with no gaps, like 4, 5, 6, 7 or Monday, Tuesday, Wednesday.

Conversion graph (10) Graph showing a relationship between two quantities, e.g. *litres* and *gallons*.

Coordinates (2, 30) Two values giving the position of a point on a graph or grid. Sometimes called an *ordered pair*.

Correlation The degree of linkage between two or more sets of data. (See *scatter graph*.)

D

Decade 10 years.

Decagon A *plane* figure with 10 sides and 10 angles.

Decimal fraction (9, 19, 21) Part of a whole one; shown with a decimal point, e.g. 0·5, 0·25.

Decimal places (19, 21) Number of figures to the right of the decimal point, e.g. 2·374 has 3 decimal places.

Degrees Used to measure the amount of turn in an angle. A whole turn is divided into 360 degrees (360°).

Denominator The bottom number in a common *fraction*.

Deposit Part of the cost of something you are buying, paid to show you intend to buy it. Also an amount paid into a savings account.

Depreciation Loss of value, e.g. the decreasing value of an ageing car.

Diagonal A straight line inside and from corner to corner of a polygon.

Diameter A *chord* of a circle that passes through the centre.

Die The singular of dice.

Digit sum (6) Example 348 → 3 + 4 + 8 = 15 → 1 + 5 = **6**.

Direct proportion (13) When two quantities decrease or increase at the same rate.
Example A recipe serves 8 people; **halve** the recipe to serve **half** the people.

E

Equilateral Equal sided. An equilateral *triangle* has equal sides and equal angles.

Equivalence Equal amounts shown in different ways.
Example $\frac{3}{6} = \frac{1}{2} = 0{\cdot}5 = 50\%$.

Estimation An approximate calculation, as in estimating the size of a field.

Evaluate Finding the answer as accurately as possible.

Exchange rate (24) As in \$1·80 = £1.

Express the answer As in 'express the answer in *metres*', meaning 'give the answer in metres'.

F

Factors (6) A number that divides into another number without leaving a remainder.
Example The *set of* factors of 12 is {1, 2, 3, 4, 6, 12}.

Fahrenheit A temperature scale where 32 °F marks the freezing point and 212 °F the boiling point of water.

Feet *Imperial* measure of length. About 30 cm.

Formula Example πr^2 is the formula for finding the *area* of a circle.

Fractions (9, 11, 19, 21, 22) *Common (vulgar) fraction*, e.g. $\frac{1}{2}$; *decimal fraction*, e.g. 0·5; *percentage fraction*, e.g. 50%.

Fractional probability (32) Showing the chance, or probability, of something in fractional form, e.g. one chance in two → $\frac{1}{2}$.

Frequency The number of times something happens.

G

Gallons An *imperial* measure of liquid capacity. 8 *pints* = 1 gallon.

Gram *Metric* measurement of weight. 1000 g = 1 kg.

Greater than Shown by the *symbol* >, e.g. 8 > 3 ('eight is greater than 3).

Gross — 144; also gross pay: pay before deductions.

H

Hectare — An *area* of 10 000 m^2.

Heptagon — *Plane* figure with 7 sides.

Hexagon — *Plane* figure with 6 sides.

Hire purchase (HP) (20, 22) — A method of buying something over a period of time, usually by paying a *deposit* followed by monthly payments.

Horizontal — 'Across the page'; as in the horizontal *axis*; horizon.

I

Imperial — A British system of measurement, with units like feet, pounds, pints.

Improper fraction — A common *fraction* showing more than 1, e.g. $\frac{5}{2}$.

Inches — *Imperial* measure of length; 12″ = 1 foot; 1″ = 2·54 cm.

Inclusive — '1 to 10 inclusive' means include 1 and 10.

Index — As in 5^2, where we call the small raised 2 the index or the power.

Inequalities — $<$ means 'smaller or less than';
$>$ means 'greater or more than';
$\neq$ means 'is not equal to'.

Infinite — Having no end, e.g. the set of even numbers, {2, 4, 6, 8 . . .}.

Inflation — Where rising prices make money worth less, e.g. £1 in 1970 only worth 17p in 1980.

Irregular — Having unequal sides and/or unequal angles; as in an irregular *pentagon*.

Integers — The set of *positive* and *negative* whole numbers, including nought.

−3 −2 −1 0 1 2 3

Interest — Usually a charge made for borrowing money, or a reward for investing/saving money.

Isosceles — Having two equal sides; an isosceles *triangle* has two equal sides and two equal angles.

Inverse proportion (18) — One amount increases in the same *proportion* as another amount decreases. Example: a train doubling its speed ($\frac{2}{1}$) and taking $\frac{1}{2}$ the time.

K

Kilo — The *metric* prefix for 1000, as **kilo**metre (1000 metres), **kilo**gram (1000 grams).

Kilogram (31) — 1000 grams. About $2\frac{1}{4}$ *pounds* in weight.

Kilometre — 1000 *metres*. About $\frac{5}{8}$ of a *mile*.

km/h — Abbreviation for '*kilometres* per hour'. Also written as km h^{-1}.

Kite — A 4-sided shape (*quadrilateral*) with 2 pairs of equal sides, e.g.

L

Leap year — 366 days. A year whose number is a *multiple* of 4, e.g. 1980, 1984, 1988, except years divisible by 100 but not by 400, e.g. 1900.

Less than — Shown by the *symbol* $<$, e.g. $2 < 5$ ('two is less than five').

Like fractions — *Fractions* with the same *denominator*, e.g. $\frac{1}{9}$ and $\frac{2}{9}$.

Line of best fit — Drawn 'by eye' on a *scatter graph* to illustrate any *correlation*.

Line symmetry (30) — If a shape can be folded so that one part **exactly** covers the other part, then the fold is on a line of *symmetry*.

Litre — A *metric* measure of capacity, e.g. 1 *litre* of milk (about $1\frac{3}{4}$ *pints*).

Lowest common multiple (LCM) — The lowest number into which a *set of* numbers will all divide **exactly**.
Example 12 is the LCM of 1, 2, 3, 4, 6 and 12.

M

Mean (28) — Short for 'arithmetic mean', sometimes called 'the average'.
The mean of 2, 6 and 10 is $\frac{2 + 6 + 10}{3} = 6$.

Median (28) — A type of average. Half the values are above the median and half below it.
Example The median of 2, 3, 5, 7, 8 is **5**.

Metric system (31) — The system based on the *metre*. *Units* are in *multiples* of 10, as 10 mm = 1 cm, 100 cm = 1 m.

Metre — *Metric* measurement of length. About half the height of an ordinary door.
1 m = 100 cm. 1000 m = 1 km.

Midday — 12 noon; 1200 hours in *24-hour clock*.

Midnight The end of a day; 2400 or 0000 hours in *24-hour clock*.

Mile *Imperial* measurement of length; about $1\frac{3}{5}$ *kilometres*.

Mileometer A machine that records the number of *miles* travelled.

Milli The *metric* prefix for $\frac{1}{1000}$; a milligram is one-thousandth of a gram. 1000 mg = 1 g.

Millilitre (ml) One-thousandth ($\frac{1}{1000}$) of a *litre*.

Millimetre (mm) One-thousandth ($\frac{1}{1000}$) of a *metre*.

Million 1 000 000 (one thousand thousands).

Minute Measurement of time: 1 min = 60 seconds.

m.p.h. *Miles* per hour.

Mixed number A number made up from an *integer* and a *common fraction*, e.g. $4\frac{2}{3}$.

Mode (28) A type of average. The value that occurs most often.

N

Nearest As in, 'Give your answer to the nearest *metre*,' etc.
Example 5 m 60 cm is nearer to 6 metres than to 5 metres.

Negative Numbers below *zero*, e.g. −2, −4·5.

Net The *plane* shape that can be folded to make a solid.
Example A cube can be made from this net →

Network A diagram of connected lines consisting of nodes, arcs and regions. Has many practical uses, e.g. transport routes, etc.

Number line The set of numbers written in order along a line. For example:

Infinity ← −5 −4 −3 −2 −1 0 1 2 3 4 5 → Infinity

Numerator The top number of a common *fraction*.

O

Obtuse An angle between 90° and 180°.

Octagon A *plane* (flat) shape with 8 sides.

Odd Numbers that do not divide exactly by 2. The *set of* odd numbers is {1, 3, 5, 7 . . .}.

Order of magnitude Example Where a list of numbers have to be written in size order, from the smallest to the largest.

Ordered pair Another name for the *coordinates* of a point, e.g. (2, 3).

Order of rotational symmetry (30)	See *rotational symmetry*.

P

Parallel	Lines which are the same distance apart, e.g. the opposite sides of a rectangle. The symbols are // or ↗↗.
Parallelogram	A *quadrilateral* with *parallel* and equal opposite sides.
Pentagon	A *plane* shape with 5 sides.
Percentage (22)	A fraction with a *denominator* of 100. Example 50% = $\frac{50}{100} = \frac{1}{2}$.
Perimeter	The distance around a shape. Example A *square* has 5 cm sides; its perimeter is 4 × 5 cm = 20 cm.
Perpendicular	Where a line is at right-angles to another line → ⊥; *plane* surfaces may be perpendicular, as a wall to a pavement.
'Pi'	The number of times the *diameter* of a circle divides into the *circumference*. It is not an exact number, so it is represented by the *symbol* π. π is often taken as $3\frac{1}{7}$ or 3·14.
Pictogram (5)	A chart showing information by means of picture *symbols*.
Pie-chart (22)	A chart showing information by means of dividing a circle into *sectors*. Example 25% (a $\frac{1}{4}$) of something could be shown by a *sector* with a 90° angle (360° ÷ 4 = 90°)
Pints	An *imperial* measure of liquid capacity. Just over $\frac{1}{2}$ a *litre*.
Place value	The value of a figure according to its place in a number, e.g. in 5·5 one 5 is 5 units, the other is 5 tenths.
Plan	A view from above, or any design for something. Example A plan of a building drawn to a *scale* of 1 : 50.
Plane shapes	Shapes with flat surfaces. Triangles and squares are examples of plane shapes.
Plotting	Placing the position of a point on a graph by its distances from the x and y axes.
Point symmetry (30)	A figure has point *symmetry* if it looks the same after a rotation of 180°.
Polygon	Any *plane* (flat) figure with three or more straight sides, e.g. a *triangle*.
Positive	Above *zero*, e.g. 2 and 4·5.

p.m.	*Post* meridiem, meaning after midday.
Pound sterling	A British unit of money (£1).
Pound (weight)	An *imperial* measure of weight. Just under $\frac{1}{2}$ a *kilogram*. Abbreviated to lb.
Post	As in post-war (after the war).
Pre	As in pre-war (before the war).
Prime number	A number with only 1 and itself as *factors*, e.g. 2, 3, 5, 7, 11, etc.
Prism	A three-dimensional shape with a regular cross-section (the same shape all the way through). Examples: a cylinder, a cuboid.
Probability line (32)	Probabilities shown on a scale from 0 to 1.
Product	The result of a multiplication, e.g. 35 is the product of 5 × 7.
Program	A set of instructions as in 'computer program'.
Proportional division (16)	Divided in a given *ratio*. Example £36 divided in the ratio 1 : 3 gives £9 and £27.
Proportionate bar-chart (35)	Various proportions of a whole represented on one bar.
Protractor	An instrument used for drawing and measuring angles.

Q

Quadrilateral	Any *plane* shape with 4 straight sides, e.g. a *square* or a rectangle.
Quadrant	A quarter of a circle.
Questionnaire	A list of questions designed to find out certain views, facts etc.

R

Radius	A straight line from the middle to the *circumference* of a circle. Half a *diameter*. The plural of radius is radii.
Ratio (13)	Comparing two or more amounts or shares, e.g. 2 : 3 : 4 (total of 9 equal parts or shares).
Raw data	The basic, unordered information collected in a statistical survey.
Reciprocal	The inverse of a number. Example $\frac{1}{3}$ is the reciprocal of 3.

Recurring decimal	A decimal fraction with a figure, or figures, that recur over and over again. Examples $0{\cdot}\dot{3}$ (meaning 0·333 333 3 . . .), $0{\cdot}1\dot{4}\dot{5}$ (meaning 0·145 454 545 . . .)
Regular shape	A shape with equal sides and equal angles. Example A regular *pentagon* has all five sides and five angles equal.
Root	Usually referring to the '*square root*', i.e. the number that multiplies by itself to make the given number. Example $\sqrt{36} = 6$, read as 'The *square root* of 36 is 6'.
Rotational symmetry (30)	A shape has rotational symmetry if it can be turned and seem to be unchanged and in the same position. The order of rotational symmetry is the number of times it 'fits into itself' in a complete turn. A square has rotational symmetry of order 4.

S

Scale	Example A map might be drawn to a scale of 1 cm to 1 km, meaning 1 cm on the map represents 1 km of the *real* distance.
Scalene	A scalene *triangle* has all sides and angles of different sizes.
Seconds	60 s = 1 min. 3600 s = 1 hour.
Sector	Part of a circle between two *radii*.
Segment	Part of a circle cut off by a *chord*.
Semicircle	Half of a circle cut off by a *diameter*.
Sequence	A set of numbers connected by a pattern or a rule. Example 2, 4, 6, 8, . . .
Set of	A collection of items, usually having something in common, e.g. the set of even numbers.
Square	A *quadrilateral* with four equal sides and four right-angles.
Square metre	A measurement of *area* consisting of a *square* with each side 1 *metre* long; abbreviation 1 m^2 (one square metre).
Square numbers	The first three square whole numbers are: **1** (1×1), **4** (2×2), **9** (3×3).
Square root	See *root*.
Stationary	At rest, no movement. Shown on a travel graph as a *horizontal* (flat) section of line.
Stick graph	Values represented on a graph by *vertical* (stick) lines.
Sum of	Adding values to find a total, e.g. the sum of 2, 8 and 9 is $2 + 8 + 9 = 19$.

Supersonic	Faster than the speed of sound, which is approximately 760·98 m.p.h. at sea-level at 15 °C.
Survey	To find out peoples' opinions, attitudes, etc., or to measure land as in Ordnance Survey.
Symbol	A sign, character, etc. that represents something. Examples +, =, ∴, √, etc.
Symmetry (30)	See *line symmetry*, *order of rotational symmetry* and *point symmetry*.

T

Tally marks	A method of counting *frequencies*, e.g. ~~IIII~~ represents 5.
Tangent	A straight line that touches but does not cross a circle, as in ○
Tariff	A table of prices.
Tonne	A *metric* measure of weight; 1000 kg = 1 tonne.
Top-heavy	As in an *improper fraction*, e.g. $\frac{7}{3}$.
Triangle	A *polygon* with three sides and three angles. The *sum of* the angles is 180°.
Triangular numbers	Numbers that can be represented as a triangle of dots. 1, 3 and 6 are the first three triangular numbers.
Trundle wheel	A revolving circle on a handle, used for measuring distances.
Twenty-four hour clock (7)	The system of dividing a day into 24 hours. Examples 7:35 a.m. = 0735; 7:35 p.m. = 1935.
Two-way table	A table of information that can be totalled two ways. Example: an order list for a Chinese take-away.

U

Unbiased	Not favouring any particular outcome. As in unbiased (balanced) die.
Unlike common fractions	*Common fractions* with different *denominators*, e.g. $\frac{1}{2}$, $\frac{1}{4}$, $\frac{1}{3}$.
Units	Ones.

V

Value Added Tax	VAT. A government tax added to the cost of various things. In 1988 the tax was 15%.
Vertex	A corner of a shape. The plural is vertices.

Vertical axis The upright reference line on a graph; the *y axis* on certain graphs.

Vulgar A *common fraction* that is not top-heavy.

W

Whole number Not involving a *fraction*; also called an *integer*.

Y

Yard An *imperial* measure of length; 3 feet = 1 yard. Just under a *metre* in length.

Z

Zero Nought.

Acknowledgements

Cover design by Peter Theodosiou
Diagrams by Sherrington Foster
Cartoons by John Hawkwood, Impress International
Text layout by Peter Ducker

Photographs and copyright illustrations by permission of:
Survival International (p.10), The Image Bank (p.25), Science Photo Library (p.32), A. G. Langham (pp.33, 44 right, 128 right, 158), Trustees of the Science Museum (p.38 centre), Ferranti plc (p.38 bottom), British Petroleum (pp.42, 59), Biophoto Associates (p.44 top left), Colorsport (p.44 bottom), Vauxhall Motors (p.78), British Airways (p.82), Cathedral Gifts Ltd (p.84), Ideal Home magazine (pp.85, 161), Trustees of the British Museum (p.112), French Government Tourist Office (p.114), Picturepoint (p.128, left and middle), NHPA/Stephen Dalton (p.188), NHPA (pp.189, 190), NHPA/John Shaw (p.191), British Rail (p.248), Post Office (pp.248, 249)

Puzzles reproduced by permission of:
Scottish Curriculum Development Service, from *Practical Mathematics in Schools* (**Which class?**, p.87)
Tarquin Publications, Diss, Norfolk, from *Can you Solve These?*, David Wells (**Coming and going**, p.143, **Half-full**, p.202, **Rooms**, p.203)
Basil Blackwell, Oxford, from *Sources of Mathematical Discovery*, Lorraine Mottershead (**Topology**, p.143)

Examination questions reproduced by permission of the following examination boards:
Northern Examining Association (NEA)
Midland Examining Group (MEG)
Welsh Joint Education Committee (WJEC)
London and East Anglian Group (LEAG)
Southern Examining Group (SEG)

Sources of other information:
The Building Societies Association (p.9), BBC (pp.37, 247), BP plc (p.41), National Food Survey 1982 (p.135), Department of Roman Antiques, British Museum (p.148), Social Trends, Central Statistical Office (pp.237, 239, 243), British Rail (pp.247–249), Post Office (pp.248–250)